Experiment Central

Understanding Scientific Principles
Through Projects

Experiment Central

Understanding Scientific Principles
Through Projects
Second Edition

VOLUME 6: SP-Z

M. Rae Nelson
Kristine Krapp, editor

U·X·L
A part of Gale, Cengage Learning

GALE
CENGAGE Learning

Detroit • New York • San Francisco • New Haven, Conn • Waterville, Maine • London

GALE
CENGAGE Learning™

Experiment Central
Understanding Scientific
Principles Through Projects
Second Edition
M. Rae Nelson

Project Editor: Kristine Krapp

Managing Editor: Debra Kirby

Rights Acquisition and Management:
Margaret Abendroth, Robyn Young

Composition: Evi Abou-El-Seoud, Mary
Beth Trimper

Manufacturing: Wendy Blurton

Product Manager: Julia Furtaw

Product Design: Jennifer Wahi

© 2010 Gale, Cengage Learning

For product information and technology assistance, contact us at
Gale Customer Support, 1-800-877-4253.
For permission to use material from this text or product,
submit all requests online at **www.cengage.com/permissions.**
Further permissions questions can be e-mailed to
permissionrequest@cengage.com

Cover photographs: Images courtesy of Dreamstime, Photos.com, and
iStockPhoto.

Library of Congress Cataloging-in-Publication Data

Experiment central : understanding scientific principles through projects. --
2nd ed. / M. Rae Nelson, Kristine Krapp, editors.   p. cm. --
  Includes bibliographical references and index.
   ISBN 978-1-4144-7613-1 (set) -- ISBN 978-1-4144-7614-8 (vol. 1) --
ISBN 978-1-4144-7615-5 (vol. 2) -- ISBN 978-1-4144-7616-2 (vol. 3) --
ISBN 978-1-4144-7617-9 (vol. 4) -- ISBN 978-1-4144-7618-6 (vol. 5) --
ISBN 978-1-4144-7619-3 (vol. 6)
   1. Science--Experiments--Juvenile literature. I. Nelson, M. Rae. II. Krapp,
Kristine M.

Q164.E96 2010
507.8--dc22   2009050304

Gale
27500 Drake Rd.
Farmington Hills, MI, 48331-3535

978-1-4144-7613-1 (set)   1-4144-7613-2 (set)
978-1-4144-7614-8 (vol. 1)   1-4144-7614-0 (vol. 1)
978-1-4144-7615-5 (vol. 2)   1-4144-7615-9 (vol. 2)
978-1-4144-7616-2 (vol. 3)   1-4144-7616-7 (vol. 3)
978-1-4144-7617-9 (vol. 4)   1-4144-7617-5 (vol. 4)
978-1-4144-7618-6 (vol. 5)   1-4144-7618-3 (vol. 5)
978-1-4144-7619-3 (vol. 6)   1-4144-7619-1 (vol. 6)

This title is also available as an e-book.
ISBN-13: 978-1-4144-7620-9 (set)
ISBN-10: 1-4144-7620-5 (set)
Contact your Gale sales representative for ordering information.

Printed by China Translation & Printing Services Limited,
Guangdong Province, China. 1st printing. 05/2010
1 2 3 4 5 6 7 14 13 12 11 10

Table of Contents

Experiment Central, 2nd edition

Experiment Central, 2nd edition

Experiment Central, 2nd edition

Experiment Central, 2nd edition

Experiment Central, 2nd edition

Experiment Central, 2nd edition

Reader's Guide

Experiment Central: Understanding Scientific Principles Through Projects
provides in one resource a wide variety of science experiments covering
nine key science curriculum fields—astronomy, biology, botany, chemistry, ecology, food science, geology, meteorology, and physics—spanning
the earth sciences, life sciences, and physical sciences.

Experiment Central, 2nd edition combines, expands, and updates the
original four-volume and two-volume UXL sets. This new edition includes
20 new chapters, 60 new experiments, and more than 35 enhanced experiments. Each chapter explores a scientific subject and offers experiments
or projects that utilize or reinforce the topic studied. Chapters are alphabeti-
cally arranged according to scientific concept, including: Air and
Water Pollution, Color, Eclipses, Forensic Science, Genetics, Magnetism,
Mountains, Periodic Table, Renewable Energy, Storms and Water Cycle.
Two to three experiments or projects are included in each chapter.

Entry format

Chapters are presented in a standard, easy-to-follow format. All chapters
open with an explanatory overview section designed to introduce students
to the scientific concept and provide the background behind a concept s
discovery or important figures who helped advance the study of the field.

Each experiment is divided into eight standard sections to help
students follow the experimental process clearly from beginning to end.
Sections are:

- Purpose/Hypothesis
- Level of Difficulty

- Materials Needed
- Approximate Budget
- Timetable
- Step-by-Step Instructions
- Summary of Results
- Change the Variables

Chapters also include a "Design Your Own Experiment" section that allows students to apply what they have learned about a particular concept and to create their own experiments. This section is divided into:

- How to Select a Topic Relating to this Concept
- Steps in the Scientific Method
- Recording Data and Summarizing the Results
- Related Projects

Special Features

A "Words to Know" sidebar provides definitions of terms used in each chapter. A cumulative glossary collected from all the "Words to Know" sections is included in the beginning of each volume.

The "Experiments by Scientific Field" section categorizes experiments by scientific curriculum area. This section cumulates all experiments across the six-volume series.

The Parent's and Teacher's Guide recommends that a responsible adult always oversee a student's experiment and provides several safety guidelines for all students to follow.

Standard sidebars accompany experiments and projects.

- "What Are the Variables?" explains the factors that may have an impact on the outcome of a particular experiment.
- "How to Experiment Safely" clearly explains any risks involved with the experiment and how to avoid them.
- "Troubleshooter's Guide" presents problems that a student might encounter with an experiment, possible causes of the problem, and ways to remedy the problem.

Over 450 photos enhance the text; approximately 450 custom illustrations show the steps in the experiments.

Four indexes cumulate information from all the experiments in this six-volume set, including:

- Budget Index categorizes the experiments by approximate cost.
- Level of Difficulty Index lists experiments according to "easy," "moderate," or "difficult," or a combination thereof.
- Timetable Index categorizes each experiment by the amount of time needed to complete it, including setup and follow-through time.
- General Subject Index provides access to all major terms, people, places, and topics covered in the set.

Acknowledgments

The author wishes to acknowledge and thank Laurie Curtis, teacher/ researcher; Cindy O'Neill, science educator; and Joyce Nelson, chemist, for their contributions to this edition as consultants.

Comments and Suggestions

We welcome your comments on *Experiment Central*. Please write: Editors, *Experiment Central*, U*X*L, 27500 Drake Rd. Farmington Hills, MI 48331-3535; call toll-free: 1-800-347-4253; or visit us at www.gale.cengage.com.

Parent's and Teacher's Guide

The experiments and projects in *Experiment Central* have been carefully constructed with issues of safety in mind, but your guidance and supervision are still required. Following the safety guidelines that accompany each experiment and project (found in the "How to Experiment Safely" sidebar box), as well as putting to work the safe practices listed below, will help your child or student avoid accidents. Oversee your child or student during experiments, and make sure he or she follows these safety guidelines:

- Always wear safety goggle is there is any possiblity of sharp objects, small particles, splashes of liquid, or gas fumes getting in someone's eyes.
- Always wear protective gloves when handling materials that could irritate the skin.
- Never leave an open flame, such as a lit candle, unattended. Never wear loose clothing around an open flame.
- Follow instructions carefully when using electrical equipment, including batteries, to avoid getting shocked.
- Be cautious when handling sharp objects or glass equipment that might break. Point scissors away from you and use them carefully.
- Always ask for help in cleaning up spills, broken glass, or other hazardous materials.
- Always use protective gloves when handling hot objects. Set them down only on a protected surface that will not be damaged by heat.

- Always wash your hands thoroughly after handling material that might contain harmful microorganisms, such as soil and pond water.

- Do not substitute materials in an experiment without asking a knowledgeable adult about possible reactions.

- Do not use or mix unidentified liquids or powders. The result might be an explosion or poisonous fumes.

- Never taste or eat any substances being used in an experiment.

- Always wear old clothing or a protective apron to avoid staining your clothes.

Experiments by Scientific Field

Chapter name in brackets, followed by experiment name. The numeral before the colon indicates volume; numbers after the colon indicate page number.

CHEMISTRY

Experiment Central, 2nd edition

ECOLOGY

FOOD SCIENCE

GEOLOGY

Experiment Central, 2nd edition

Words to Know

Abdomen: The third segment of an insect body.

Abscission: Barrier of special cells created at the base of leaves in autumn.

Absolute dating: The age of an object correlated to a specific fixed time, as established by some precise dating method.

Acceleration: The rate at which the velocity and/or direction of an object is changing with respect to time.

Acid: Substance that when dissolved in water is capable of reacting with a base to form salts and release hydrogen ions.

Acid rain: A form of precipitation that is significantly more acidic than neutral water, often produced as the result of industrial processes and pollution.

Acoustics: The science concerned with the production, properties, and propagation of sound waves.

Acronym: A word or phrase formed from the first letter of other words.

Active solar energy system: A solar energy system that uses pumps or fans to circulate heat captured from the Sun.

Additive: A chemical compound that is added to foods to give them some desirable quality, such as preventing them from spoiling.

Adhesion: Attraction between two different substances.

Adhesive: A substance that bonds or adheres two substances together.

Aeration: Mixing a gas, like oxygen, with a liquid, like water.

Aerobic: A process that requires oxygen.

Aerodynamics: The study of the motion of gases (particularly air) and the motion and control of objects in the air.

Agar: A nutrient rich, gelatinous substance that is used to grow bacteria.

Air: Gaseous mixture that covers Earth, composed mainly of nitrogen (about 78%) and oxygen (about 21%) with lesser amounts of argon, carbon dioxide, and other gases.

Air density: The ratio of the mass of a substance to the volume it occupies.

Air mass: A large body of air that has similar characteristics.

Air pressure: The force exerted by the weight of the atmosphere above a point on or above Earth's surface.

Alga/Algae: Single-celled or multicellular plants or plant-like organisms that contain chlorophyll, thus making their own food by photosynthesis. Algae grow mainly in water.

Alignment: Adjustment in a certain direction or orientation.

Alkali metals: The first group of elements in the periodic table, these metals have a single electron in the outermost shell.

Alkaline: Having a pH of more than 7.

Alleles: One version of the same gene.

Alloy: A mixture of two or more metals with properties different from those metals of which it is made.

Amine: An organic compound derived from ammonia.

Amino acid: One of a group of organic compounds that make up proteins.

Amnesia: Partial or total memory loss.

Amperage: A measurement of current. The common unit of measure is the ampere or amp.

Amphibians: Animals that live on land and breathe air but return to the water to reproduce.

Amplitude: The maximum displacement (difference between an original position and a later position) of the material that is vibrating. Amplitude can be thought of visually as the highest and lowest point of a wave.

Anaerobic: A process that does not require oxygen.

Anal fin: Fin on the belly of a fish, used for balance.

Anatomy: The study of the structure of living things.

Anemometer: A device that measures wind speed.

Angiosperm: A flowering plant that has its seeds produced within an ovary.

Animalcules: Life forms that Anton van Leeuwenhoek named when he first saw them under his microscope; they later became known as protozoa and bacteria.

Anther: The male reproductive organs of the plant, located on the tip of a flower's stamen.

Anthocyanin: Red pigment found in leaves, petals, stems, and other parts of a plant.

Antibiotic: A substance produced by or derived from certain fungi and other organisms, that can destroy or inhibit the growth of other microorganisms.

Antibiotic resistance: The ability of microorganisms to change so that they are not killed by antibiotics.

Antibody: A protein produced by certain cells of the body as an immune (disease-fighting) response to a specific foreign antigen.

Antigen: A substance that causes the production of an antibody when injected directly into the body.

Antioxidants: Used as a food additive, these substances can prevent food spoilage by reducing the food's exposure to air.

Aquifer: Underground layer of sand, gravel, or spongy rock that collects water.

Arch: A curved structure that spans an opening and supports a weight above the opening.

Artesian well: A well in which water is forced out under pressure.

Asexual reproduction: A reproductive process that does not involve the union of two individuals in the exchange of genetic material.

Astronomers: Scientists who study the positions, motions, and composition of stars and other objects in the sky.

Astronomy: The study of the physical properties of objects and matter outside Earth's atmosphere.

Atmosphere: Layers of air that surround Earth.

Atmospheric pressure: The pressure exerted by the atmosphere at Earth's surface due to the weight of the air.

Atom: The smallest unit of an element, made up of protons and neutrons in a central nucleus surrounded by moving electrons.

Atomic mass: Also known as atomic weight, the average mass of the atoms in an element; the number that appears under the element symbol in the periodic table.

Atomic number: The number of protons (or electrons) in an atom; the number that appears over the element symbol in the periodic table.

Atomic symbol: The one- or two-letter abbreviation for a chemical element.

Autotroph: An organism that can build all the food and produce all the energy it needs with its own resources.

Auxins: A group of plant hormones responsible for patterns of plant growth.

Axis: An imaginary straight line around which an object, like a planet, spins or turns. Earth's axis is a line that goes through the North and South Poles.

Bacteria: Single-celled microorganisms that live in soil, water, plants, and animals that play a key role in the decay of organic matter and the cycling of nutrients. Some are agents of disease.

Bacteriology: The scientific study of bacteria, their characteristics, and their activities as related to medicine, industry, and agriculture.

Barometer: An instrument for measuring atmospheric pressure, used especially in weather forecasting.

Base: Substance that when dissolved in water is capable of reacting with an acid to form salts and release hydrogen ions; has a pH of more than 7.

Base pairs: In DNA, the pairing of two nucleotides with each other: adenine (A) with thymine (T), and guanine (G) with cytosine (C).

Beam: A straight, horizontal structure that spans an opening and supports a weight above the opening.

Bedrock: Solid layer of rock lying beneath the soil and other loose material.

Beriberi: A disease caused by a deficiency of thiamine and characterized by nerve and gastrointestinal disorders.

Biochemical oxygen demand (BOD5): The amount of oxygen micro-organisms use over a five-day period in 68°F (20°C) water to decay organic matter.

Biodegradable: Capable of being decomposed by biological agents.

Biological variables: Living factors such as bacteria, fungi, and animals that can affect the processes that occur in nature and in an experiment.

Bioluminescence: The chemical phenomenon in which an organism can produce its own light.

Biomass: Organic materials that are used to produce usable energy.

Biomes: Large geographical areas with specific climates and soils, as well as distinct plant and animal communities that are interdependent.

Biomimetics: The development of materials that are found in nature.

Biopesticide: Pesticide produced from substances found in nature.

Bivalve: Bivalves are characterized by shells that are divided into two parts or valves that completely enclose the mollusk like the clam or scallop.

Blanching: A cooking technique in which the food, usually vegetables and fruits, are briefly cooked in boiling water and then plunged into cold water.

Blood pattern analysis: The study of the shape, location, and pattern of blood in order to understand how it got there.

Blueshift: The shortening of the frequency of light waves toward the blue end of the visible light spectrum as they travel towards an observer; most commonly used to describe movement of stars towards Earth.

Boiling point: The temperature at which a substance changes from a liquid to a gas or vapor.

Bond: The force that holds two atoms together.

Bone joint: A place in the body where two or more bones are connected.

Bone marrow: The spongy center of many bones in which blood cells are manufactured.

Bone tissue: A group of similar cells in the bone with a common function.

Bony fish: The largest group of fish, whose skeleton is made of bone.

Boreal: Northern.

Botany: The branch of biology involving the scientific study of plant life.

Braided rivers: Wide, shallow rivers with multiple channels and pebbly islands in the middle.

Buoyancy: The tendency of a liquid to exert a lifting effect on a body immersed in it.

By-product: A secondary substance produced as the result of a physical or chemical process, in addition to the main product.

Calcium carbonate: A substance that is secreted by a mollusk to create the shell it lives in.

Calibration: To standardize or adjust a measuring instrument so its measurements are correct.

Cambium: The tissue below the bark that produces new cells, which become wood and bark.

Camouflage: Markings or coloring that help hide an animal by making it blend into the surrounding environment.

Cancellous bone: Also called spongy bone, the inner layer of a bone that has cells with large spaces in between them filled with marrow.

Canning: A method of preserving food using airtight, vacuum-sealed containers and heat processing.

Capillary action: The tendency of water to rise through a narrow tube by the force of adhesion between the water and the walls of the tube.

Caramelization: The process of heating sugars to the point at which they break down and lead to the formation of new compounds.

Carbohydrate: A compound consisting of carbon, hydrogen, and oxygen found in plants and used as a food by humans and other animals.

Carbonic acid: A weak acid that forms from the mixture of water and carbon dioxide.

Carnivore: A meat-eating organism.

Carotene: Yellow-orange pigment in plants.

Cartilage: The connective tissue that covers and protects the bones.

Cartilaginous fish: The second largest group of fish whose skeleton is made of cartilage

Cast: In paleontology, the fossil formed when a mold is later filled in by mud or mineral matter.

Catalase: An enzyme found in animal liver tissue that breaks down hydrogen peroxide into oxygen and water.

Catalyst: A compound that starts or speeds up the rate of a chemical reaction without undergoing any change in its own composition.

Caudal fin: Tail fin of a fish used for fast swimming.

Cave: Also called cavern, a hollow or natural passage under or into the ground large enough for a person to enter.

Celestial bodies: Describing planets or other objects in space.

Cell membrane: The layer that surrounds the cell, but is inside the cell wall, allowing some molecules to enter and keeping others out of the cell.

Cell theory: All living things have one or more similar cells that carry out the same functions for the living process.

Cell wall: A tough outer covering over the cell membrane of bacteria and plant cells.

Cells: The basic unit for living organisms; cells are structured to perform highly specialized functions.

Centrifugal force: The apparent force pushing a rotating body away from the center of rotation.

Centrifuge: A device that rapidly spins a solution so that the heavier components will separate from the lighter ones.

Centripetal force: Rotating force that moves towards the center or axis.

Cerebral cortex: The outer layer of the brain.

Channel: A shallow trench carved into the ground by the pressure and movement of a river.

Chemical change: The change of one or more substances into other substances.

Chemical energy: Energy stored in chemical bonds.

Chemical property: A characteristic of a substance that allows it to undergo a chemical change. Chemical properties include flammability and sensitivity to light.

Chemical reaction: Any chemical change in which at least one new substance is formed.

Chemosense: A sense stimulated by specific chemicals that cause the sensory cell to transmit a signal to the brain.

Chitin: Substance that makes up the exoskeleton of crustaceans.

Chlorophyll: A green pigment found in plants that absorbs sunlight, providing the energy used in photosynthesis, or the conversion of carbon dioxide and water to complex carbohydrates.

Chloroplasts: Small structures in plant cells that contain chlorophyll and in which the process of photosynthesis takes place.

Chromatography: A method for identifying the components of a substance based on their characteristic colors.

Chromosome: A structure of DNA found in the cell nucleus.

Cilia: Hairlike structures on olfactory receptor cells that sense odor molecules.

Circuit: The complete path of an electric current including the source of electric energy.

Circumference: The distance around a circle.

Clay: Type of soil comprising the smallest soil particles.

Cleavage: The tendency of a mineral to split along certain planes.

Climate: The average weather that a region experiences over a long period.

Coagulation: The clumping together of particles in a mixture, often because the repelling force separating them is disrupted.

Cohesion: Attraction between like substances.

Cold blooded: When an animals body temperature rises or falls to match the environment.

Collagen: A protein in bone that gives the bone elasticity.

Colloid: A mixture containing particles suspended in, but not dissolved in, a dispersing medium.

Colony: A mass of microorganisms that have been bred in a medium.

Colorfast: The ability of a material to keep its dye and not fade or change color.

Coma: Glowing cloud of gas surrounding the nucleus of a comet.

Combustion: Any chemical reaction in which heat, and usually light, is produced. It is commonly the burning of organic substances during which oxygen from the air is used to form carbon dioxide and water vapor.

Comet: An icy body orbiting in the solar system, which partially vaporizes when it nears the Sun and develops a diffuse envelope of dust and gas as well as one or more tails.

Comet head: The nucleus and the coma of a comet.

Comet nucleus: The core or center of a comet. (Plural: Comet nuclei.)

Comet tail: The most distinctive feature of comets; comets can display two basic types of tails: one gaseous and the other largely composed of dust.

Compact bone: The outer, hard layer of the bone.

Complete metamorphosis: Metamorphosis in which a larva becomes a pupa before changing into an adult form.

Composting: The process in which organic compounds break down and become dark, fertile soil called humus.

Compression: A type of force on an object where the object is pushed or squeezed from each end.

Concave: Hollowed or rounded inward, like the inside of a bowl.

Concave lens: A lens that is thinner in the middle than at the edges.

Concentration: The amount of a substance present in a given volume, such as the number of molecules in a liter.

Condensation: The process by which a gas changes into a liquid.

Conduction: The flow of heat through a solid.

Conductivity: The ability of a material to carry an electrical current.

Conductor: A substance able to carry an electrical current.

Cones: Cells in the retina that can perceive color.

Confined aquifer: An aquifer with a layer of impermeable rock above it where the water is held under pressure.

Coniferous: Refers to trees, such as pines and firs, that bear cones and have needle-like leaves that are not shed all at once.

Conservation of energy: The law of physics that states that energy can be transformed from one form to another, but can be neither created nor destroyed.

Constellations: Patterns of stars in the night sky. There are eighty-eight known constellations.

Continental drift: The theory that continents move apart slowly at a predictable rate.

Contract: To shorten, pull together.

Control experiment: A set-up that is identical to the experiment but is not affected by the variable that will be changed during the experiment.

Convection: The circulatory motion that occurs in a gas or liquid at a nonuniform temperature owing to the variation of its density and the action of gravity.

Convection current: A circular movement of a fluid in response to alternating heating and cooling.

Convex: Curved or rounded outward, like the outside of a ball.

Convex lens: A lens that is thicker in the middle than at the edges.

Coprolites: The fossilized droppings of animals.

Coriolis force: A force that makes a moving object appear to travel in a curved path over the surface of a spinning body.

Corona: The outermost atmospheric layer of the Sun.

Corrosion: An oxidation-reduction reaction in which a metal is oxidized (reacted with oxygen) and oxygen is reduced, usually in the presence of moisture.

Cotyledon: Seed leaves, which contain the stored source of food for the embryo.

Crater: An indentation caused by an object hitting the surface of a planet or moon.

Crest: The highest point reached by a wave.

Cross-pollination: The process by which pollen from one plant pollinates another plant of the same species.

Crust: The hard outer shell of Earth that floats upon the softer, denser mantle.

Experiment Central, 2nd edition

Crustacean: A type of arthropod characterized by hard and thick skin, and having shells that are jointed. This group includes the lobster, crab, and crayfish.

Crystal: Naturally occurring solid composed of atoms or molecules arranged in an orderly pattern that repeats at regular intervals.

Crystal faces: The flat, smooth surfaces of a crystal.

Crystal lattice: The regular and repeating pattern of the atoms in a crystal.

Cultures: Microorganisms growing in prepared nutrients.

Cumulonimbus cloud: The parent cloud of a thunderstorm; a tall, vertically developed cloud capable of producing heavy rain, high winds, and lightning.

Current: The flow of electrical charge from one point to another.

Currents: The horizontal and vertical circulation of ocean waters.

Cyanobacteria: Oxygen-producing, aquatic bacteria capable of manufacturing its own food; resembles algae.

Cycles: Occurrence of events that take place on a regular, repeating basis.

Cytology: The branch of biology concerned with the study of cells.

Cytoplasm: The semifluid substance inside a cell that surrounds the nucleus and other membrane-enclosed organelles.

Decanting: The process of separating a suspension by waiting for its heavier components to settle out and then pouring off the lighter ones.

Decibel (dB): A unit of measurement for the amplitude of sound.

Deciduous: Plants that lose their leaves during some season of the year, and then grow them back during another season.

Decompose: To break down into two or more simpler substances.

Decomposition: The breakdown of complex molecules of dead organisms into simple nutrients that can be reutilized by living organisms.

Decomposition reaction: A chemical reaction in which one substance is broken down into two or more substances.

Deficiency disease: A disease marked by a lack of an essential nutrient in the diet.

Degrade: Break down.

Dehydration: The removal of water from a material.

Denaturization: Altering an enzyme so it no longer works.

Density: The mass of a substance divided by its volume.

Density ball: A ball with the fixed standard of 1.0 gram per milliliter, which is the exact density of pure water.

Deoxyribonucleic acid (DNA): Large, complex molecules found in the nuclei of cells that carry genetic information for an organism's development; double helix. (Pronounced DEE-ox-see-rye-bo-noo-klay-ick acid)

Dependent variable: The variable in an experiment whose value depends on the value of another variable in the experiment.

Deposition: Dropping of sediments that occurs when a river loses its energy of motion.

Desert: A biome with a hot-to-cool climate and dry weather.

Desertification: Transformation of arid or semiarid productive land into desert.

Dewpoint: The point at which water vapor begins to condense.

Dicot: Plants with a pair of embryonic seeds that appear at germination.

Diffraction: The bending of light or another form of electromagnetic radiation as it passes through a tiny hole or around a sharp edge.

Diffraction grating: A device consisting of a surface into which are etched very fine, closely spaced grooves that cause different wavelengths of light to reflect or refract (bend) by different amounts.

Diffusion: Random movement of molecules that leads to a net movement of molecules from a region of high concentration to a region of low concentration.

Disinfection: Using chemicals to kill harmful organisms.

Dissolved oxygen: Oxygen molecules that have dissolved in water.

Distillation: The process of separating liquids from solids or from other liquids with different boiling points by a method of evaporation and condensation, so that each component in a mixture can be collected separately in its pure form.

DNA fingerprinting: A technique that uses DNA fragments to identify the unique DNA sequences of an individual.

DNA replication: The process by which one DNA strand unwinds and duplicates all its information, creating two new DNA strands that are identical to each other and to the original strand.

DNA (deoxyribonucleic acid): Large, complex molecules found in nuclei of cells that carry genetic information for an organism's development.

Domain: Small regions in iron that possess their own magnetic charges.

Dominant gene: A gene that passes on a certain characteristic, even when there is only one copy (allele) of the gene.

Doppler effect: The change in wavelength and frequency (number of vibrations per second) of either light or sound as the source is moving either towards or away from the observer.

Dormant: A state of inactivity in an organism.

Dorsal fin: The fin located on the back of a fish, used for balance.

Double helix: The shape taken by DNA (deoxyribonucleic acid) molecules in a nucleus.

Drought: A prolonged period of dry weather that damages crops or prevents their growth.

Dry cell: A source of electricity that uses a non-liquid electrolyte.

Dust tail: One of two types of tails a comet may have, it is composed mainly of dust and it points away from the Sun.

Dye: A colored substance that is used to give color to a material.

Dynamic equilibrium: A situation in which substances are moving into and out of cell walls at an equal rate.

Earthquake: An unpredictable event in which masses of rock suddenly shift or rupture below Earth's surface, releasing enormous amounts of energy and sending out shockwaves that sometimes cause the ground to shake dramatically.

Eclipse: A phenomenon in which the light from a celestial body is temporarily cut off by the presence of another.

Ecologists: Scientists who study the interrelationship of organisms and their environments.

Ecosystem: An ecological community, including plants, animals and microorganisms, considered together with their environment.

Efficiency: The amount of power output divided by the amount of power input. It is a measure of how well a device converts one form of power into another.

Effort: The force applied to move a load using a simple machine.

Elastomers: Any of various polymers having rubbery properties.

Electric charge repulsion: Repulsion of particles caused by a layer of negative ions surrounding each particle. The repulsion prevents coagulation and promotes the even dispersion of such particles through a mixtures.

Electrical energy: Kinetic energy resulting from the motion of electrons within any object that conducts electricity.

Electricity: A form of energy caused by the presence of electrical charges in matter.

Electrode: A material that will conduct an electrical current, usually a metal; used to carry electrons into or out of a battery.

Electrolyte: Any substance that, when dissolved in water, conducts an electric current.

Electromagnetic spectrum: The complete array of electromagnetic radiation, including radio waves (at the longest-wavelength end), microwaves, infrared radiation, visible light, ultraviolet radiation, X rays, and gamma rays (at the shortest-wavelength end).

Electromagnetism: A form of magnetic energy produced by the flow of an electric current through a metal core. Also, the study of electric and magnetic fields and their interaction with charges and currents.

Electron: A subatomic particle with a single negative electrical change that orbits the nucleus of an atom.

Electroplating: The process of coating one metal with another metal by means of an electrical current.

Electroscope: A device that determines whether an object is electrically charged.

Element: A pure substance composed of just one type of atom that cannot be broken down into anything simpler by ordinary chemical means.

Elevation: Height above sea level.

Elliptical: An orbital path which is egg-shaped or resembles an elongated circle.

Elongation: The percentage increase in length that occurs before a material breaks under tension.

Embryo: The seed of a plant, which through germination can develop into a new plant.

Embryonic: The earliest stages of development.

Endothermic reaction: A chemical reaction that absorbs heat or light energy, such as photosynthesis, the production of food by plant cells.

Energy: The ability to cause an action or to perform work.

Entomology: The study of insects.

Environmental variables: Nonliving factors such as air temperature, water, pollution, and pH that can affect processes that occur in nature and in an experiment.

Enzyme: Any of numerous complex proteins produced by living cells that act as catalysts, speeding up the rate of chemical reactions in living organisms.

Enzymology: The science of studying enzymes.

Ephemerals: Plants that lie dormant in dry soil for years until major rainstorms occur.

Epicenter: The location where the seismic waves of an earthquake first appear on the surface, usually almost directly above the focus.

Equilibrium: A balancing or canceling out of opposing forces, so that an object will remain at rest.

Erosion: The process by which topsoil is carried away by water, wind, or ice action.

Ethnobotany: The study of how cultures use plants in everyday life.

Eukaryotic: Multicellular organism whose cells contain distinct nuclei, which contain the genetic material. (Pronounced yoo-KAR-ee-ah-tic)

Euphotic zone: The upper part of the ocean where sunlight penetrates, supporting plant life, such as phytoplankton.

Eutrophication: The process by which high nutrient concentrations in a body of water eventually cause the natural wildlife to die.

Evaporation: The process by which liquid changes into a gas.

Exoskeleton: A hard outer covering on animals, which provide protection and structure.

Exothermic reaction: A chemical reaction that releases heat or light energy, such as the burning of fuel.

Experiment: A controlled observation.

Extremophiles: Bacteria that thrive in environments too harsh to support most life forms.

False memory: A memory of an event that never happened or an altered memory from what happened.

Family: A group of elements in the same column of the periodic table or in closely related columns of the table. A family of chemical compounds share similar structures and properties.

Fat: A type of lipid, or chemical compound used as a source of energy, to provide insulation and to protect organs in an animal body.

Fat-soluble vitamins: Vitamins such as A, D, E, and K that can be dissolved in the fat of plants and animals.

Fault: A crack running through rock as the result of tectonic forces.

Fault blocks: Pieces of rock from Earth's crust that press against each other and cause earthquakes when they suddenly shift or rupture from the pressure.

Fault mountain: A mountain that is formed when Earth's plates come together and cause rocks to break and move upwards.

Fermentation: A chemical reaction in which enzymes break down complex organic compounds (for example, carbohydrates and sugars) into simpler ones (for example, ethyl alcohol).

Filament: In a flower, stalk of the stamen that bears the anther.

Filtration: The mechanical separation of a liquid from the undissolved particles floating in it.

Fireball: Meteors that create an intense, bright light and, sometimes, an explosion.

First law of motion (Newton's): An object at rest or moving in a certain direction and speed will remain at rest or moving in the same motion and speed unless acted upon by a force.

Fish: Animals that live in water who have gills, fins, and are cold blooded.

Fixative: A substance that mixes with the dye to hold it to the material.

Flagella: Whiplike structures used by some organisms for movement. (Singular: flagellum.)

Flammability: The ability of a material to ignite and burn.

Flower: The reproductive part of a flowering plant.

Fluid: A substance that flows; a liquid or gas.

Fluorescence: The emission of visible light from an object when the object is bombarded with electromagnetic radiation, such as ultraviolet rays. The emission of visible light stops after the radiation source has been removed.

Focal length: The distance from the lens to the point where the light rays come together to a focus.

Focal point: The point at which rays of light converge or from which they diverge.

Focus: The point within Earth where a sudden shift or rupture occurs.

Fold mountain: A mountain that is formed when Earth's plates come together and push rocks up into folds.

Food webs: Interconnected sets of food chains, which are a sequence of organisms directly dependent on one another for food.

Force: A physical interaction (pushing or pulling) tending to change the state of motion (velocity) of an object.

Forensic science: The application of science to the law and justice system.

Fortified: The addition of nutrients, such as vitamins or minerals, to food.

Fossil: The remains, trace, or impressions of a living organism that inhabited Earth more than ten thousand years ago.

Fossil fuel: A fuel such as coal, oil, or natural gas that is formed over millions of years from the remains of plants and animals.

Fossil record: The documentation of fossils placed in relationship to one another; a key source to understand the evolution of life on Earth.

Fracture: A mineral's tendency to break into curved, rough, or jagged surfaces.

Frequency: The rate at which vibrations take place (number of times per second the motion is repeated), given in cycles per second or in hertz (Hz). Also, the number of waves that pass a given point in a given period of time.

Friction: A force that resists the motion of an object, resulting when two objects rub against one another.

Front: The area between air masses of different temperatures or densities.

Fuel cell: A device that uses hydrogen as the fuel to produce electricity and heat with water as a byproduct.

Fulcrum: The point at which a lever arm pivots.

Fungi: Kingdom of various single-celled or multicellular organisms, including mushrooms, molds, yeasts, and mildews, that do not contain chlorophyll.

Funnel cloud: A fully developed tornado vortex before it has touched the ground.

Fusion: Combining of nuclei of two or more lighter elements into one nucleus of a heavier element; the process stars use to produce energy to produce light and support themselves against their own gravity.

Galaxy: A large collection of stars and clusters of stars containing anywhere from a few million to a few trillion stars.

Gastropod: The largest group of mollusks; characterized by a single shell that is often coiled in a spiral. Snails are gastropods.

Gene: A segment of a DNA (deoxyribonucleic acid) molecule contained in the nucleus of a cell that acts as a kind of code for the production of some specific protein. Genes carry instructions for the formation, functioning, and transmission of specific traits from one generation to another.

Generator: A device that converts mechanical energy into electrical energy,

Genetic engineering: A technique that modifies the DNA of living cells in order to make them change its characteristics. Also called genetic modification.

Genetic material: Material that transfers characteristics from a parent to its offspring.

Geology: The study of the origin, history and structure of Earth.

Geothermal energy: Energy from deep within Earth.

Geotropism: The tendency of roots to bend toward Earth.

Germ theory of disease: The theory that disease is caused by micro-organisms or germs, and not by spontaneous generation.

Germination: First stage in development of a plant seed.

Gibbous moon: A phase of the Moon when more than half of its surface is lighted.

Gills: Special organ located behind the head of a fish that takes in oxygen from the water.

Glacier: A large mass of ice formed from snow that has packed together and which moves slowly down a slope under its own weight.

Global warming: Warming of Earth's atmosphere as a result of an increase in the concentration of gases that store heat, such as carbon dioxide.

Glucose: A simple sugar broken down in cells to produce energy.

Gnomon: The perpendicular piece of the sundial that casts the shadow.

Golgi body: An organelles that sorts, modifies, and packages molecules.

Gravity: Force of attraction between objects, the strength of which depends on the mass of each object and the distance between them.

Greenhouse effect: The warming of Earth's atmosphere due to water vapor, carbon dioxide, and other gases in the atmosphere that trap heat radiated from Earth's surface.

Greenhouse gases: Gases that absorb infrared radiation and warm the air before the heat energy escapes into space.

Greenwich Mean Time (GMT): The time at an imaginary line that runs north and south through Greenwich, England, used as the standard for time throughout the world.

Groundwater: Water that soaks into the ground and is stored in the small spaces between the rocks and soil.

Group: A vertical column of the periodic table that contains elements possessing similar chemical characteristics.

H

Hardwood: Wood from angiosperm, mostly deciduous, trees.

Heartwood: The inner layers of wood that provide structure and have no living cells.

Heat: A form of energy produced by the motion of molecules that make up a substance.

Heat capacity: The measure of how well a substance stores heat.

Heat energy: The energy produced when two substances that have different temperatures are combined.

Heliotropism: The tendency of plants to turn towards the Sun throughout the day.

Herbivore: A plant-eating organism.

Hertz (Hz): The unit of measurement of frequency; a measure of the number of waves that pass a given point per second of time.

Heterogeneous: Different throughout.

Heterotrophs: Organisms that cannot make their own food and that must, therefore, obtain their food from other organisms.

High air pressure: An area where the air is cooler and more dense, and the air pressure is higher than normal.

Hippocampus: A part of the brain associated with learning and memory.

Homogenous: The same throughout.

Hormones: Chemicals produced in the cells of plants and animals that control bodily functions.

Hue: The color or shade.

Humidity: The amount of water vapor (moisture) contained in the air.

Humus: Fragrant, spongy, nutrient-rich decayed plant or animal matter.

Hydrologic cycle: Continual movement of water from the atmosphere to Earth's surface through precipitation and back to the atmosphere through evaporation and transpiration.

Hydrologists: Scientists who study water and its cycle.

Hydrology: The study of water and its cycle.

Hydrometer: An instrument that determines the specific gravity of a liquid.

Hydrophilic: A substance that is attracted to and readily mixes with water.

Hydrophobic: A substance that is repelled by and does not mix with water.

Hydropower: Energy produced from capturing moving water.

Hydrotropism: The tendency of roots to grow toward a water source.

Hypertonic solution: A solution with a higher concentration of materials than a cell immersed in the solution.

Hypha: Slender, cottony filaments making up the body of multicellular fungi. (Plural: hyphae)

Hypothesis: An idea in the form of a statement that can be tested by observation and/or experiment.

Hypotonic solution: A solution with a lower concentration of materials than a cell immersed in the solution.

Igneous rock: Rock formed from the cooling and hardening of magma.

Immiscible: Incapable of being mixed.

Imperfect flower: Flowers that have only the male reproductive organ (stamen) or the female reproductive organs (pistil).

Impermeable: Not allowing substances to pass through.

Impurities: Chemicals or other pollutants in water.

Inclined plane: A simple machine with no moving parts; a slanted surface.

Incomplete metamorphosis: Metamorphosis in which a nymph form gradually becomes an adult through molting.

Independent variable: The variable in an experiment that determines the final result of the experiment.

Indicator: Pigments that change color when they come into contact with acidic or basic solutions.

Inertia: The tendency of an object to continue in its state of motion.

Infrared radiation: Electromagnetic radiation of a wavelength shorter than radio waves but longer than visible light that takes the form of heat.

Inner core: Very dense, solid center of Earth.

Inorganic: Not containing carbon; not derived from a living organism.

Insect: A six-legged invertebrate whose body has three segments.

Insoluble: A substance that cannot be dissolved in some other substance.

Insulated wire: Electrical wire coated with a non-conducting material such as plastic.

Insulation: A material that is a poor conductor of heat or electricity.

Insulator: A material through which little or no electrical current or heat energy will flow.

Interference fringes: Bands of color that fan out around an object.

Internal skeleton: An animal that has a backbone.

Invertebrate: An animal that lacks a backbone or internal skeleton.

Ion: An atom or groups of atoms that carry an electrical charge—either positive or negative—as a result of losing or gaining one or more electrons.

Ion tail: One of two types of tails a comet may have, it is composed mainly of charged particles and it points away from the Sun.

Ionic conduction: The flow of an electrical current by the movement of charged particles, or ions.

Isobars: Continuous lines that connect areas with the same air pressure.

Isotonic solutions: Two solutions that have the same concentration of solute particles and therefore the same osmotic pressure.

Jawless fish: The smallest group of fishes, who lacks a jaw.

Kinetic energy: The energy of an object or system due to its motion.

Kingdom: One of the five classifications in the widely accepted classification system that designates all living organisms into animals, plants, fungi, protists, and monerans.

Labyrinth: A lung-like organ located above the gills that allows the fish to breathe in oxygen from the air.

Lactobacilli: A strain of bacteria.

Landfill: A method of disposing of waste materials by placing them in a depression in the ground or piling them in a mound. In a sanitary landfill, the daily deposits of waste materials are covered with a layer of soil.

Larva: Immature form (wormlike in insects; fishlike in amphibians) of an organism capable of surviving on its own. A larva does not resemble the parent and must go through metamorphosis, or change, to reach its adult stage.

Lava: Molten rock that occurs at the surface of Earth, usually through volcanic eruptions.

Lava cave: A cave formed from the flow of lava streaming over solid matter.

Leach: The movement of dissolved minerals or chemicals with water as it percolates, or oozes, downward through the soil.

Leaching: The movement of dissolved chemicals with water that is percolating, or oozing, downward through the soil.

Leavening agent: A substance used to make foods like dough and batter to rise.

Leeward: The side away from the wind or flow direction.

Lens: A piece of transparent material with two curved surfaces that bend rays of light passing through it.

Lichen: An organism composed of a fungus and a photosynthetic organism in a symbiotic relationship.

Lift: Upward force on the wings of an aircraft created by differences in air pressure on top of and underneath the wings.

Ligaments: Tough, fibrous tissue connecting bones.

Light: A form of energy that travels in waves.

Light-year: Distance light travels in one year in the vacuum of space, roughly 5.9 trillion miles (9.5 trillion kilometers).

The Local Group: A cluster of thirty galaxies, including the Milky Way, pulled together by gravity.

Long-term memory: The last category of memory in which memories are stored away and can last for years.

Low air pressure: An area where the air is warmer and less dense, and the air pressure is lower than normal.

Luminescent: Producing light through a chemical process.

Luminol: A compound used to detect blood.

Lunar eclipse: An eclipse that occurs when Earth passes between the Sun and the Moon, casting a shadow on the Moon.

Luster: A glow of reflected light; a sheen.

Machine: Any device that makes work easier by providing a mechanical advantage.

Macrominerals: Minerals needed in relatively large quantities.

Macroorganisms: Visible organisms that aid in breaking down organic matter.

Magma: Molten rock deep within Earth that consists of liquids, gases, and particles of rocks and crystals. Magma underlies areas of volcanic activity and at Earth's surface is called lava.

Magma chambers: Pools of bubbling liquid rock that are the source of energy causing volcanoes to be active.

Magma surge: A swell or rising wave of magma caused by the movement and friction of tectonic plates, which heats and melts rock, adding to the magma and its force.

Magnet: A material that attracts other like materials, especially metals.

Magnetic circuit: A series of magnetic domains aligned in the same direction.

Magnetic field: The space around an electric current or a magnet in which a magnetic force can be observed.

Magnetism: A fundamental force in nature caused by the motion of electrons in an atom.

Maillard reaction: A reaction caused by heat and sugars and resulting in foods browning and flavors.

Mammals: Animals that have a backbone, are warm blooded, have mammary glands to feed their young and have or are born with hair.

Mantle: Thick dense layer of rock that underlies Earth's crust and overlies the core; also soft tissue that is located between the shell and an animal's inner organs. The mantle produces the calcium carbonate substance that create the shell of the animal.

Manure: The waste matter of animals.

Mass: Measure of the total amount of matter in an object. Also, an object's quantity of matter as shown by its gravitational pull on another object.

Matter: Anything that has mass and takes up space.

Meandering river: A lowland river that twists and turns along its route to the sea.

Medium: A material that contains the nutrients required for a particular microorganism to grow.

Melting point: The temperature at which a substance changes from a solid to a liquid.

Memory: The process of retaining and recalling past events and experiences.

Meniscus: The curved surface of a column of liquid.

Metabolism: The process by which living organisms convert food into energy and waste products.

Metamorphic rock: Rock formed by transformation of pre-existing rock through changes in temperature and pressure.

Metamorphosis: Transformation of an immature animal into an adult.

Meteor: An object from space that becomes glowing hot when it passes into Earth's atmosphere; also called shooting star.

Meteor shower: A group of meteors that occurs when Earth's orbit intersects the orbit of a meteor stream.

Meteorites: A meteor that is large enough to survive its passage through the atmosphere and hit the ground.

Meteoroid: A piece of debris that is traveling in space.

Meteorologist: Scientist who studies the weather and the atmosphere.

Microbiology: Branch of biology dealing with microscopic forms of life.

Microclimate: A unique climate that exists only in a small, localized area.

Microorganisms: Living organisms so small that they can be seen only with the aid of a microscope.

Micropyle: Seed opening that enables water to enter easily.

Microvilli: The extension of each taste cell that pokes through the taste pore and first senses the chemicals.

Milky Way: The galaxy in which our solar system is located.

Mimicry: A characteristic in which an animal is protected against predators by resembling another, more distasteful animal.

Mineral: An inorganic substance found in nature with a definite chemical composition and structure. As a nutrient, it helps build bones and soft tissues and regulates body functions.

Mixture: A combination of two or more substances that are not chemically combined with each other and that can exist in any proportion.

Mnemonics: Techniques to improve memory.

Mold: In paleontology, the fossil formed when acidic water dissolves a shell or bone around which sand or mud has already hardened.

Molecule: The smallest particle of a substance that retains all the properties of the substance and is composed of one or more atoms.

Mollusk: An invertebrate animal usually enclosed in a shell, the largest group of shelled animals.

Molting: A process by which an animal sheds its skin or shell.

Monocot: Plants with a single embryonic leaf at germination.

Monomer: A small molecule that can be combined with itself many times over to make a large molecule, the polymer.

Moraine: Mass of boulders, stones, and other rock debris carried along and deposited by a glacier.

Mordant: A substance that fixes the dye to the material.

Mountain: A landform that stands well above its surroundings; higher than a hill.

Mucus: A thick, slippery substance that serves as a protective lubricant coating in passages of the body that communicate with the air.

Multicellular: Living things with many cells joined together.

Muscle fibers: Stacks of long, thin cells that make up muscle; there are three types of muscle fiber: skeletal, cardiac, and smooth.

Mycelium: In fungi, the mass of threadlike, branching hyphae.

Nanobots: A nanoscale robot.

Nanometer: A unit of length; this measurement is equal to one-billionth of a meter.

Nanotechnology: Technology that involves working and developing technologies on the nanometer (atomic and molecular) scale.

Nansen bottles: Self-closing containers with thermometers that draw in water at different depths.

Nebula: Bright or dark cloud, often composed of gases and dust, hovering in the space between the stars.

Nectar: A sweet liquid, found inside a flower, that attracts pollinators.

Neutralization: A chemical reaction in which the mixing of an acidic solution with a basic (alkaline) solution results in a solution that has the properties of neither an acid nor a base.

Neutron: A subatomic particle with a mass of about one atomic mass unit and no electrical charge that is found in the nucleus of an atom.

Newtonian fluid: A fluid that follows certain properties, such as the viscosity remains constant at a given temperature.

Niche: The specific location and place in the food chain that an organism occupies in its environment.

Noble gases: Also known as inert or rare gases; the elements argon, helium, krypton, neon, radon, and xenon, which are nonreactive gases and form few compounds with other elements.

Non-Newtonian fluid: A fluid whose property do not follow Newtonian properties, such as viscosity can vary based on the stress.

Nonpoint source: An unidentified source of pollution, which may actually be a number of sources.

Nucleation: The process by which crystals start growing.

Nucleotide: The basic unit of a nucleic acid. It consists of a simple sugar, a phosphate group, and a nitrogen-containing base. (Pronounced noo-KLEE-uh-tide.)

Nucleus: The central part of the cell that contains the DNA; the central core of an atom, consisting of protons and (usually) neutrons.

Nutrient: A substance needed by an organism in order for it to survive, grow, and develop.

Nutrition: The study of the food nutrients an organism needs in order to maintain well-being.

Nymph: An immature form in the life cycle of insects that go through an incomplete metamorphosis.

Objective lens: In a refracting telescope, the lens farthest away from the eye that collects the light.

Oceanographer: A person who studies the chemistry of the oceans, as well as their currents, marine life, and the ocean floor.

Oceanography: The study of the chemistry of the oceans, as well as their currents, marine life, and the ocean bed.

Olfactory: Relating to the sense of smell.

Olfactory bulb: The part of the brain that processes olfactory (smell) information.

Olfactory epithelium: The patch of mucous membrane at the top of the nasal cavity that contains the olfactory (smell) nerve cells.

Olfactory receptor cells: Nerve cells in the olfactory epithelium that detect odors and transmit the information to the brain.

Oort cloud: Region of space beyond our solar system that theoretically contains about one trillion inactive comets.

Optics: The study of the nature of light and its properties.

Orbit: The path followed by a body (such as a planet) in its travel around another body (such as the Sun).

Organelle: A membrane-enclosed structure that performs a specific function within a cell.

Organic: Containing carbon; also referring to materials that are derived from living organisms.

Oscillation: A repeated back-and-forth movement.

Osmosis: The movement of fluids and substances dissolved in liquids across a semipermeable membrane from an area of its greater concentration to an area of its lesser concentration until all substances involved reach a balance.

Outer core: A liquid core that surrounds Earth's solid inner core; made mostly of iron.

Ovary: In a plant, the base part of the pistil that bears ovules and develops into a fruit.

Ovule: Structure within the ovary that develops into a seed after fertilization.

Oxidation: A chemical reaction in which oxygen reacts with some other substance and in which ions, atoms, or molecules lose electrons.

Oxidation state: The sum of an atom's positive and negative charges.

Oxidation-reduction reaction: A chemical reaction in which one substance loses one or more electrons and the other substance gains one or more electrons.

Oxidizing agent: A chemical substance that gives up oxygen or takes on electrons from another substance.

Paleontologist: Scientist who studies the life of past geological periods as known from fossil remains.

Papain: An enzyme obtained from the fruit of the papaya used as a meat tenderizer, as a drug to clean cuts and wounds, and as a digestive aid for stomach disorders.

Papillae: The raised bumps on the tongue that contain the taste buds.

Parent material: The underlying rock from which soil forms.

Partial solar/lunar eclipse: An eclipse in which our view of the Sun/Moon is only partially blocked.

Particulate matter: Solid matter in the form of tiny particles in the atmosphere. (Pronounced par-TIK-you-let.)

Passive solar energy system: A solar energy system in which the heat of the Sun is captured, used, and stored by means of the design of a building and the materials from which it is made.

Pasteurization: The process of slow heating that kills bacteria and other microorganisms.

Peaks: The points at which the energy in a wave is maximum.

Pectin: A natural carbohydrate found in fruits and vegetables.

Pectoral fin: Pair of fins located on the side of a fish, used for steering.

Pedigree: A diagram that illustrates the pattern of inheritance of a genetic trait in a family.

Pelvic fin: Pair of fins located toward the belly of a fish, used for stability.

Pendulum: A free-swinging weight, usually consisting of a heavy object attached to the end of a long rod or string, suspended from a fixed point.

Penicillin: A mold from the fungi group of microorganisms; used as an antibiotic.

Pepsin: Digestive enzyme that breaks down protein.

Percolate: To pass through a permeable substance.

Perfect flower: Flowers that have both male and female reproductive organs.

Period: A horizontal row in the periodic table.

Periodic table: A chart organizing elements by atomic number and chemical properties into groups and periods.

Permeable: Having pores that permit a liquid or a gas to pass through.

Permineralization: A form of preservation in which mineral matter has filled in the inner and outer spaces of the cell.

Pest: Any living thing that is unwanted by humans or causes injury and disease to crops and other growth.

Pesticide: Substance used to reduce the abundance of pests.

Petal: Leafy structure of a flower just inside the sepals; they are often brightly colored and have many different shapes.

Petrifaction: Process of turning organic material into rock by the replacement of that material with minerals.

pH: A measure of the acidity or alkalinity of a solution referring to the concentration of hydrogen ions present in a liter of a given fluid. The pH scale ranges from 0 (greatest concentration of hydrogen ions and therefore most acidic) to 14 (least concentration of hydrogen ions and therefore most alkaline), with 7 representing a neutral solution, such as pure water.

Pharmacology: The science dealing with the properties, reactions, and therapeutic values of drugs.

Phases: Changes in the portion of the Moon's surface that is illuminated by light from the Sun as the Moon revolves around Earth.

Phloem: The plant tissue that carries dissolved nutrients through the plant.

Phosphorescence: The emission of visible light from an object when the object is bombarded with electromagnetic radiation, such as ultraviolet rays. The object stores part of the radiation energy and the emission of visible light continues for a period ranging from a fraction of a second to several days after the radiation source has been removed.

Photoelectric effect: The phenomenon in which light falling upon certain metals stimulates the emission of electrons and changes light into electricity.

Photosynthesis: Chemical process by which plants containing chlorophyll use sunlight to manufacture their own food by converting carbon dioxide and water to carbohydrates, releasing oxygen as a by-product.

Phototropism: The tendency of a plant to grow toward a source of light.

Photovoltaic cells: A device made of silicon that converts sunlight into electricity.

Physical change: A change in which the substance keeps its molecular identity, such as a piece of chalk that has been ground up.

Physical property: A characteristic that you can detect with your senses, such as color and shape.

Physiologist: A scientist who studies the functions and processes of living organisms.

Phytoplankton: Microscopic aquatic plants that live suspended in the water.

Pigment: A substance that displays a color because of the wavelengths of light that it reflects.

Pili: Short projections that assist bacteria in attaching to tissues.

Pistil: Female reproductive organ of flowers that is composed of the stigma, style, and ovary.

Pitch: A property of a sound, determined by its frequency; the highness or lowness of a sound.

Plant extract: The juice or liquid essence obtained from a plant by squeezing or mashing it.

Plasmolysis: Occurs in walled cells in which cytoplasm, the semifluid substance inside a cell, shrivels and the membrane pulls away from the cell wall when the vacuole loses water.

Plates: Large regions of Earth's surface, composed of the crust and uppermost mantle, which move about, forming many of Earth's major geologic surface features.

Platform: The horizontal surface of a bridge on which traffic travels.

Pnematocysts: Stinging cells.

Point source: An identified source of pollution.

Pollen: Dust-like grains or particles produced by a plant that contain male sex cells.

Pollinate: The transfer of pollen from the male reproductive organs to the female reproductive organs of plants.

Pollination: Transfer of pollen from the male reproductive organs to the female reproductive organs of plants.

Pollinator: Any animal, such as an insect or bird, that transfers the pollen from one flower to another.

Pollution: The contamination of the natural environment, usually through human activity.

Polymer: Chemical compound formed of simple molecules (known as monomers) linked with themselves many times over.

Polymerization: The bonding of two or more monomers to form a polymer.

Polyvinyl acetate: A type of polymer that is the main ingredient of white glues.

Pore: An opening or space.

Potential energy: The energy of an object or system due to its position.

Precipitation: Any form of water that falls to Earth, such as rain, snow, or sleet.

Predator: An animal that hunts another animal for food.

Preservative: An additive used to keep food from spoiling.

Primary colors: The three colors red, green, and blue; when combined evenly they produce white light and by combining varying amounts can produce the range of colors.

Prism: A piece of transparent material with a triangular cross-section. When light passes through it, it causes different colors to bend different amounts, thus separating them into a rainbow of colors.

Probe: The terminal of a voltmeter, used to connect the voltmeter to a circuit.

Producer: An organism that can manufacture its own food from nonliving materials and an external energy source, usually by photosynthesis.

Product: A compound that is formed as a result of a chemical reaction.

Prokaryote: A cell without a true nucleus, such as a bacterium.

Prominences: Masses of glowing gas, mainly hydrogen, that rise from the Sun's surface like flames.

Propeller: Radiating blades mounted on a rapidly rotating shaft, which moves aircraft forward.

Protein: A complex chemical compound consisting of many amino acids attached to each other that are essential to the structure and functioning of all living cells.

Protists: Members of the kingdom Protista, primarily single-celled organisms that are not plants or animals.

Proton: A subatomic particle with a single positive charge that is found in the nucleus of an atom.

Protozoa: Single-celled animal-like microscopic organisms that live by taking in food rather than making it by photosynthesis. They must live in the presence of water.

Pulley: A simple machine made of a cord wrapped around a wheel.

Pupa: The insect stage of development between the larva and adult in insects that go through complete metamorphosis.

Radiation: Energy transmitted in the form of electromagnetic waves or subatomic particles.

Radicule: Seed's root system.

Radio wave: Longest form of electromagnetic radiation, measuring up to 6 miles (9.6 kilometers) from peak to peak.

Radioisotope dating: A technique used to date fossils, based on the decay rate of known radioactive elements.

Radiosonde balloons: Instruments for collecting data in the atmosphere and then transmitting that data back to Earth by means of radio waves.

Radon: A radioactive gas located in the ground; invisible and odorless, radon is a health hazard when it accumulates to high levels inside homes and other structures where it is breathed.

Rain shadow: Region on the side of the mountain that receives less rainfall than the area windward of the mountain.

Rancidity: Having the condition when food has a disagreeable odor or taste from decomposing oils or fats.

Reactant: A compound present at the beginning of a chemical reaction.

Reaction: Response to an action prompted by stimulus.

Recessive gene: A gene that produces a certain characteristic only two both copies (alleles) of the gene are present.

Recycling: The use of waste materials, also known as secondary materials or recyclables, to produce new products.

Redshift: The lengthening of the frequency of light waves toward the red end of the visible light spectrum as they travel away from an observer; most commonly used to describe movement of stars away from Earth.

Reduction: A process in which a chemical substance gives off oxygen or takes on electrons.

Reed: A tall woody perennial grass that has a hollow stem.

Reflection: The bouncing of light rays in a regular pattern off the surface of an object.

Reflector telescope: A telescope that directs light from an opening at one end to a concave mirror at the far end, which reflects the light back to a smaller mirror that directs it to an eyepiece on the side of the tube.

Refraction: The bending of light rays as they pass at an angle from one transparent or clear medium into a second one of different density.

Refractor telescope: A telescope that directs light through a glass lens, which bends the light waves and brings them to a focus at an eyepiece that acts as a magnifying glass.

Relative age: The age of an object expressed in relation to another like object, such as earlier or later.

Relative density: The density of one material compared to another.

Rennin: Enzyme used in making cheese.

Resistance: A partial or complete limiting of the flow of electrical current through a material. The common unit of measure is the ohm.

Respiration: The physical process that supplies oxygen to living cells and the chemical reactions that take place inside the cells.

Resultant: A force that results from the combined action of two other forces.

Retina: The light-sensitive part of the eyeball that receives images and transmits visual impulses through the optic nerve to the brain.

Ribosome: A protein composed of two subunits that functions in protein synthesis (creation).

Rigidity: The amount an object will deflect when supporting a weight. The less it deflects for a given amount of weight, the greater its rigidity.

River: A main course of water into which many other smaller bodies of water flow.

Rock: Naturally occurring solid mixture of minerals.

Rods: Cells in the retina that are sensitive to degrees of light and movement.

Root hairs: Fine, hair-like extensions from the plant's root.

Rotate: To turn around on an axis or center.

Runoff: Water that does not soak into the ground or evaporate, but flows across the surface of the ground.

Salinity: The amount of salts dissolved in water.

Saliva: Watery mixture with chemicals that lubricates chewed food.

Sand: Granular portion of soil composed of the largest soil particles.

Sapwood: The outer wood in a tree, which is usually a lighter color.

Saturated: In referring to solutions, a solution that contains the maximum amount of solute for a given amount of solvent at a given temperature.

Saturation: The intensity of a color.

Scanning tunneling microscope: A microscope that can show images of surfaces at the atomic level by scanning a probe over a surface.

Scientific method: Collecting evidence and arriving at a conclusion under carefully controlled conditions.

Screw: A simple machine; an inclined plane wrapped around a cylinder.

Scurvy: A disease caused by a deficiency of vitamin C, which causes a weakening of connective tissue in bone and muscle.

Sea cave: A cave in sea cliffs, formed most commonly by waves eroding the rock.

Second law of motion (Newton's): The force exerted on an object is proportional to the mass of the object times the acceleration produced by the force.

Sediment: Sand, silt, clay, rock, gravel, mud, or other matter that has been transported by flowing water.

Sedimentary rock: Rock formed from compressed and solidified layers of organic or inorganic matter.

Sedimentation: A process during which gravity pulls particles out of a liquid.

Seed crystal: Small form of a crystalline structure that has all the facets of a complete new crystal contained in it.

Seedling: A small plant just starting to grow into its mature form.

Seismic belt: Boundaries where Earth's plates meet.

Seismic waves: Vibrations in rock and soil that transfer the force of an earthquake from the focus into the surrounding area.

Seismograph: A device that detects and records vibrations of the ground.

Seismology: The study and measurement of earthquakes.

Seismometer: A seismograph that measures the movement of the ground.

Self-pollination: The process in which pollen from one part of a plant fertilizes ovules on another part of the same plant.

Semipermeable membrane: A thin barrier between two solutions that permits only certain components of the solutions, usually the solvent, to pass through.

Sensory memory: Memory that the brain retains for a few seconds.

Sepal: The outermost part of a flower; typically leaflike and green.

Sexual reproduction: A reproductive process that involves the union of two individuals in the exchange of genetic material.

Shear stress: An applied force to a give area.

Shell: A region of space around the center of the atom in which electrons are located; also, a hard outer covering that protects an animal living inside.

Short-term memory: Also known as working memory, this memory was transferred here from sensory memory.

Sidereal day: The time it takes for a particular star to travel around and reach the same position in the sky; about four minutes shorter than the average solar day.

Silt: Medium-sized soil particles.

Simple machine: Any of the basic structures that provide a mechanical advantage and have no or few moving parts.

Smog: A form of air pollution produced when moisture in the air combines and reacts with the products of fossil fuel combustion. Smog is characterized by hazy skies and a tendency to cause respiratory problems among humans.

Softwood: Wood from coniferous trees, which usually remain green all year.

Soil: The upper layer of Earth that contains nutrients for plants and organisms; a mixture of mineral matter, organic matter, air, and water.

Soil horizon: An identifiable soil layer due to color, structure, and/or texture.

Soil profile: Combined soil horizons or layers.

Solar collector: A device that absorbs sunlight and collects solar heat.

Solar day: Called a day, the time between each arrival of the Sun at its highest point.

Solar eclipse: An eclipse that occurs when the Moon passes between Earth and the Sun, casting a shadow on Earth.

Solar energy: Any form of electromagnetic radiation that is emitted by the Sun.

Solubility: The tendency of a substance to dissolve in some other substance.

Soluble: A substance that can be dissolved in some other substance.

Solute: The substance that is dissolved to make a solution and exists in the least amount in a solution, for example sugar in sugar water.

Solution: A mixture of two or more substances that appears to be uniform throughout except on a molecular level.

Solvent: The major component of a solution or the liquid in which some other component is dissolved, for example water in sugar water.

Specific gravity: The ratio of the density of a substance to the density of pure water.

Specific heat capacity: The energy required to raise the temperature of 1 kilogram of the substance by 1 degree Celsius.

Speleologist: One who studies caves.

Speleology: Scientific study of caves and their plant and animal life.

Spelunkers: Also called cavers, people who explore caves for a hobby.

Spiracles: The openings on an insects side where air enters.

Spoilage: The condition when food has taken on an undesirable color, odor, or texture.

Spore: A small, usually one-celled, reproductive body that is capable of growing into a new organism.

Stalactite: Cylindrical or icicle-shaped mineral deposit projecting downward from the roof of a cave. (Pronounced sta-LACK-tite.)

Stalagmite: Cylindrical or icicle-shaped mineral deposit projecting upward from the floor of a cave. (Pronounced sta-LAG-mite.)

Stamen: Male reproductive organ of flowers that is composed of the anther and filament.

Standard: A base for comparison.

Star: A vast clump of hydrogen gas and dust that produces great energy through fusion reactions at its core.

Static electricity: A form of electricity produced by friction in which the electric charge does not flow in a current but stays in one place.

Stigma: Top part of the pistil upon which pollen lands and receives the male pollen grains during fertilization.

Stomata: Pores in the epidermis (surface) of leaves.

Storm: An extreme atmospheric disturbance, associated with strong damaging winds, and often with thunder and lightning.

Storm chasers: People who track and seek out storms, often tornadoes.

Stratification: Layers according to density; applies to fluids.

Streak: The color of the dust left when a mineral is rubbed across a rough surface.

Style: Stalk of the pistil that connects the stigma to the ovary.

Subatomic: Smaller than an atom. It usually refers to particles that make up an atom, such as protons, neutrons, and electrons.

Sublime: The process of changing a solid into a vapor without passing through the liquid phase.

Substrate: The substance on which an enzyme operates in a chemical reaction.

Succulent: Plants that live in dry environments and have water storage tissue.

Sundial: A device that uses the position of the Sun to indicate time.

Supersaturated: Solution that is more highly concentrated than is normally possible under given conditions of temperature and pressure.

Supertaster: A person who is extremely sensitive to specific tastes due to a greater number of taste buds.

Supplements: A substance intended to enhance the diet.

Surface area: The total area of the outside of an object; the area of a body of water that is exposed to the air.

Surface tension: The attractive force of molecules to each other on the surface of a liquid.

Surface water: Water in lakes, rivers, ponds, and streams.

Suspension: A temporary mixture of a solid in a gas or liquid from which the solid will eventually settle out.

Swim bladder: Located above the stomach, takes in air when the fish wants to move upwards and releases air when the fish wants to move downwards.

Symbiosis: A pattern in which two or more organisms live in close connection with each other, often to the benefit of both or all organisms.

Synthesis reaction: A chemical reaction in which two or more substances combine to form a new substance.

Synthesize: To make something artificially, in a laboratory or chemical plant, that is generally not found in nature.

Synthetic: A substance that is synthesized, or manufactured, in a laboratory; not naturally occurring.

Synthetic crystals: Artificial or manmade crystals.

Taiga: A large land biome mostly dominated by coniferous trees.

Taste buds: Groups of taste cells located on the papillae that recognize the different tastes.

Taste pore: The opening at the top of the taste bud from which chemicals reach the taste cells.

Tectonic: Relating to the forces and structures of the outer shell of Earth.

Tectonic plates: Huge flat rocks that form Earth's crust.

Telescope: A tube with lenses or mirrors that collect, transmit, and focus light.

Temperate: Mild or moderate weather conditions.

Temperature: The measure of the average energy of the molecules in a substance.

Tendon: Tough, fibrous connective tissue that attaches muscle to bone.

Tensile strength: The force needed to stretch a material until it breaks.

Terminal: A connection in an electric circuit; usually a connection on a source of electric energy such as a battery.

Terracing: A series of horizontal ridges made in a hillside to reduce erosion.

Testa: A tough outer layer that protects the embryo and endosperm of a seed from damage.

Theory of special relativity: Theory put forth by Albert Einstein that time is not absolute, but it is relative according to the speed of the observer's frame of reference.

Thermal conductivity: A number representing a material's ability to conduct heat.

Thermal energy: Kinetic energy caused by the movement of molecules due to temperature.

Thermal inversion: A region in which the warmer air lies above the colder air; can cause smog to worsen.

Thermal pollution: The discharge of heated water from industrial processes that can kill or injure water life.

Thiamine: A vitamin of the B complex that is essential to normal metabolism and nerve function.

Thigmotropism: The tendency for a plant to grow toward a surface it touches.

Third law of motion (Newton's): For every action there is an equal and opposite reaction.

Thorax: The middle segment of an insect body; the legs and wings are connected to the thorax.

Tides: The cyclic rise and fall of seawater.

Titration: A procedure in which an acid and a base are slowly mixed to achieve a neutral substance.

Topsoil: The uppermost layers of soil containing an abundant supply of decomposed organic material to supply plants with nutrients.

Tornado: A violently rotating, narrow column of air in contact with the ground and usually extending from a cumulonimbus cloud.

Total solar/lunar eclipse: An eclipse in which our view of the Sun/Moon is totally blocked.

Toxic: Poisonous.

Trace element: A chemical element present in minute quantities.

Trace minerals: Minerals needed in relatively small quantities.

Translucent: Permits the passage of light.

Transpiration: Evaporation of water in the form of water vapor from the stomata on the surfaces of leaves and stems of plants.

Troglobite: An animal that lives in a cave and is unable to live outside of one.

Troglophile: An animal that lives the majority of its life cycle in a cave but is also able to live outside of the cave.

Trogloxene: An animal that spends only part of its life cycle in a cave and returns periodically to the cave.

Tropism: The growth or movement of a plant toward or away from a stimulus.

Troposphere: The lowest layer of Earth's atmosphere, ranging to an altitude of about 9 miles (15 km) above Earth's surface.

Trough: The lowest point of a wave. (Pronounced trawf.)

Tsunami: A large wave of water caused by an underwater earthquake.

Tuber: An underground, starch-storing stem, such as a potato.

Tundra: A treeless, frozen biome with low-lying plants.

Turbine: A spinning device used to transform mechanical power from energy into electrical energy.

Turbulence: Air disturbance that affects an aircraft's flight.

Turgor pressure: The force that is exerted on a plant's cell wall by the water within the cell.

Tyndall effect: The effect achieved when colloidal particles reflect a beam of light, making it visible when shined through such a mixture.

Ultraviolet: Electromagnetic radiation (energy) of a wavelength just shorter than the violet (shortest wavelength) end of the visible light spectrum and thus with higher energy than the visible light.

Unconfined aquifer: An aquifer under a layer of permeable rock and soil.

Unicellular: Living things that have one cell. Protozoans are unicellular, for example.

Unit cell: The basic unit of the crystalline structure.

Universal law of gravity: The law of physics that defines the constancy of the force of gravity between two bodies.

Updraft: Warm, moist air that moves away from the ground.

Upwelling: The process by which lower-level, nutrient-rich waters rise upward to the ocean's surface.

Vacuole: An enclosed, space-filling sac within plant cells containing mostly water and providing structural support for the cell.

Van der Waals' force: An attractive force between two molecules based on the positive and negative side of the molecule.

Variable: Something that can affect the results of an experiment.

Vegetative propagation: A form of asexual reproduction in which plants are produced that are genetically identical to the parent.

Velocity: The rate at which the position of an object changes with time, including both the speed and the direction.

Veneer: Thin slices of wood.

Viable: The capability of developing or growing under favorable conditions.

Vibration: A regular, back-and-forth motion of molecules in the air.

Viscosity: The measure of a fluid's resistance to flow; its flowability.

Visible spectrum: The range of individual wavelengths of radiation visible to the human eye when white light is broken into its component colors as it passes through a prism or by some other means.

Vitamin: A complex organic compound found naturally in plants and animals that the body needs in small amounts for normal growth and activity.

Volatilization: The process by which a liquid changes (volatilizes) to a gas.

Volcano: A conical mountain or dome of lava, ash, and cinders that forms around a vent leading to molten rock deep within Earth.

Voltage: Also called potential difference; a measurement of the amount of electric energy stored in a mass of electric charges compared to the energy stored in some other mass of charges. The common unit of measure is the volt.

Voltmeter: An instrument for measuring the amperage, voltage, or resistance in an electrical circuit.

Volume: The amount of space occupied by a three-dimensional object; the amplitude or loudness of a sound.

Vortex: A rotating column of a fluid such as air or water.

Waste stream: The waste materials generated by the population of an area, or by a specific industrial process, and removed for disposal.

Water (hydrologic) cycle: The constant movement of water molecules on Earth as they rise into the atmosphere as water vapor, condense into droplets and fall to land or bodies of water, evaporate, and rise again.

Water clock: A device that uses the flow of water to measure time.

Water table: The level of the upper surface of groundwater.

Water vapor: Water in its gaseous state.

Water-soluble vitamins: Vitamins such as C and the B-complex vitamins that dissolve in the watery parts of plant and animal tissues.

Waterline: The highest point to which water rises on the hull of a ship. The portion of the hull below the waterline is under water.

Wave: A means of transmitting energy in which the peak energy occurs at a regular interval; the rise and fall of the ocean water.

Wavelength: The distance between the peak of a wave of light, heat, or other form of energy and the next corresponding peak.

Weather: The state of the troposphere at a particular time and place.

Weather forecasting: The scientific predictions of future weather patterns.

Weathered: Natural process that breaks down rocks and minerals at Earth's surface into simpler materials by physical (mechanical) or chemical means.

Wedge: A simple machine; a form of inclined plane.

Weight: The gravitational attraction of Earth on an object; the measure of the heaviness of an object.

Wet cell: A source of electricity that uses a liquid electrolyte.

Wetlands: Areas that are wet or covered with water for at least part of the year.

Wheel and axle: A simple machine; a larger wheel(s) fastened to a smaller cylinder, an axle, so that they turn together.

Work: The result of a force moving a mass a given distance. The greater the mass or the greater the distance, the greater the work involved.

Xanthophyll: Yellow pigment in plants.

Xerophytes: Plants that require little water to survive.

Xylem: Plant tissue consisting of elongated, thick-walled cells that transport water and mineral nutrients. (Pronounced ZY-lem.)

Yeast: A single-celled fungi that can be used to as a leavening agent.

Space Observation

People's fascination with space goes back hundreds of years to simple stargazing and trying to understand the heavens. Today's astronomers use a wealth of tools to study space. Most astronomers are involved in measuring things, such as the speed, distance, and mass of objects in the universe. Knowing these facts can lead to further knowledge, such as the object's origin or composition. To measure things astronomers use observations and laws of the universe.

Much of what we know about space comes from the study of light given off by objects in space. The change from observing objects with the naked eye to powerful instruments was one of the major advances in astronomy. Telescopes are one of the main tools astronomers use to gather light. Understanding the physical laws of how light and objects move also fueled astronomers' knowledge of the universe. Merging the visual data with calculations has led to awesome findings on stars, planets, galaxies, and solar systems that are far, far away.

Mountains on the Moon Peer through the right telescope on Earth and it is possible to view something in space that is a billion light years away—just one light year is about 5,865,696,000,000 miles (9,460,800,000,000 kilometers)! The telescope was the first ground-breaking tool used in astronomy. With the telescope, astronomers could study the motions of celestial objects that were previously undetectable.

The telescope was invented in the Netherlands in the early 1600s. Soon afterwards, Italian scientist Galileo Galilei (1564–1642) became the first person to use this new instrument to study the sky. He made a series of remarkable discoveries. Among his observations was that the Moon had mountains and craters on it and was not smooth as previously believed. He observed four bright objects orbiting or revolving around Jupiter, what is now known as Jupiter's moons. He also saw that the Sun

One of the largest optical telescopes in the world is the W. M. Keck telescope in Hawaii. It measures 33 feet (10 meters) in diameter. © ROGER RESSMEYER/ CORBIS.

The Hubble Space Telescope was launched into space in 1990 and has transmitted up-close views of celestial objects that are billions of light years away. UPI/BETTMANN.

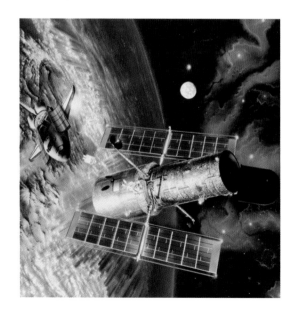

had spots, which rotated. His observations led him to conclude that objects rotated and that they revolved around other objects.

In modern day astronomers use telescopes of all shapes and sizes. Some are located on Earth and others sit in space. One of the most famous telescopes in space is the Hubble Space Telescope. The Hubble was launched into space in 1990 and has transmitted up-close views of celestial objects that are billions of light years away.

How they work In the way that they collect and magnify the light, telescopes make objects appear larger than they are. There are two basic types of telescopes: refractor telescopes and reflector telescopes. Each goes about enlarging an image in different ways. The amount of light a telescope can collect relates to the size of the lens or mirror used to gather light. Telescopes that have a larger lens or mirror will generally collect more light, and so will detect much fainter objects.

The Galileo-style of telescope is a refractor telescope and it uses two types of lenses to gather and bend or refract the light. The lens in the front of the telescope, the objective lens, gathers the light from the object. In a refracting telescope the objectives lens is a convex lens, a lens that is thicker in the middle and curves outward. Convex lenses make objects appear larger but blurry. This is the type of lens used in a magnifying glass.

In one type of refractor telescope the second lens, called the eyepiece lens, uses a smaller concave lens. A concave lens caves or curves inward in the middle. This focuses the light from the objective lens and magnifies it. A long tube, or series of tubes, holds the lenses in place at the correct distance from one another.

The reflector telescope uses mirrors instead of lenses to collect light. The primary mirror that collects and focuses the light is usually a concave mirror. The light reflects off the primary mirror to another mirror, which directs the light to the eyepiece. Each type of telescope has strengths and weaknesses. Most of the largest telescopes

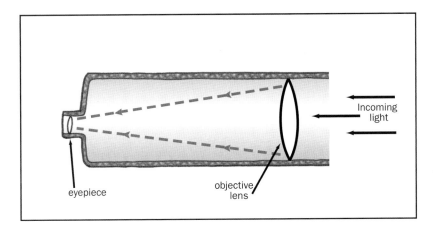

A refractor telescope uses two types of lenses to gather and bend or refract the light. GALE GROUP.

in the world are reflectors. Large mirrors cost less and are easier to support than lenses.

The deeper astronomers look into space, the farther back in time they are looking. It takes so long for light traveling through space to reach Earth that astronomers scanning the edges of the universe are seeing objects as they were billions of years ago.

Shifty light Astronomers take observations gathered from telescopes and apply their knowledge of how light travels to theorize on the past, present, and future behavior of objects in space. The Doppler effect or Doppler shift is one way that astronomers make measurements on the light they observe. Astronomers use the Doppler effect to calculate the speed of an object and its movements.

Although they are not visible, light energy travels in waves. Water and sound energy also travel in waves. A wave is a vibrational disturbance that

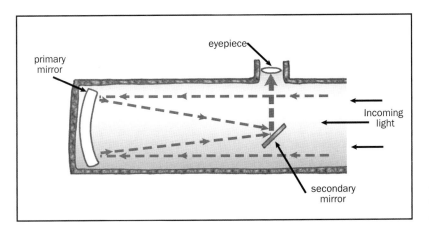

A reflector telescope uses mirrors instead of lenses to collect light. GALE GROUP.

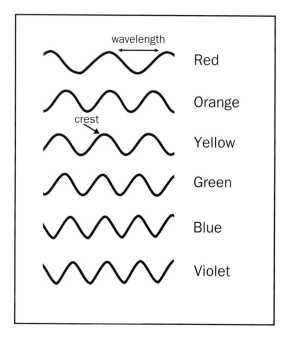

Light travels in waves; each color has its own wavelength.
GALE GROUP.

When an object approaches a person, waves bunch together and there is a blueshift; when an object recedes, waves spread out and there is a redshift.
GALE GROUP.

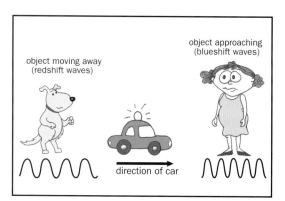

travels through a material or space. Light waves can travel through matter or a vacuum, such as space. Every wave has a high point called a crest. The distance from one crest to the next crest is called the wavelength.

Visible light is made up of seven basic colors—red, orange, yellow, green, blue, indigo, and violet. Each color has its own unique wavelength. For example, blue light waves are shorter than red light waves. The frequency is the number of waves that pass a point in space during any time interval. What a person sees as color is actually the frequency of the light. Because red has a longer wavelength, something red has a lower frequency than something blue.

The Doppler shift occurs because there is an apparent shift in the wavelength depending on whether an object is moving towards or away from the observer. As objects in space move away, or recede, from Earth, the wavelengths appear stretched or longer. This is called a redshift, because the light appears to have a lower frequency. If the object moves towards Earth, the wavelengths appear compressed or shorter. This makes the light appear to have a higher frequency and a blueshift occurs.

In a vacuum, such as space, all the wavelengths in light travel at one speed. If scientists know the amount and colors of light that an object gives off, they can measure the amount of color shift. Since the wavelength of each color is known, the color shift will determine the direction and speed of the object.

The Doppler effect can be used by astronomers to gather information about how fast stars, galaxies, and other astronomical objects move toward or away from Earth. Using the Doppler shift, astronomers calculated that the more distant galaxies are moving away from Earth more rapidly than the ones that are closer. This finding led to the theory that the universe is expanding, and to the origins of the solar system.

In the following two experiments you will explore the Doppler effect and telescopes.

WORDS TO KNOW

Blueshift: The shortening of the frequency of light waves toward the blue end of the visible light spectrum as they travel towards an observer; most commonly used to describe movement of stars towards Earth.

Concave lens: A lens that is thinner in the middle than at the edges.

Control experiment: A setup that is identical to the experiment, but is not affected by the variable that acts on the experimental group.

Convex lens: A lens that is thicker in the middle than at the edges.

Crest: The highest point reached by a wave.

Doppler effect: The change in wavelength and frequency (number of vibrations per second) of either light or sound as the source is moving either towards or away from the observer.

Focal length: The distance from the lens to the point where the light rays come together to a focus.

Frequency: The rate at which vibrations take place (number of times per second the motion is repeated), given in cycles per second or in hertz (Hz). Also, the number of waves that pass a given point in a given period of time.

Hypothesis: An idea in the form of a statement that can be tested by observation and/or experiment.

Objective lens: In a refracting telescope, the lens farthest away from the eye that collects the light.

Redshift: The lengthening of the frequency of light waves toward the red end of the visible light spectrum as they travel away from an observer; most commonly used to describe movement of stars away from Earth.

Reflector telescope: A telescope that directs light from an opening at one end to a concave mirror at the far end, which reflects the light back to a smaller mirror that directs it to an eyepiece on the side of the tube.

Refractor telescope: A telescope that directs light through a glass lens, which bends the light waves and brings them to a focus at an eyepiece that acts as a magnifying glass.

Telescope: A tube with lenses or mirrors that collect, transmit, and focus light.

Variable: Something that can affect the results of an experiment.

Wave: A motion in which energy and momentum are carried away from some source; a wave repeats itself in space and time with little or no change.

Wavelength: The distance between the crest of a wave of light, heat, or energy and the next corresponding crest.

EXPERIMENT 1

Telescopes: How do different combinations of lenses affect the image?

Purpose/Hypothesis Telescopes take advantage of the properties of light to enlarge and focus images. The basic design of a telescope aligns two lenses a set distance from each other. In general, the objective lens is relatively large in diameter so that it can gather light; the eyepiece is smaller and stronger. For this experiment, you will test different combinations of convex (curving outward) and concave (curving inward) lenses. If possible, try to gather several different strengths and sizes of lenses; the listed sizes are only suggestions. Check the Further Readings section for places to find lenses.

The objective lens will always be a convex lens. This lens should be larger in diameter and weaker than the eyepiece lens. The thinner a lens is in the center, the weaker it is. Use an eyepiece lens that is smaller and more powerful than the objective lens. You can determine a lens' power by its focal length, the distance required by the lens to bring the light to a focus. In general, as the focal length of a lens decreases, the power of the lens increases. You will use both a convex and a concave eyepiece lens. Cardboard, or construction paper, tubes that slide in and out from each other will hold the lenses. The distance between the two lenses should be about the sum of the focal lengths of the lenses.

Using a convex and a concave lens will produce a right-side-up image. Using two convex lenses will produce an upside-down image. (When viewing celestial objects, astronomers do not care that much whether the object is upside down or not.)

You can also calculate the magnification power of your telescope if you know the focal lengths of your lenses. The magnification power equals the focal length of the objective lens divided by the focal length of the eyepiece lens. For example, if the focal length of the objective lens is 50 centimeters, and the focal length of the eyepiece is 5 centimeters, your telescope will magnify the object ten times the actual size of the object. If the focal length of that same telescope had a focal length of 1 centimeter, the telescope would magnify the object 50 times its actual size.

Before you begin, make an educated guess about the outcome of this experiment based on your knowledge of telescopes. This educated guess, or prediction, is your hypothesis. A hypothesis should explain these things:

Powerful telescopes allow scientists to observe parts of space that the human eye never could, such as this cluster of thousands of stars. SPACE TELESCOPE SCIENCE INSTITUTE

- the topic of the experiment
- the variable you will change
- the variable you will measure
- what you expect to happen

A hypothesis should be brief, specific, and measurable. It must be something you can test through further investigation. Your experiment will prove or disprove whether your hypothesis is correct. Here is one possible hypothesis for this experiment: "Two convex lenses will produce a larger but blurrier image than a convex and a concave lens combination."

In this case, the variable you will change is the type of eyepiece lens. The variable you will measure is the size and sharpness of the image produced.

Level of Difficulty Moderate.

Materials Needed

1. 1 convex lens for the objective lens (can be about 2 to 4 inches [5 to 10 centimeters] in diameter, and over 500 millimeters in focal length). (Lenses are available from scientific supply houses and hobby stores. You could also try to find lenses around the house, such as from magnifying glasses or old eyeglasses, as well as asking an eyeglass store if they have any lenses they are going to discard.)
2. 1 convex lens for the eyepiece, smaller in diameter than the objective lens (can be 1 to 1.5 inches [2.5 to 3.5 centimeters] in diameter, focal length of less than 20 to 50 millimeters)
3. 1 concave lens for the eyepiece, (can be 1 to1.5 inches [2.5 to 3.5 centimeters] in diameter, focal length of less than 20 to 50 millimeters)
4. sturdy tape, such as masking tape
5. scissors
6. ruler
7. 2 cardboard tubes, one that slides inside the other: The tubes should be about the same size as the lenses. If you do not have tubes, you can roll up thick construction paper and tape to make them.

What Are the Variables?

Variables are anything that might affect the results of an experiment. Here are the main variables in this experiment:

- the thickness of the lens
- the size of the lens
- the curvature of the lens
- the distance between the lenses

In other words, the variables in this experiment are everything that might affect the magnified image. If you change more than one variable at the same time, you will not be able to tell which variable had the most effect on seeing the image.

8. helper
9. picture or news article to view
10. other concave and convex lenses of different sizes (optional)

Approximate Budget $15.

Timetable 1 hour.

Step-by-Step Instructions

1. Tape the picture or printed piece of paper on a wall.
2. Begin with the smaller, stronger convex lens to use as the eyepiece, and the larger, less powerful convex lens for the objective lens. Hold the objective lens towards the picture at arms length.
3. Hold the eyepiece near your eye, in front of the objective lens.
4. Move the eyepiece closer and farther away to the objective lens while focusing on the picture.
5. When the object is in focus, have your helper measure the distance between the two lenses. (If you know the focal length of your lenses, the distance of the tubes should about equal the sum of the focal lengths of the lenses.)
6. Place the smaller tube inside the larger tube. The tubes should fit snugly inside each other, with the inner tube able to slide. Extend the tubes and cut them so the combined length of the tubes is slightly greater than the distance between the lenses. If you are rolling tubes out of thick construction paper, make sure you roll the paper into tubes where the openings are roughly equal to the size of the lenses.
7. Tape the objective lens to the far end of the telescope, and the eyepiece lens to the near side.
8. Look at the picture through the telescope, sliding the tubes until the object comes into focus.
9. Note whether the image is right side up or inverted, and the relative size of the image.
10. Remove the eyepiece lens and repeat Steps 2 through 7 using the concave lens as the eyepiece.

Step 7: Tape the objective lens to the far end of the telescope, and the eyepiece lens to the near side. GALE GROUP.

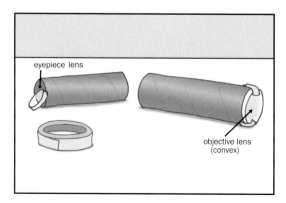

eyepiece lens

objective lens
(convex)

11. If you have other lenses of differing sizes and thickness, repeat the process to compare the results. Old glasses and magnifying glasses are a couple inexpensive sources for lenses. Record whether the lens is thicker or thinner than the one you already used when you note the results. If you know the focal lengths of the lenses, calculate the magnification power.

Summary of Results Was your hypothesis correct? What does sliding the inner tube in and out do to the image? If you tried using other lenses, how did these compare to the first set? Think about what change the eyepiece made in the appearance of the image once you placed it in front of the objective lens. If you want to continue the project to view celestial objects, go outside at night. Pick one particular light in the night sky and compare the image using each of the telescopes.

Change the Variables To change the variables in this experiment you can change the type of lens you use, the thickness of the lens, or the length between the lenses.

Modify the Experiment You can simplify this experiment by testing two magnifying glasses by themselves. Try to find two magnifying glasses that are different sizes. If you do not have two magnifying glasses, you can use other lenses around the house, such as eyeglasses. You need to make sure that one of the lenses is convex (thicker in the middle).

Find a well-lit object or picture that you can focus on. Hold the more powerful magnifying glass up close to your eye. This is the eyepiece lens. Hold the weaker magnifying glass between the eyepiece lens and the object. This lens should be convex. Move this lens back and forth until the object become clear and in focus. How does moving the lens change the look of the object? What happens when you take the lens away and only look through the eyepiece lens? Keep the eyepiece lens the same and experiment with convex lenses you can find that are different strengths. How does this magnify the object?

Troubleshooter's Guide

Below is a problem that may arise during this experiment, some possible causes, and some ways to remedy the problem.

Problem: The picture is blurry.

Possible cause: The distance between the two lenses may be too short or long. The distance should be equal to the sum of the focal lengths of the two lenses. Building a telescope involves some trial and error to get the correct distance and focus. Take careful measurements when holding the lenses up and try to gather several different lenses to investigate telescopes thoroughly.

What Are the Variables?

Variables are anything that might affect the results of an experiment. Here are the main variables in this experiment:

- the sound
- the speed of the object (in this case, the bicycle)
- the direction the object is moving—either towards or away from the person holding the microphone

In other words, the variables in this experiment are everything that might affect the sound of the noise maker. If you change more than one variable at the same time, you will not be able to tell which variable had the most effect on the distance and speed of the object.

EXPERIMENT 2

Doppler Effect: How can waves measure the distance and speed of objects?

Purpose/Hypothesis Astronomers use the Doppler effect to determine whether an object in space is moving towards or away from Earth and how fast it is moving. However, the Doppler effect was first discovered using sound waves, not light waves. The perception of both light and sound is from the waves emitted. Waves coming from an object moving away from an observer have a lower frequency than those from an object moving toward the observer.

In sound, pitch is determined by how many waves per second reach the ear. The more sound waves a person hears, the higher the pitch. When an object moves toward a person, it takes less and less time for each wave to reach the person. The waves crowd together. The person gets more waves per second and it results in an increase in pitch. When the sound moves away from a person, the waves spread out. A person gets fewer waves per second and the person hears a decrease in pitch.

In this experiment, you will determine how the Doppler effect relates to sound waves. You will record the sound of an alarm clock or noise-making device that is approaching and moving past you at varying speeds. You can then draw conclusions about the relative distance and speed of the object from listening to the increase and decrease in pitch.

Before you begin, make an educated guess about the outcome of this experiment based on your knowledge of the Doppler effect and waves. This educated guess, or prediction, is your hypothesis. A hypothesis should explain these things:

- the topic of the experiment
- the variable you will change
- the variable you will measure
- what you expect to happen

A hypothesis should be brief, specific, and measurable. It must be something you can test through further investigation. Your experiment will prove or disprove whether your hypothesis is correct. Here is one possible hypothesis for this experiment: "The object moving at the fastest speed will emit a pitch that quickly increases, then decreases, as it passes a stationary person."

In this case, the variable you will change is the speed of the moving object. The variable you will measure is the pitch of the sound.

Conducting a control experiment will help you isolate each variable and measure the changes in the dependent variable. Only one variable will change between the control and the experimental setup, and that is the movement of a noisy object. For the control in this experiment you will record the sound of an unmoving object, which will release its sound waves at a steady pitch.

Level of Difficulty Easy.

Materials Needed

- an assistant to help perform experiment
- bicycle
- wind-up alarm clock with continuous sound or other portable noise-making appliance, such as a kitchen timer
- tape recorder with microphone
- helper

Approximate Budget $0 (assuming that you have the tape recorder and bike).

Timetable 20 minutes.

Step-by-Step Instructions

1. For the control: Stand at the side of a low-traffic area with the tape recorder. Start the alarm clock or buzzer and record the noise as you hold it for about five to 10 seconds. When finished recording, say the word "control" into the microphone to identify what is happening on the tape.

> ### How to Experiment Safely
>
> Be careful when biking. Find an empty area with little or no traffic before you begin.

Step 3: Tape record the sound of the alarm clock as it approaches and moves past you.
GALE GROUP.

Troubleshooter's Guide

Below is a problem that may arise during this experiment, a possible cause, and a way to remedy the problem.

Problem: There was no difference between the "Slow" tone and the "Fast" tone.

Possible cause: The biker may not have been riding at a significantly slower speed that the fast speed. Try biking at two different speeds as you steadily count, matching your counting to each pedal rotation. Practice for the slow and fast speeds, then repeat the experiment.

2. One person will hold the tape recorder and one will ride the bike. Have your helper (or you) walk a set distance away with the tape recorder; when the biker is ready to ride, he or she should turn the alarm clock or buzzer on.

3. The person at the side of the road begins tape recording, as the biker slowly rides the bike past the tape recorder. The biker should keep at a steady, slow pace, by counting the rotations of each pedal.

4. Say the word "Slow" into the microphone after the bike stops.

5. Repeat the bike ride, returning to the set distance, this time riding at a steady quick pace past the tape recorder with the alarm clock on.

6. Say the word "Fast" into the microphone after the bike stops.

7. Turn off the noise and listen to the tape recordings.

Summary of Results Write a brief description of each recording. How did the control sound compare to the fast sound? Did you hear the sound increasing in pitch? By using the data on both the fast and slow sounds, and the set distance, what conclusions can you draw on the relative speed at which each object was traveling? How does this help you draw conclusions on the relative distance the object was from you? Write a summary of the experimental results and how these results relate to astronomical measurements.

Change the Variables You can change the variable in this experiment by changing the speed of the moving object. You can physically throw the sound maker, or move it around in a ball or a string. You can also see what happens when the person with the microphone runs alongside the bike at the same speed.

Design Your Own Experiment

How to Select a Topic Relating to this Concept There are many types of tools and theories astronomers use for space measurements. You can further experiment with the telescope and the Doppler effect, or explore other tools.

Check the Further Readings section and talk with your science or physics teacher to learn more about space measurements. You may also want to visit a planetarium or science museum to get some ideas. There are also many amateur astronomy groups and organizations you could join.

Steps in the Scientific Method To conduct an original experiment, you need to plan carefully and think things through. Otherwise, you might not be sure what question you are answering, what you are or should be measuring, or what your findings prove or disprove.

Here are the steps in designing an experiment:

- State the purpose of—and the underlying question behind—the experiment you propose to do.
- Recognize the variables involved and select one that will help you answer the question at hand.
- State your hypothesis, an educated guess about the answer to your question.
- Decide how to change the variable you selected.
- Decide how to measure your results.

Recording Data and Summarizing the Results Your data could include charts and graphs to display your data. If included, they should be clearly labeled and easy to read. You may also want to include photographs and drawings of your experimental setup and results, which will help other people visualize the steps in the experiment.

If you are preparing an exhibit, you may want to display your results, such as any experimental setup you designed. If you have completed a nonexperimental project, explain clearly what your research question was and illustrate your findings.

Related Projects Space observations and calculations is a broad topic with many related projects. Every day, astronomers are learning new information produced from tools on Earth and in space. There are many different types of telescopes with varying combinations of lenses and mirrors. You can explore the strengths and weaknesses of the different types. Once you have built a standard telescope, you can experiment with building telescopes of varying powers and materials.

You could explore the data from telescopes and how humans' view of space has changed over the past several centuries. A project related to space measurement could involve identifying stars with a telescope that you have constructed. You could also look at how computer calculations have influenced people's knowledge of space. The Doppler effect also has many commonplace usages that you could examine.

For More Information

Freudenrich, Craig. "How Telescopes Work." *How Stuff Works.* http://science. howstuffworks.com/telescope1.htm (accessed on February 3, 2008). Simple explanation of telescopes.

"Galileo's Biography." *The Galileo Project.* http://galileo.rice.edu/bio/index. html (accessed on February 8, 2008). Details of Galileo's life and work.

"How Telescopes Work." *Yes Mag.* http://www.yesmag.bc.ca/how_work/ telescope.html (accessed on February 8, 2008). Brief, clear explanation of how telescopes work, with references.

Kerrod, Robin. *The Night Sky.* Austin, TX: Raintree Steck-Vaughn Publishers, 2002. A look at the history of the exploration of the sky, with graphics and illustrations.

"Telescopes." *Astro-Tom.com.* http://www.astro-tom.com/telescopes/ telescopes.htm (accessed on February 8, 2008). Explanation of telescopes along with lots of other astronomy information.

Stars

The first myth about the stars in the night sky probably came from the Chinese 5,000 years ago. They described stars as a heavenly river. The two brightest stars lived on either side of the river. They were known as Vega, a princess who wove beautiful clothes, and Altair, a herdsman. One night each year, a bridge of birds would span the river, allowing Vega and Altair to meet.

We now know that stars are not princesses, herdsmen, gods, or goddesses, but vast clumps of hydrogen gas and dust that exist in space millions of miles (kilometers) away. Scientists who study the positions, motions, and composition of stars, planets and other objects in space are known as astronomers.

Galileo Galilei confirmed that a huge collection of stars make up the Milky Way. CORBIS CORP.

What's up there? Ancient people were intrigued by what we now call the Milky Way. What was this band of light that stretched across the skies, they wondered. According to Greek legend, droplets of milk spilt upwards when Juno breastfed the infant Hercules. That's why this light became known as the Milky Way.

Democritus, a Greek philosopher, realized the truth in the fifth century B.C.E. He suggested that countless stars, too faint to be seen individually, make up the Milky Way. In 1609, when the Italian astronomer Galileo Galilei (1564–1642) focused the telescope he had made, the immense number of stars he saw staggered him. Galileo confirmed that the Milky Way is made up of innumerable stars grouped in clusters.

A star is born How does a star begin? First, hydrogen, helium, dust, and ashes of stars that

The Orion Nebula is the birthplace of at least 700 young stars. PHOTO RESEARCHERS INC.

Sirius is the brightest star in the sky. PHOTO RESEARCHERS INC.

have died form swirling nebula, the Latin word for "cloud." When a dense accumulation of these nebula gathers, the mass becomes a spawning ground for stars. As this mass of gas and dust heats up, gravity causes it to clump together, and a new star is formed. But only after nuclear fusion takes place at the star's core does it produce enough light for us to see it. This process takes about 50 million years.

A star stays in the same spot during its lifetime. We do see stars in different positions over the course of a month, but this apparent movement of the stars is caused by Earth moving around the Sun. Certain stars lie in patterns called constellations. Of the eighty-eight constellation patterns, some form shapes that look like animals, women, warriors, or objects. Constellation patterns sparked the star myths told by ancient people.

Astronomers use light-years to measure the distance between stars. A light-year is the distance light travels in one year: roughly 5.9 trillion miles (9.5 trillion kilometers). How vast are the distances between stars? The star Proxima Centuri is 25 trillion miles (40 trillion kilometers) away—or 4.29 light-years. And that's the closest star.

The brightest and the biggest Sirius, 8.6 light-years away, is the brightest star in the sky, twenty-six times brighter than the Sun, which is also a star. How was this determined? In 1912, astronomer Henrietta Swan Leavitt (1868–1921) discovered that stars increase and fade in brightness over time. By studying a sequence of photographs of stars, analyzing their changes, and applying mathematical formulas, Leavitt came up with a way for astronomers to calculate the true brightness of stars.

Stars are just one part of a galaxy, which also includes gas, dust, and planets, all drawn together by gravity. The Milky Way is not the only galaxy. The Andromeda Galaxy, which has about 300 trillion stars, and the Milky Way, with about 200 billion stars, are the two biggest and most important in a cluster of thirty galaxies called The Local Group. Improved technologies are helping astronomers detect galaxies that were

WORDS TO KNOW

Astronomers: Scientists who study the positions, motions, and composition of stars and other objects in the sky.

Constellations: Patterns of stars in the night sky. There are eighty-eight known constellations.

Fusion: Combining of nuclei of two or more lighter elements into one nucleus of a heavier element; the process stars use to produce energy to produce light and support themselves against their own gravity.

Galaxy: A large collection of stars and clusters of stars containing anywhere from a few million to a few trillion stars.

Light-year: Distance light travels in one year in the vacuum of space, roughly 5.9 trillion miles (9.5 trillion kilometers).

Milky Way: The galaxy in which our solar system is located.

Nebula: Bright or dark cloud, often composed of gases and dust, hovering in the space between the stars.

Star: A vast clump of hydrogen gas and dust that produces great energy through fusion reactions at its core.

The Local Group: A cluster of thirty galaxies, including the Milky Way, pulled together by gravity.

---

unknown just decades ago. Scientists estimate that there are over 100 billion galaxies in the visible universe.

The two projects that follow will help you learn more about the stars over our heads.

PROJECT 1

Tracking Stars: Where is Polaris?

Purpose/Hypothesis Stars do not move in space, but the planets, including Earth, rotate on their axis and revolve around stars like our Sun. While stars appear to be in different places in the sky from one night to the next, what has really happened is that Earth has shifted its position.

In this project, you will use a camera to follow the stars. Normally when a picture is taken, the film is exposed to light for only a fraction of a second. In this experiment, the film will be exposed for 1200 seconds. To obtain a clear picture and avoid over-exposing the film, you must take the pictures at night in dark surroundings (no overhead lighting including street lights) with a clear sky and a view of the North Star (Polaris).

Level of Difficulty Moderate, because of the camera operation.

How to Experiment Safely

This project poses no hazards. However, you might ask a knowledgeable adult to help you operate the camera.

Materials Needed

- single-lens reflex 35-mm manual camera, such as a Pentax K-1000 (your school may use this type in photography classes)
- 1 roll 35-mm film, 1000 speed, 12 to 24 exposures
- shutter bulb (Keeps the shutter open for prolonged exposures. You can purchase one in a photography store.)
- tripod stand for camera
- compass (optional)
- ruler and protractor

Approximate Budget Less than $20 for film and shutter bulb. (Try to borrow all other supplies.)

Timetable 1 to 2 hours.

Step-by-Step Instructions

1. Properly load the film in the camera. If necessary, ask for help.
2. Set the shutter speed to the manual setting (M). Some cameras have a different symbol. Use the setting that keeps the shutter open as long as you press the shutter button.

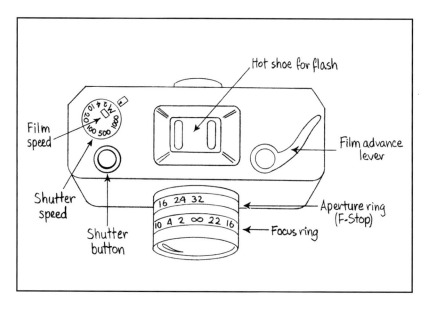

Steps 2 to 5: Parts of a camera.
GALE GROUP.

3. Set the film speed at 1000.

4. Attach the shutter bulb by screwing the end into the shutter button.

5. Set the aperture to the highest number.

6. Screw the tripod into the bottom of the camera

7. Set the tripod on firm ground.

8. Locate Polaris, the North Star, in the northern sky, using the pointer stars of the Big Dipper.

9. Position the camera so the North Star is visible through the eyepiece.

10. Squeeze the bulb to open the shutter. Hold it open by adjusting the screw near the bulb.

11. Leave the shutter open for one hour.

12. Close the shutter by loosening the screw or releasing the bulb.

13. Advance the film and repeat steps 10 through 12 on different nights.

14. Remove the roll of film and get it developed.

15. Using a pen, draw lines on each photo from the North Star (the only star that did not move) to the ends of one or two star trails.

16. Using a compass, measure the angle of the two lines. The angle should measure 15 degrees for each hour the film is exposed.

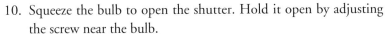
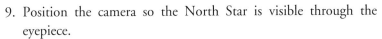

Step 8: Locate Polaris, the North Star, in the northern sky, using the pointer stars of the Big Dipper. GALE GROUP.

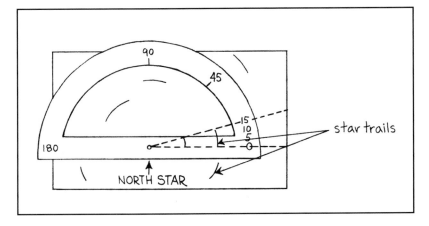

Step 16: Compass over photo with lines drawn to North Star from an angle. GALE GROUP.

Troubleshooter's Guide

Here is a problem that may arise during this project, some possible causes, and ways to remedy the problem.

Problem: The photo is too hazy, and the star trails are not visible.

Possible causes: The sky was not clear enough, or there were too many lights that overexposed the film. Try the project again, away from houses and streets.

Summary of Results Record your angle measurements and the date on each photo. All angles should be 15 degrees for each hour of exposure because Earth revolves 15 degrees each hour. What seemed to happen to all the stars except the North Star? How can you explain this?

PROJECT 2

Tracking the Motion of the Planets: Can a planet be followed?

Purpose/Hypothesis Planets sometimes reflect light from the Sun, which makes them shine like stars. But unlike the stationary stars, Earth and the other planets move through the sky as they orbit the Sun. As the other planets orbit the Sun, Earth continues through its orbit. The combination of these movements can make the apparent path of the planets in Earth's sky resemble an s-shaped pattern. In this project, you will examine this phenomenon.

Level of Difficulty Moderate. (You need to be familiar with the star positions.)

Steps 3 to 5: Example of plotting the position of a planet on Day 1 and 2, related to the Orion Constellation. GALE GROUP.

Materials Needed

- a star map for your area and time of the year
- binoculars or telescope (optional)

Approximate Budget $2 for a star map. (Consult local papers or magazines for current monthly maps.)

Timetable 15 to 20 minutes per night for 10 to 15 nights.

Step-by-Step Instructions

1. Examine your local star map. Most star maps should be held upside down and over your head.
2. Choose a planet that should be visible in your night sky. Locate its position on the map.
3. With or without using binoculars, try to find this planet in the night sky. Planets are usually the brightest objects in the sky and do not twinkle like stars.
4. On your star map, record the position and time you located the planet.
5. Repeat this procedure every night for 10 to 15 nights.
6. Connect the marks on the star map and trace the path of the planet.

How to Experiment Safely

Always stay on level ground when star gazing. Have an adult with you.

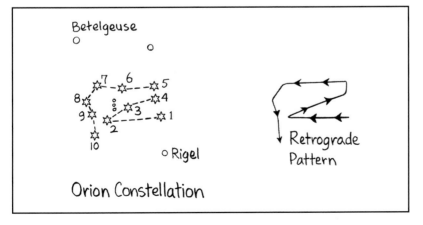

Step 6: Example of graphing a planet's motion relative to the Orion Constellation. GALE GROUP.

Troubleshooter's Guide

Here are some problems that may arise during this project, some possible causes, and ways to remedy the problems.

Problem: You cannot see the planets or stars.

Possible cause: The sky is too overcast. Try coming out again an hour or two later.

Problem: You cannot find the new position of the planet.

Possible cause: You might be unfamiliar with the night sky. Ask a knowledgeable adult for help, or look on the Internet for a daily star map. Locate the planet and transfer its position to your star map.

Summary of Results Record your results on a star map like the one illustrated. Be sure to label each star and the daily positions of the planet. After 10 to 15 nights of observations, were you able to notice the motion of the planet among the stars?

Design Your Own Experiment

How to Select a Topic Relating to this Concept Space is an infinite frontier sparsely filled with objects. Comets, stars, meteors, asteroids, moons, and planets are just a few of the objects visible in space. Before you begin making observations or experimenting, ask yourself questions. What is an asteroid? What is the difference between a meteor and a meteorite?

Check the Further Readings section and talk with your science teacher or school or community media specialist to start gathering information on star questions that interest you.

Steps in the Scientific Method To do an original experiment, you need to plan carefully and think things through. Otherwise, you might not be sure what question you are answering, what you are or should be measuring, or what your findings prove or disprove.

Here are the steps in designing an experiment:

- State the purpose of—and the underlying question behind—the experiment you propose to do.

- Recognize the variables involved, and select one that will help you answer the question at hand.

- State a testable hypothesis, an educated guess about the answer to your question.

- Decide how to change the variable you selected.

- Decide how to measure your results.

Example of apparent motion of star and planets. GALE GROUP.

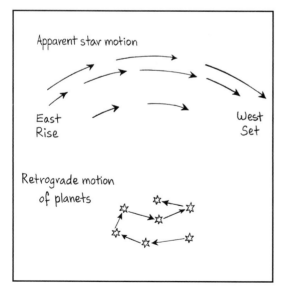

Recording Data and Summarizing the Results As a scientist investigating a question, you must gather information and share it with others. Observations, researched facts, and data can be diagrammed or charted. Once you have gathered your information, study it, draw a conclusion, and share your results with others.

Related Projects Binoculars and telescopes can improve your view of the nighttime sky. When choosing a topic such as comets, make sure you have the proper instruments to observe the object. You may want to choose a phenomenon or event that is easily observed, such as a meteor shower. When a meteor shower is predicted, you might try to calculate the number of shooting stars you see in one hour.

For More Information

Matloff, Gregory L. *The Urban Astronomer.* New York: John Wiley, 1991. Describes interesting objects you can see in a city sky.

McSween, Jr., Harry Y. *Stardust to Planets.* New York: St. Martin's Press, 1993. Provides a good survey of the solar system.

National Aeronautics and Space Administration. *NASA: For Students.* http://www.nasa.gov/audience/forstudents/index.html (accessed on January 10, 2008).

Van Cleave, Janice. *Astronomy for Every Kid.* New York: John Wiley, 1991. Outlines more than one hundred simple experiments that demonstrate the principles of astronomy.

85

Static Electricity

You experiment with static electricity every time you shuffle across a rug and touch a metal door handle. Static electricity is a form of electricity produced by friction (the rubbing of one object against another) in which the electric charge does not flow in a current but stays in one place.

Electricity is a form of energy caused by the presence of electrical charges in matter. Matter is anything that has mass and takes up space. All matter, including you and this book, is made of tiny particles called atoms. An atom is the smallest particle of which an element can exist. Each atom, in turn, contains positively charged protons in its nucleus, or center core, and negatively charged electrons orbiting around its nucleus.

How does an object become electrically charged? An increase or decrease in the number of electrons in an object gives it an electrical charge. When an object gains electrons, it becomes negatively charged. When it loses electrons, it becomes positively charged.

In some materials, such as copper and silver, electrons can move around freely. These "free" electrons make these two metals good conductors. A conductor is a substance that is able to carry an electrical current. In other materials, electrons are tightly bound to their atoms. These materials, such as glass, rubber, and dry wood, do not conduct electricity easily, so they are good insulators and can be used as protective layers around conductors.

Some materials have a stronger attraction for electrons than other materials. When two different materials are rubbed together, electrons move from the material that has the weaker attraction for them to the material that has the stronger attraction. For example, a balloon will usually not stick to a sheet of paper. However, you can make it stick by rubbing them together. As you rub, electrons move from the paper, which has a weak attraction for electrons, to the balloon, which has a stronger

before rubbing

after rubbing

Rubbing does not create new electrons. It just causes them to move from the paper to the balloon. GALE GROUP.

attraction. Because the paper has lost some electrons, it now is positively charged. The balloon has gained electrons, so it is now negatively charged.

When it comes to electrical charges, opposites attract. A material with a positive charge attracts a material with a negative charge, and vice versa. However, materials that both have a positive charge repel (are resistant to) each other, as do materials that both have a negative charge.

When you place the negatively charged balloon near the positively charged paper, they will now cling together. As they cling, however, some of the electrons move from the balloon back to the paper. When the electrons are evenly distributed again, the balloon and paper are no longer electrically charged, so they will stop clinging together.

What is static electricity? As you placed the charged balloon near the charged paper, you might have seen or heard a small crackle of static electricity. When an object with a strong negative charge is placed near one with a strong positive charge, the attraction of these opposites is so

Benjamin Franklin was the first to use the words "positive" and "negative" to describe electric charges. PHOTO RESEARCHERS INC.

great that the air between them becomes electrically charged. It forms a path over which the electrons can move. As the electrons jump from the negative object to the positive one, they create static electricity. After the jump, the electrons are balanced again, so both objects lose their electrical charge.

American scientist and political leader Benjamin Franklin (1706–1790) was one of the first to experiment with static electricity. You may remember his famous and dangerous kite experiments with lightning, which is a form of static electricity.

Scientists still do not know exactly how lightning occurs, but they do know that a negative charge in one cloud repels electrons on the ground beneath it or in another cloud. As these electrons are repelled, the surface of the ground or the other cloud facing the negative cloud ends up with an excess of protons, giving it a positive charge. When the difference between the negative and positive charges reaches a certain point, lightning flashes from the negatively charged cloud to the positively charged ground or to the other cloud. This powerful burst of static electricity balances the electrons at both locations.

Lightning is a form of static electricity. PETER ARNOLD INC.

In the first experiment, you will build an electroscope, a device that determines whether an object is electrically charged, and you will use it to test objects for electrical charges. In the second experiment, you will determine whether wool or nylon creates a stronger electrical charge.

EXPERIMENT 1

Building an Electroscope: Which objects are electrically charged?

Purpose/Hypothesis In this experiment, you will build an electroscope and use it to determine whether objects have an electric charge. An electroscope has two metal strips that hang down. When you hold a negatively charged object near the strips, the excess electrons move into

WORDS TO KNOW

Atom: The smallest unit of an element, made up of protons and neutrons in a central nucleus surrounded by moving electrons.

Conductor: A substance able to carry an electrical current.

Control experiment: A setup that is identical to the experiment but is not affected by the variable that will be changed during the experiment.

Current: A flow of electrical charge from one point to another.

Electricity: A form of energy caused by the presence of electrical charges in matter.

Electron: A subatomic particle with a single electrical charge that orbits around the nucleus of an atom.

Electroscope: A device that determines whether an object is electrically charged.

Friction: The rubbing of one object against another.

Hypothesis: An idea in the form of a statement that can be tested by observation and/or experiment.

Insulator: A material through which little or no electrical current will flow.

Matter: Anything that has mass and takes up space.

Nucleus: The central core of an atom, consisting of protons and (usually) neutrons.

Proton: A subatomic particle with a single positive charge that is found in the nucleus of an atom.

Static electricity: A form of electricity produced by friction in which the electric charge does not flow in a current but stays in one place.

Variable: Something that can affect the results of an experiment.

---

the strips, causing them both to have a negative charge. Because they both have the same charge, they will repel each other and move apart. When you remove the charged object, the strips will lose their negative charge and hang down, as before.

An electroscope responds in the same way if a positively charged object is brought near the strips. The positively charged object attracts electrons from the strips, giving them both a positive charge. This time the strips move apart because they are both positively charged.

Before you begin, make an educated guess about the outcome of this experiment based on your knowledge of static electricity. This educated guess, or prediction, is your hypothesis. A hypothesis should explain these things:

- the topic of the experiment
- the variable you will change

How to Experiment Safely

Be careful in handling the glass materials and in using the scissors.

- the variable you will measure
- what you expect to happen

A hypothesis should be brief, specific, and measurable. It must be something you can test through observation. Your experiment will prove or disprove whether your hypothesis is correct. Here is one possible hypothesis for this experiment: "A glass test tube and a plastic comb that have been rubbed will hold an electric charge, but identical objects that have not been rubbed will not hold a charge."

In this case, the variable you will change is whether the objects have been rubbed, and the variable you will measure, using the electroscope, is the electric charge of the objects. You expect the objects to have a charge only after they have been rubbed.

The unrubbed objects will serve as a control experiment, showing whether the objects have an electric charge if they have not been rubbed. If only the rubbed objects have an electric charge, you will know your hypothesis is correct.

Level of Difficulty Easy/moderate.

Materials Needed

- 1 wide-mouth jar
- cardboard circle cut to cover the jar opening
- 2 strips of aluminum foil, each 0.5 inches x 2 inches (1.3 centimeters x 5 centimeters)
- large paper clip
- sharpened pencil
- masking tape
- scissors
- clean, dry cloth
- 2 identical pairs of objects to test, such as two glass test tubes and two plastic combs

What Are the Variables?

Variables are anything that might affect the results of an experiment. Here are the main variables in this experiment:

- whether the experimental and control objects are identical
- which objects are rubbed
- how long and in what manner the objects are rubbed
- whether the test objects touch each other (keep those you rubbed—the experimental objects—separate from those you did not rub—the control objects—so electrons will not move from one to the other before you test them)
- the humidity level of the air (electric charges can leak away in humid air and change the results of your experiment)

In other words, the variables in this experiment are everything that might affect the electric charges of the objects. If you change more than one variable, you will not be able to tell which variable had the most effect on each object's electric charge.

Steps 2 and 3: Preparing aluminum foil strip and paper clip. GALE GROUP.

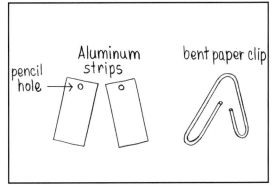

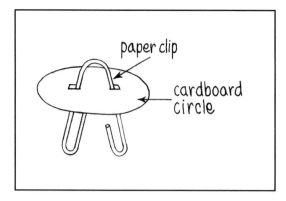

Step 4: Set-up of cardboard circle and paper clip. GALE GROUP.

Approximate Budget $0 to $5. The materials should be available in most households.

Timetable 15 minutes to build the electroscope; 10 minutes to test the objects.

Step-by-Step Instructions

1. Choose a day with low humidity to do your experiment. (If the air feels damp, it has just rained, or you seem to perspire easily, the humidity is too high for this experiment.)

2. Use the pencil to make a small hole in one end of each foil strip.

3. Open the paper clip so that it becomes a loop with two hooks at the bottom.

4. Use the scissors to cut two slots in the cardboard circle. Slip the sides of the paper clip into the slots.

5. Hang each foil strip on a paper clip hook. If the strips do not move freely, enlarge the holes in them.

Reaction Chart	
Control Object 1	Reaction of aluminum strips:
Control Object 2	Reaction of aluminum strips:
Experimental (rubbed) Object 1	Reaction of aluminum strips:
Experimental (rubbed) Object 2	Reaction of aluminum strips:

Step 8: Recording chart for Experiment 1. GALE GROUP.

6. Use masking tape to secure the cardboard circle to the top of the jar. Your electroscope is ready to use.

7. Hold one of the control objects near the top of the paper clip loop that is sticking out of the cardboard circle. Do not touch the clip with the object.

8. Move the object away. Use a chart such as the one illustrated to record whether the aluminum strips moved apart.

9. Repeat Steps 7 and 8 with the other control object.

10. Rub one test object vigorously with the dry cloth and repeat Steps 7 and 8.

11. Rub the other test object vigorously with the cloth and repeat Steps 7 and 8.

Summary of Results Use the data on your chart to create a line or bar graph of your findings. Then study your chart and graph and decide whether your hypothesis was correct. Did the aluminum strips move apart only for the rubbed objects? What does this show? Write a paragraph summarizing your findings and explaining whether they support your hypothesis.

Change the Variables You can vary this experiment in several ways. For example, use different pairs of objects, including copper or silver objects that are good conductors. You can also put an object that you know has a positive charge near the paper clip. For example, you might use paper after it has been rubbed against a balloon. Do the aluminum strips respond in the same way?

Troubleshooter's Guide

Below are some problems that may arise during this experiment, some possible causes, and ways to remedy the problems.

Problem: The aluminum strips did not move for any objects.

Possible causes:

1. The air is too humid. Wait for a drier day and try again.

2. The holes in the strips are too small, preventing movement. Enlarge the holes and try again.

3. The test objects were not charged. Rub them longer or try rubbing them with a wool scarf.

Problem: The strips moved for all of the objects.

Possible cause: The control objects were charged accidentally. Touch them to something metal to release any electric charge in them and test them again.

EXPERIMENT 2

Measuring a Charge: Does nylon or wool create a stronger static electric charge?

Purpose/Hypothesis In this experiment, you will create an electric charge in nylon, which is a synthetic fiber, and in wool, a natural fiber. Then you

What Are the Variables?

Variables are anything that might affect the results of an experiment. Here are the main variables in this experiment:

- the types of cloth used and the size of the pieces
- whether the pairs of control and experimental cloth squares are identical
- which cloth squares are rubbed
- how long the cloth squares are rubbed and what they are rubbed against
- whether the rubbed cloth squares touch anything before they are tested
- the humidity level of the air (electric charges can leak away in humid air and change the results of your experiment)

In other words, the variables in this experiment are everything that might affect the strength of the static electric charge. If you change more than one variable, you will not be able to tell which one had the most effect on the strength of the static charge.

will measure the strength of each charge, using the electroscope you built in Experiment 1 or using an alternative procedure.

Before you begin, make an educated guess about the outcome of this experiment based on your understanding of static electricity. This educated guess, or prediction, is your hypothesis. A hypothesis should explain these things:

- the topic of the experiment
- the variable you will change
- the variable you will measure
- what you expect to happen

A hypothesis should be brief, specific, and measurable. It must be something you can test through observation. Your experiment will prove or disprove whether your hypothesis is correct. Here is one possible hypothesis for this experiment: "Wool will create a stronger static electric charge than nylon."

In this case, the variable you will change is the material being rubbed, and the variable you will measure is the strength of the electrostatic charge, as measured on your electroscope. You expect the wool will have a stronger charge.

As a control experiment, you will also test squares of wool and nylon that have not been rubbed. The control experiment will determine whether these unrubbed cloth squares also have a charge and, if so, how strong it is. If the rubbed wool has a stronger charge than the rubbed nylon and if the unrubbed cloth squares have little or no static charge, you will know your hypothesis is correct.

Level of Difficulty Easy/moderate.

Materials Needed

- two 5-inch (12.7-centimeter) squares of wool
- two 5-inch (12.7-centimeter) squares of nylon
- plastic comb

Chart of Reactions

Control wool square	Reaction of aluminum strips:	Width between bottom of strips:
Control nylon square	Reaction of aluminum strips:	Width between bottom of strips:
Experimental (rubbed) wool square	Reaction of aluminum strips:	Width between bottom of strips:
Experimental (rubbed) nylon square	Reaction of aluminum strips:	Width between bottom of strips:

Step 2: Recording chart for Experiment 2. GALE GROUP.

Step 3: Hold an empty margarine container about 1 inch (2.5 centimeters) above the lid of cereal. GALE GROUP.

- electroscope from Experiment 1 (or a clean, empty margarine tub with a clear lid and some dry, lightweight cereal, such as puffed rice)
- ruler

Approximate Budget $3 for cloth. (The other materials should be available in most households.)

Timetable 20 minutes.

Step-by-Step Instructions To use an electroscope to measure the strength of a static charge:

1. Choose a dry day to do your experiment. Be careful not to rub the control squares of cloth against anything.
2. Place the control wool square near the paper clip loop. Observe the response of the aluminum strips. If they move, use the ruler to estimate the distance between the lower edges of the two strips. Record

Troubleshooter's Guide

Below are some problems that may arise during this experiment, some possible causes, and ways to remedy the problems.

Problem: None of the cloth squares held a static charge.

Possible causes:

1. The air is too humid. Wait for a drier day and try again.
2. The experimental squares were not charged. Rub them longer, making sure to rub both kinds of cloth in the same way.

Problem: All of the cloth squares held a charge.

Possible cause: The control squares might have been charged accidentally as you prepared for your experiment. Touch them to something metal to release any electric charge in them and test them again.

Problem: The pieces of cereal flew all around.

Possible cause: The cereal had already been charged, perhaps by being shaken and rubbed inside the box. Try a different box of cereal and try not to let the pieces rub together.

the results on a chart like the one illustrated.

3. Repeat Step 2 with the control nylon square.

4. Rub the experimental wool square vigorously against the comb. Then, without touching the cloth to anything, hold it near the paper clip loop. Observe and record how the aluminum strips respond.

5. Repeat Step 4 using the experimental nylon square, rubbing it in the same way and as long as you rubbed the wool square.

To use an alternative testing procedure: Rubbing a plastic margarine container with a cloth square will give the container a static electric charge that will draw lightweight cereal toward the container. Rubbing causes electrons to leave the cloth and move to the plastic tub. The negatively charged tub then repels the electrons in the cereal and attracts the protons, drawing the cereal upward.

1. Choose a day with low humidity for your experiment.

2. Place about 15 pieces of cereal in the tub lid.

3. As a control experiment, hold the empty margarine container about 1 inch (2.5 centimeters) above the lid of cereal. Observe whether any cereal pieces move upward toward the bottom of the container, and record your findings on a chart.

4. With one hand inside the container, rub the outside vigorously with a square of wool. Then remove the wool and hold the container above the cereal. Record how the cereal pieces respond and how many respond.

5. Repeat Step 4 with the nylon square, rubbing in the same way and for the same length of time. Record the results.

Summary of Results Use the data on your charts to create a line or bar graph of your findings. Then study your charts and graph and decide whether your hypothesis was correct. Did the wool square create more static electricity than the nylon square, either causing the aluminum strips to move farther apart or causing more cereal to cling to the bottom of the margarine container? Did the unrubbed cloth squares exert no noticeable static charge, according to your electroscope? Or did the unrubbed container not pull the cereal upward? Write a paragraph summarizing your findings and explaining whether they support your hypothesis.

Change the Variables You can change the variables and conduct other interesting experiments. For example, use different kinds of synthetic and natural fabrics, such as rayon, polyester knit, cotton, or silk. You can also change the length of time you rub a cloth square to see if the strength of the electric charge increases the longer you rub.

An electroscope can determine whether an object holds an electric charge. PETER ARNOLD INC.

Another way to vary the experiment is to rub a cloth square against the plastic comb, and hold the comb near the paper clip in the electroscope instead of the cloth. The comb should also hold a static charge, although it will be negative, while the cloth should be positive. (The electroscope should respond in the same way because both aluminum strips will still receive the same kind of charge and move apart.)

Instead of using cereal in the alternative electroscope design, you can put salt and pepper or tiny pieces of paper in the margarine container.

Modify the Experiment This experiment tested whether nylon or wool has a stronger static electric charge. You can make this experiment more challenging by testing a variety of materials and creating a Triboelectric Series. Triboelectricity relates to electricity that comes from friction. A Triboelectric Series is a list of materials showing which are more likely to let go of their negative charges (electrons) and becomes positively charged, and which are more likely to attract electrons and becomes negatively charged. Some materials, such as steel, are not likely to give up electrons at all. If a material does not have a charge, it is called neutral.

You will first need to gather a variety of materials found in the house, such as leather, glass, wool, paper, plastic, wood, and plastic wrap. You can also test your hair and skin. Test each object with the electroscope as described in the experiment, and measure the distance between the aluminum strips. Write up a summary of your results. When you are done, you can see how your Tribolectric Series compares to others.

The electroscope in this experiment will show that there is a charge, not whether the charge is positive or negative. You can carry this experiment even further by exploring the charge of each material. Knowing what you do about static electricity and electricity, how would you sort which of the items in your Tribolectric Series are positively or negatively charged? If you start out with an item that you know has a certain charge, how would that help?

Design Your Own Experiment

How to Select a Topic Relating to this Concept You can explore many other aspects of static electricity. For example, why does static electricity occur in some situations and not in others? What kinds of materials are more likely to have a positive or a negative charge? How does the humidity in the air affect static electricity? How do static charges affect electrical equipment?

As you consider possible experiments, be sure to discuss them with your science teacher or another knowledgeable adult before trying them. While static electricity usually involves a small electric charge (except for lightning!), experiments with electricity are potentially dangerous. NEVER experiment with lightning or the electric current that comes from electrical outlets.

Check the Further Readings section and talk with your science teacher or school or community media specialist to start gathering information on static electricity questions that interest you.

Steps in the Scientific Method To do an original experiment, you need to plan carefully and think things through. Otherwise, you might not be sure what question you are answering, what you are or should be measuring, or what your findings prove or disprove.

Here are the steps in designing an experiment:

- State the purpose of—and the underlying question behind—the experiment you propose to do.
- Recognize the variables involved, and select one that will help you answer the question at hand.
- State a testable hypothesis, an educated guess about the answer to your question.
- Decide how to change the variable you selected.
- Decide how to measure your results.

Recording Data and Summarizing the Results In the static electricity experiments, your raw data might include not only charts and graphs of the responses of control and electrically charged objects, but also drawings or photographs of these responses.

If you display your experiment, make clear your beginning question, the variable you changed, the variable you measured, the results, and your conclusions. You might include photographs or drawings of the steps of the experiment. Explain what materials you used, how long each step took, and other basic information.

Related Projects You can undertake a variety of projects related to static electricity. For example, you might explore products that claim to stop static cling on clothes. Does one product work better than another? You might see how many times you can transfer a static charge from one object to another, or if you can use static electricity to move objects without touching them.

For More Information

Bonnet, Robert. *Science Fair Projects with Electricity and Electronics.* New York: Sterling Publishing, 1996. Outlines nearly fifty projects designed for science fairs.

Energy Information Administration. "Electricity: A Secondary Energy Source." *Energy Kid's Page.* http://www.eia.doe.gov/kids/energyfacts/sources/electricity.html (accessed on February 12, 2008). Explanation of electricity includes information on static electricity.

Garner, Robert. *Science Projects about Electricity and Magnets.* Hillside, NJ: Enslow Publishers, 1994. Provides detailed explanations of projects and the concepts they demonstrate.

Gibson, Gary. *Understanding Electricity.* Brookfield, CT: Copper Beech Books, 1995. Explains basic concepts and includes experiments.

Kurtus, Ron. "School for Champions." *Materials that Cause Static Electricity.* http://www.school-for-champions.com/science/static_materials.htm (accessed on February 9, 2008). List and explanation of the Triboelectric Series.

Van Cleave, Janice. *Spectacular Science Projects: Electricity.* New York: Wiley & Sons, 1994. Describes twenty science projects, explaining how to carry them out and what they prove.

Wood, Robert. *Electricity and Magnetism FUNdamentals.* New York: Learning Triangle Press, 1997. Offers instructions for experiments on the nature of electricity and magnetism and the relationship between them.

Storms

Right now, at least one area of the world is experiencing some type of powerful storm. Storms are periods of extreme bad weather that can bring powerful winds and torrential rains. Storms can rip buildings apart, toss cars through the air, cause deaths, and spark forest fires. Every day there are as many as fifty thousand storms occurring throughout the world. They can stretch for hundreds of miles, or remain isolated to a few hundred yards. Either way, storms can cause enormous devastation. Some of the more common types of storms are thunderstorms, tornadoes and hailstorms.

How air works Storms all begin by the movement of air. Air is made up of a mixture of different gases, mainly oxygen and nitrogen with about four times as much nitrogen. Air is constantly moving around as it changes temperatures. The movement of air causes wind. (For more details on how air works, see Air chapter.)

When air gets warmer its particles start to move about quickly and expand. The warm air particles take up more room in a given space. This makes the warm air rise because it is lighter than the air around it. Cooler air particles move closer together and take up less room. That makes cooler air heavier than the air around it and causes it to sink. As the Sun heats the air around Earth's surface, this warm air moves upwards and the cooler air sinks. The faster that air is warmed and rises, the faster the winds.

Clouds a brewing Thunderstorms need three basic ingredients to form. The first is moisture in the air or water vapor, which forms clouds and rain. The second is a column of unstable air, which provides relatively warm, moist air on the bottom layers with cold, dry air high above it. And lastly, a thunderstorm needs some kind of force to lift the air upwards.

When the moist, warm air rises it eventually meets colder air and begins to cool. That forms the beginning of a cloud. Inside a cloud,

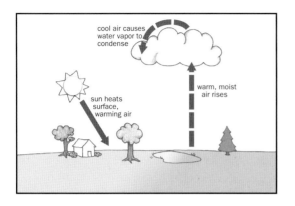

cool air causes water vapor to condense

sun heats surface, warming air

warm, moist air rises

The process of cloud formation.
GALE GROUP.

currents of air move up and down quickly. This air is filled with tiny particles of dust. Water vapor is pushed upwards by the warm air. When it comes into contact with cooler air, the water vapor condenses. Condensation is when a gas (or vapor) changes into a liquid. The condensed drops of water will then surround a dust particle. Clouds form where millions of water-dust droplets gather together. Each of the particles in a cloud has a positive and a negative electrical charge.

These small, puffy clouds grow increasingly larger as more warm air rises from the ground. If the cloud gets large enough, it may continue to rise into the ever-colder air. Strong winds can blow the top of the cloud downwind, and this gives the top of the cloud an anvil shape. This thunderstorm cloud is called a cumulonimbus cloud and it can extend upwards for miles.

Shocking sights, loud noises To be called a thunderstorm there must be thunder. Thunder is caused by lightning, and lightning begins in the cumulonimbus clouds. Lightning is an intense discharge of electricity. Scientists estimate that about a hundred lightning flashes occur each second around the world. The electricity flowing within a lightning bolt is so powerful that it can kill instantly, split trees, and spark fires. The average flash of lightning could turn on a 100-watt light bulb for more than three months.

As a storm advances, strong winds blow the particles of dust and water in the cloud and cause them to hit each other. Each particle contains positive and negative charges, which are attracted to each other under normal conditions, but collisions cause the positive and negative charges to separate. Positive charges tend to move towards the top of a cloud and negative charges move towards the bottom. Both types of charges hold energy. Charges that are alike repel each other and charges that are opposites pull together. When enough charges and time build up, the negative charge in the cloud reach out towards the positive charges on the ground. The result is a burst of electricity, or a lightning bolt.

Every lightning flash produces thunder. In just a fraction of a second a lightning flash can heat up the air to 50,000°F (28,000°C)—a temperature hotter that the surface of the Sun. The burst of heat causes the air molecules around it to expand quickly away from the lightning's flash. As this hot air cools, it contracts. This quick expansion and contraction of air causes the air molecules to shake or vibrate, making sound waves that create the sound of thunder.

Thunder and lightning occur simultaneously, yet people will always see lightning before they hear thunder because light and sound travel at different speeds. Light travels at about 186,000 miles per second (299,800 kilometers per second). The speed of sound is only about 0.2 miles per second (0.3 kilometers per second). That means a person will see lightning almost instantly, but won't hear the thunder for several seconds. Knowing this allows any storm watcher to calculate the distance of the lightning strike. Count the number of seconds between the lightning and the thunder, and divide the number of seconds by five to calculate the miles distance; divide the number of seconds by three to calculate the kilometers distance.

Lightning forms when the negative charges in the cloud are attracted to the positive charges on the ground. GALE GROUP.

Twisting about Tornadoes are swirling columns of air that have enormous power. They have a short life span, from a few minutes to over an hour, yet are one of the most ferocious storms. They develop on land

Fujita Tornado Scale

F-Scale	Winds	Type of Damage
F0	40-72 mph 64-116 km/h	MINIMAL DAMAGE: Some damage to chimneys, TV antennas, roof shingles, trees and windows.
F1	73-112 mph 117-180 km/h	MODERATE DAMAGE: Automobiles overturned, carports destroyed, trees uprooted.
F2	113-157 mph 181-253 km h	MAJOR DAMAGE: Roofs blown off homes, sheds and outbuildings demolished, mobile homes overturned.
F3	158-206 mph 254-332 km/h	SEVERE DAMAGE: Exterior walls and roofs blown off homes. Metal buildings collapsed or are severely damaged. Forests and farmland flattened.
F4	207-260 mph 333-418 km/h	DEVASTATING DAMAGE: Few walls, if any, standing in well-built homes. Large steel and concrete missiles thrown far distances.
F5	261-318 mph 419-512 km/h	INCREDIBLE DAMAGE: Homes leveled with all debris removed. Schools, motels, and other larger structures have considerable damage with exterior walls and roofs gone.

Developed by Dr. T. Theodore Fujita in 1971, the Fujita Tornado Scale, or F-Scale, classifies tornadoes according to the damage caused. GALE GROUP.

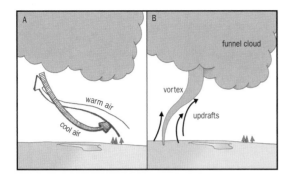

The formation of a tornado. (A) formation of vortex; (B) when the funnel cloud touches the ground it becomes a tornado. GALE GROUP.

and come from the energy released in a thunderstorm. This energy is concentrated in a small area, such as the size of a football field, and moves across the ground at speeds of 20 to 40 miles per hour (32 to 64 kilometers per hour). On average, the United States gets about a thousand tornadoes each year. The most violent tornadoes can reach wind speeds of over 250 miles per hour (400 kilometers per hour) and can slice a path of destruction more than 1 mile (1.6 kilometers) wide and 50 miles (80 kilometers) long.

Tornadoes are often called "twisters" because of their rapidly spinning, funnel-shaped clouds. Only a small percentage of thunderstorms will turn into a tornado, and scientists have different theories on what exactly causes a tornado to form. One widespread theory says tornadoes form mainly due to wind. When winds at two different heights move at two different speeds this can create a horizontal spinning column of air.

Thunderstorms supply the rising warm air or updrafts that a tornado needs to form. The updraft tilts the spinning air from the horizontal to the vertical direction. This whirling air is called a vortex and it causes the funnel cloud to form. When the warm air gets pulled up and meets the cold air, the moisture in the air condenses. Water droplets get swept into

Using special equipment, storm chasers gather data on tornadoes to help scientists learn more about this powerful, destructive form of storm.
© CORBIS SYGMA

the mass of whirling air, starting at the top of the vortex where the temperature is lowest. This begins to form the tornado's visible funnel cloud.

Strong updrafts will cause the funnel cloud to narrow, which causes it to spin faster. This principle works much as an ice skater spinning. When an ice skater brings his or her arms closer to the body, he or she will spin faster.

The funnel extends downwards from the cloud to the land as a tornado forms. A funnel cloud that touches land becomes a tornado. Some funnel clouds are hard to spot until they strike. As they pick up dirt and other materials from the ground these materials swirl about and cause the funnel cloud to darken and become more visible.

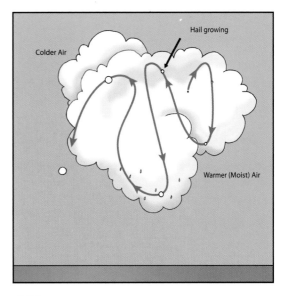

The formation of hail stones.
ILLUSTRATION BY TEMAH NELSON.

Scientists are still working to answer several questions on tornadoes. One of the key questions is why updrafts in some thunderstorms become twisting funnel clouds, while those in similar thunderstorms do not. Some of the people who are helping to answer questions on tornadoes and other storms are storm chasers. Storm chasers seek out storms for study or adventure. They often use special equipment and can capture the spectacular sights and sounds of these violent storms.

Hailstorms Hailstorms, like lightening and tornadoes, are a product of strong thunderstorms. Hail can create massive damage to property and crops, and harm people who are caught in them. Hail tends to fall along paths, which can vary in size from a few acres to larger areas 10 miles (16 kilometers) wide by 100 miles (160 kilometers) long.

Hail is formed during thunderstorms when tiny particles are swept into strong currents of rising and falling air in a storm cloud. The particle, called the nucleus, can be dust, salt, pollutants or ice crystals. The nucleus attracts water droplets around it that freeze as it moves into colder temperatures. A gust of downward moving air causes the nucleus to move into warmer temperatures where it picks up more water. The water forms into ice when an updraft (rising air) lifts it higher. The cycle of moving down and up through the air, gaining water that freezes, creates layers of ice. The longer the cycle continues, the larger the hail stone.

WORDS TO KNOW

Air: Gaseous mixture that envelopes Earth, composed mainly of nitrogen (about 78%) and oxygen (about 21%) with lesser amounts of argon, carbon dioxide, and other gases.

Condense: When a gas or vapor changes to a liquid.

Control experiment: A setup that is identical to the experiment, but is not affected by the variable that acts on the experimental group.

Cumulonimbus cloud: The parent cloud of a thunderstorm; a tall, vertically developed cloud capable of producing heavy rain, high winds, and lightning.

Updraft: A strong current of upward moving air.

Funnel cloud: A fully developed tornado vortex before it has touched the ground.

Hypothesis: An idea in the form of a statement that can be tested by observation and/or experiment.

Storm: An extreme atmospheric disturbance, associated with strong damaging winds, and often with thunder and lightning.

Storm chasers: People who track and seek out storms, often tornadoes.

Tornado: A violently rotating, narrow column of air in contact with the ground and usually extending from a cumulonimbus cloud.

Updraft: Warm, moist air that moves away from the ground.

Variable: Something that can affect the results of an experiment.

Vortex: A rotating column of a fluid such as air or water.

Water vapor: The change of water from a liquid to a gas.

The size of a hailstone, generally, is also determined by the strength of the updraft. The stronger the updraft, the more ice layers will accumulate as it travels up and down in the cloud. The hailstone will eventually fall to earth when it becomes too heavy to stay in the air. Most hailstones are smaller than a dime and often melt before they reach the ground. However, severe thunderstorms can produce extremely large hailstones, golf ball size and larger.

EXPERIMENT 1

Lightning Sparks: Explore how separating charges causes an attraction between objects

Purpose/Hypothesis Lightning that is produced during a storm is simply a massive electric spark, which is called static electricity. Friction causes the particles to separate into positive and negative charges. These opposite charges attract one another, and when the electric charges are separated they look for a way to get back together. In a storm, the jump of numerous negative charges reaching out towards the positive charges produces a bolt of lighting. A miniature version of static electricity will produce sparks and an attraction between charged objects.

In this experiment you will explore what happens when you cause charges to separate. You will use friction to create electrical charges on a balloon, and observe how three different objects react to these charges. The three objects you will use are: salt and pepper, water, and another balloon.

Before you begin, make an educated guess about the outcome of this experiment based on your knowledge of lightning and charges. This educated guess, or prediction, is your hypothesis. A hypothesis should explain these things:

- the topic of the experiment
- the variable you will change
- the variable you will measure
- what you expect to happen

A hypothesis should be brief, specific, and measurable. It must be something you can test through further investigation. Your experiment will prove or disprove whether your hypothesis is correct. Here is one possible hypothesis for this experiment: "If enough charges are separated, the balloon will attract different objects and create electricity."

In this case, the variable you will change is the separation of the negative and positive charges on the balloon. The variable you will measure is how the balloon's charges are attracted to other objects.

Having a control experiment will help you isolate each variable and measure the changes in the dependent variable. Only one variable will change between the control and the experimental setup, and that is the amount of charged particles. At the end of the experiment you will compare the charged balloon with the neutrally charged balloon.

Level of Difficulty Easy.

What Are the Variables?

Variables are anything that might affect the results of an experiment. Here are the main variables in this experiment:

- the object that is charged
- the degree of friction
- the material that produces the friction
- the distance from the balloon to the objects

In other words, the variables in this experiment are everything that might affect the charge of the balloon. If you change more than one variable at the same time, you will not be able to tell which variable had the most effect on the action of the charged particles.

How to Experiment Safely

This project poses little hazards, but remember you are experimenting with electricity, however small. Do not conduct this experiment if there are any flammable vapors in the air, such as gasoline from an open container.

Materials Needed

- 2 balloons
- salt and pepper
- access to sink
- small plate
- wool cloth or nylon (optional)

Approximate Budget $2.

Timetable 30 minutes.

Step-by-Step Instructions

1. Sprinkle some salt and pepper on a plate.
2. Inflate both balloons. For the control, do not rub one balloon. Place the balloon about 1 inch (2.5 centimeters) above the salt and pepper. Then place the balloon about 1 inch (2.5 centimeters) away from a trickle of water from the faucet. Note the results.
3. Rub the second balloon briskly against a piece of wool or your hair.
4. Hold this balloon about 1 inch (2.5 centimeters) above the salt and paper. Note what you see and hear.
5. Hold the balloon about 1 inch (2.5 centimeters) from a trickle of water. Note the results.
6. Darken the room. Rub both balloons against a cloth or your hair, and place them together. Note what you see and hear.
7. Place your hand gently over the section of the balloon that you rubbed. Again place the two balloons together and note the results.

Step 5: Hold the balloon close to, but not touching, the stream of water. GALE GROUP.

Summary of Results Create a data chart that describes the results of each trial. Compare the results to the control experiment. What did placing your hand over the balloon do to the charges in the balloon? Write a paragraph explaining your conclusions. Include how powerful bolts of lightning relate to this experiment.

Change the Variables You can change the variables in this experiment in several ways. You can use different types of material to create friction, and determine if this produces less or more attraction. You can also create charges on different objects, such as a comb. Try creating sparks or picking up different objects.

EXPERIMENT 2

Tornadoes: Making a violent vortex

Purpose/Hypothesis Tornadoes occur when air masses clash and result in a spinning vortex. The air in the vortex becomes stretched and narrower with time. As the shape of the funnel gradually narrows, it creates an increase in the rotation speed, resulting in a twist similar to that of a spinning skater.

In this experiment you will observe the relationship between the intensity of a vortex and its shape. You will create a vortex using water; a vortex of fluids behaves similar to that of air. A whirlpool and the water in a draining bathtub are examples of a vortex in liquids. The vortex forms when spinning water, or air, is pulled downwards, in this case by gravity. The funnel of water narrows as it is pulled down.

You will fill two bottles with water, create a vortex, and observe the water movement from one bottle to another. You will control the

Troubleshooter's Guide

Below is a problem that may arise during this experiment, a possible cause, and a way to remedy the problem.

Problem: There was no difference between the control and the experimental balloon.

Possible cause: You may not have created enough friction, in which case not enough charges would separate. Try rubbing the balloon vigorously against your hair, and repeat the experiment.

A tornado rips across the countryside in Jarrell, Texas, in May 1997. AP/WIDE WORLD

What Are the Variables?

Variables are anything that might affect the results of an experiment. Here are the main variables in this experiment:

- the size of the hole
- the shape of the bottles
- the size of the bottles
- the temperature of the liquid
- the type of liquid

In other words, the variables in this experiment are everything that might affect the vortex. If you change more than one variable at the same time, you will not be able to tell which variable had the most effect on the water's speed.

narrowness of the vortex by placing two different size holes between the two bottles. Observing small colored materials placed in the water will provide a way to measure the speed of the water's rotation.

Before you begin, make an educated guess about the outcome of this experiment based on your knowledge of tornadoes and vortexes. This educated guess, or prediction, is your hypothesis. A hypothesis should explain these things:

- the topic of the experiment
- the variable you will change
- the variable you will measure
- what you expect to happen

A hypothesis should be brief, specific, and measurable. It must be something you can test through further investigation. Your experiment will prove or disprove whether your hypothesis is correct. Here is one possible hypothesis for this experiment: "The speed of the water will increase as the vortex becomes increasingly narrow."

In this case, the variable you will change is the size of the vortex hole, and the variable you will measure is the speed of the water.

Conducting a control experiment will help you isolate each variable and measure the changes in the dependent variable. Only one variable will change between the control and each of your vortexes. For the control, you will observe the water's speed without narrowing the hole. At the end of the experiment you will compare the intensity of the control with each of the experimental vortexes.

Level of Difficulty Easy.

Materials Needed

- 2 identical 2-liter clear plastic soda bottles
- scissors
- duct tape or electrical tape
- water
- sparkles or any other small visible material that does not dissolve in water, such as oregano

- 2 washers the same outside diameter as the mouth of the bottles, one with a small center hole and one with a larger center hole
- marking pen

Approximate Budget $5.

Timetable 30 minutes.

Step-by-Step Instructions

1. Label one bottle "A" and the other "B."
2. For your control: Fill Bottle A about two-thirds full of water.
3. Sprinkle in some of the sparkles or other visible material.
4. Place bottle B upside down on top of bottle A.
5. Tape the mouths of the two bottles tightly together with the tape, aligning the openings up exactly. Test for leakage by carefully tilting the bottles.
6. Turn the bottles over so that bottle A (with the water in it) is on top of bottle B, and quickly swirl the bottles several times, just like you would spin a hula-hoop. Set the bottles down and observe the water, noting the shape and speed of the swirling water.
7. Untape the bottles and tape the washer with the larger hole to the mouth of bottle A. Do not cover the washer hole with tape.
8. Again, tape the two bottles tightly together, lining up the mouths exactly. Quickly turn the bottles over and swirl. Note the description of the shape and speed of the vortex.
9. Repeat Steps 7 and 8, taping the washer with the smaller hole to bottle A. Note the results.

Summary of Results Evaluate your results. Was your hypothesis correct? How does the water relate to the actions of a tornado? Compare the results of the two experimental trials with the control experiment. Write a summary of the

---

How to Experiment Safely

There are no safety hazards in this experiment.

Step 5: Line up the two bottles exactly and tape together. GALE GROUP.

Troubleshooter's Guide

Below are problems that may arise during this experiment, some possible causes, and some ways to remedy the problems.

Problem: There was no vortex.

Possible cause: You may not have lined up the washer exactly with the mouths of the bottles, or the tape may have covered some of the circular opening. Repeat the experiment, making sure the opening is clear.

Problem: It was difficult to gauge the speed of the vortex.

Possible cause: Determining the speed of the water is an estimate based on how quickly the sparkles are swirling. You may need to place less sparkles in the bottle. Select the same point on the bottle for every experiment to focus on the swirl.

experiment that explains your results. You may want to include drawings of the shape and speed of each vortex.

Change the Variables To alter this experiment you can change several of the variables, one at a time, and again observe the flow pattern of the water. You can use bottles of different shapes and sizes. You can also try changing the type of liquid you use and the temperature of the liquid. Would the experiment give the same results with a thick liquid substance as opposed to one that has greater flow? Different swirling techniques may also provide interesting results.

EXPERIMENT 3

Forming Hailstones: How do temperature differences affect the formation of hail?

Purpose/Hypothesis Hailstones form when a particle cycles up and down in a cloud. The extreme temperature difference between the cold, high air and the warmer air below leads to layers of ice forming around the nucleus

In this experiment, you will explore how extreme temperature differences affect the formation of a hailstone. For the extremely cold temperature, you will use dry ice. Dry ice is frozen carbon dioxide. It has a temperature of about -109°Fahrenheit (-78°Celsius). Dry ice and alcohol is a slightly warmer temper than dry ice alone. For the relatively warm temperature, you will use dry ice and water. A glass bead will act as the hail's nucleus. In one trial, you will form a hailstone by having the nucleus move through all three temperatures. In a second trial, you will only use the two relatively warm temperatures. The amount of time forming the hailstones should be approximately the same. By comparing the formation of the hailstone, you can measure the affect of temperature differences on hail formation.

Before you begin, make an educated guess about the outcome of this experiment based on your knowledge of how hail is produced in a cloud.

This educated guess, or prediction, is your hypothesis. A hypothesis should explain these things:

- the topic of the experiment
- the variable you will change
- the variable you will measure
- what you expect to happen

A hypothesis should be brief, specific, and measurable. It must be something you can test through further investigation. Your experiment will prove or disprove whether your hypothesis is correct. Here is one possible hypothesis for this experiment: "The nucleus that passes through more extreme temperatures will accumulate more ice and form a larger hailstone than the nucleus that moves through the relatively warmer temperatures."

In this case, the variable you will change is the temperatures that the nucleus will move through as it forms a hailstone. The variable you will measure is size and shape of the hailstone.

Level of Difficulty Moderate

Materials Needed

- 1 pound (0.45 kilograms) of dry ice (You will need adult help in purchasing dry ice)
- 1 cup of isopropyl alcohol (rubbing alcohol)
- 4 plastic containers
- 1 cup of water
- 2 glass beads, approximately $\frac{1}{4}$ inch (0.64 centimeters) in diameter
- thread to string the bead, approximately 10 inches (24 inches) long
- thick, insulated gloves to handle dry ice
- tongs to handle dry ice
- pencil
- clock with second hand

Approximate Budget $12

What Are the Variables?

Variables are anything that might affect the results of an experiment. Here are the variables in this experiment:

- the size of the glass bead
- the temperatures of the baths
- the time that the bead spends in the baths

In other words, the variables in this experiment are everything that might affect the accumulation of ice on the glass bead. If you change more than one variable at the same time, you will not be able to tell which variable had the most effect on the properties of the hailstone.

Step 2: Set up three temperature baths: 1) container of dry ice; 2) container of isopropyl alcohol and dry ice; and 3) a container of water and dry ice.

ILLUSTRATION BY TEMAH NELSON.

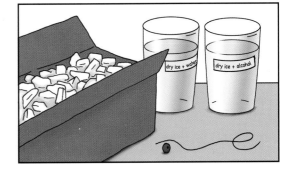

How to Experiment Safely

Dry ice is a dangerous substance, have an adult assist you in purchasing and using it during the experiment. Never touch dry ice with your bare hands. Always wear gloves and use tongs when handling.

Timetable 45 minutes.

Step-by-Step Instructions

1. Take the glass bead and string it on thread. Make sure it is securely tied onto the thread.

2. Set up three temperature baths: 1) container of dry ice; 2) container of isopropyl alcohol and dry ice; and 3) a container of water and dry ice

3. Dry ice usually comes in a cardboard box or insulated container. For the dry ice container, you can leave it in the box or container.

4. For the dry ice/alcohol mixture: Place two plastic containers inside of each other. Fill the container with one cup of isopropyl alcohol and add three to four chunks of dry ice. Make sure the mixture becomes slushy and thick, add more dry ice if needed as it melts.

5. For the dry ice/water mixture: Place two plastic containers inside of each other, as in the previous step, and add 1 cup of water. To the water add two chunks of dry ice. Mixture should become bubbly and foggy. Keep adding dry ice as it melts.

6. Place all three ice baths on a tray to protect the table or countertop.

7. To create a hailstone using three temperatures: Use the pencil to push the glass bead into the dry ice until it covers the bead. Have the bead sit in the dry ice for one minute.

8. Use the string to pull out the bead and dip it into the dry ice and alcohol mixture for 10 seconds.

9. Dip the bead into the dry ice/ water mixture for three seconds.

10. Repeat the cycle, but place the bead on top of the dry ice instead of submerging it so you do not dislocate any ice that is forming. Leave the bead in the dry ice for 30 seconds.

11. Repeat Steps 7–9 for seven to eight cycles and record your observations.

12. To create a hailstone using two temperatures: use the pencil to push a glass bead into the dry ice until it covers the bead.

Step 7: Use the pencil to push the glass bead into the dry ice until it covers the bead.

ILLUSTRATION BY TEMAH NELSON.

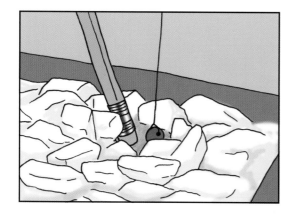

Have the bead sit in the dry ice for one minute.

13. Use the string to pull out the bead and dip it into the dry ice and alcohol mixture for 30 seconds.

14. Dip the bead into the dry ice and water mixture for three seconds.

15. Repeat the process of dipping the bead into the dry ice/alcohol and into the dry ice/water for nine to 10 cycles. The amount of time forming the two hailstones should be approximately the same.

Step 8: Use the string to pull out the bead and dip it into the dry ice and alcohol mixture for 10 seconds. ILLUSTRATION BY TEMAH NELSON.

Summary of Results Look at the two pieces of hail you formed. How do the sizes of the hailstones compare to one another? Was your hypothesis correct? How does the ice accumulate on the bead as it passes through the different temperature baths? Write a summary of the experiment that explains your results. You may want to include drawings of how the ice forms on the bead over time.

Change the Variables To alter this experiment you can change one or more of the variables. You could use a nucleus other than a glass bead, such as a pebble or small ball. If you change this variable think about what materials maintain a cold temperature: glass, plastic, metal? You can experiment with dipping the bead in the ice baths for varying lengths of time, or change the order of baths that you dip the bead into. For example, start the bead in the dry ice and alcohol bath and then place it into the dry ice and then the dry ice and water. How does this affect the build up of ice?

Design Your Own Experiment

How to Select a Topic Relating to this Concept To select a related project, you can create models of weather phenomena and collect information from observing. An experiment with storms could include observing collecting data before and during a thunderstorm. You can also use the information meteorologists and storm chasers have gathered on tornadoes. The tools used to measure storms opens up another branch of related projects.

Troubleshooter's Guide

Below are problems that may arise during this experiment, some possible causes, and some ways to remedy the problems.

Problem: Ice did not accumulate on the glass bead.

Possible cause: The bead did not get cold enough initially to sustain the formation of ice. Make sure there are still chunks of dry ice in the water bath. Keep the bead submerged in dry ice for one full minute before moving it into the alcohol and water baths.

Problem: Ice built up on the bead but was lost in water bath.

Possible cause: The water and dry ice bath serves the purpose of adding water to the bead. But if the bead is submerged in the water and dry ice too long it will melt the ice that has accumulated. Make sure that you dip the bead briefly into this bath. You can try two seconds instead of three. Also, make sure that you are replacing the dry ice that melts in the water. The dry ice serves to keep the water cold, and as it melts the temperature increases.

Check the Further Readings section and talk with your science teacher to learn more about storms. You may also want to contact a local weatherperson in your area to talk about his or her work and possible project ideas.

Steps in the Scientific Method To conduct an original experiment, you need to plan carefully and think things through. Otherwise, you might not be sure what question you are answering, what you are or should be measuring, or what your findings prove or disprove.

Here are the steps in designing an experiment:

- State the purpose of—and the underlying question behind—the experiment you propose to do.

- Recognize the variables involved and select one that will help you answer the question at hand.

- State your hypothesis, an educated guess about the answer to your question.

- Decide how to change the variable you selected.

- Decide how to measure your results.

Recording Data and Summarizing the Results If appropriate, your data should include charts and graphs. They should be clearly labeled and easy to read. You may also want to include photographs and drawings of your experimental setup and results, which will help others visualize the steps in the experiment. If you are observing or reporting on a weather phenomena, you may want to include a series of drawings or photographs taken over a set period of time. Make sure you note the time each picture occurred.

If you are preparing an exhibit, you may want to display your results, such as any experimental setup you designed. If you have completed a nonexperimental project, explain clearly what your research question was and illustrate your findings.

Related Projects You can design your own experiments on storms. Investigate methods that meteorologists use to measure storms and how these tools have changed over history. How far in advance can meteorologists predict a storm and how accurate are these predictions? You can also conduct a project related to storm safety and how people should behave in a storm. Scientists have broken down each storm into stages. You could create models of each of the stages and provide explanations for each one.

There still remain many questions about how tornadoes form. You can look at differing theories of what causes a tornado and evaluate the evidence for these theories. Where are tornadoes most likely to form and why? With lightning, there are theories on how lightning is attracted to some types of trees more than others. You can investigate what lightning hits and the cause of attraction of each object.

For More Information

"The Disaster Area." *FEMA for Kids.* http://www.fema.gov/kids/dizarea.htm (accessed on February 18, 2008). Simple instructions and explanations of storms by the Federal Emergency Management Agency.

DryiceInfo.com. www.dryiceinfo.com (accessed on February 18, 2008). Background and searchable database on where to purchase dry ice.

Grazulis, Thomas P. *Significant Tornadoes 1680–1991.* St. Johnsbury, VT: Environmental Films, 1993. Comprehensive listing of significant tornadoes and their effects.

Kahl, Jonathan, D. *Thunderbolt: Learning about Lightning.* Minneapolis, MN: Lerner Publishing Group, 1993. Simple explanations, photographs, and charts related to lightning.

Kramer, Stephen. P. *Lightning.* Minneapolis, MN: Lerner Publishing Group, 1993. Lots of illustrations and color to explain this phenomena.

Moore, Gene. *Chase Day.* www.chaseday.com/hail.html (accessed on February 18, 2008). Information and photographs of hailstorms and hailstones.

"Thunderstorms." *Met Office.* http://www.metoffice.gov.uk/education/secondary/students/thunderstorms.html (accessed on February 20, 2008). Thunderstorms leaflet includes illustrations.

"Tornadoes: The Most Ferocious Storm." *The Why Files.* http://whyfiles.org/013tornado/ (accessed on February 20, 2008). Interactive animations showing the formation and effects of a tornado.

87

Structures and Shapes

Humans have been busy building structures for almost as long as we have existed. The structures that we build, however, have changed dramatically over the last thousand years. We have learned to construct buildings that extend thousands of feet up, and we can build bridges that safely support tons of weight over immense stretches of water. What have we learned that enables us to build what our ancestors would have thought impossible?

The answer lies mainly in concepts about the nature of force and motion that Sir Isaac Newton (1642–1727) developed over three hundred years ago. Newton proposed a set of "laws" that clearly explain why and how objects move or remain still. These laws apply to the planning of structures like buildings and bridges because they must be designed to remain fixed in place and not be moved by the forces that act upon them.

Different forces can act upon one object One of Newton's laws tells us that different forces can act on a single object at the same time, as when two soccer players kick the ball at the same time. One has exerted force on the ball toward the goal; the other has exerted force in another direction. If the two players kick with precisely the same energy in exactly opposite directions, then the ball will remain motionless. Two kicks that are not equal in energy and not opposite in direction, however, will send the ball flying sideways off the field. This combined force is called a resultant.

Standing a single playing card on its edge is nearly impossible. Two cards, however, can be stood on edge quite easily. This is because the two cards can be made to exert two equal and exactly opposite forces upon each other. As long as this force stays balanced, the cards will remain standing. When different forces add up to a resultant of zero, this state is called equilibrium. If you increase the force on one side without increasing the force on the other, the resultant is no longer zero; equilibrium has

WORDS TO KNOW

Arch: A curved structure that spans an opening and supports a weight above the opening.

Beam: A straight, horizontal structure that spans an opening and supports a weight above the opening.

Compression: A type of force on an object where the object is pushed or squeezed from each end.

Equilibrium: A balancing or canceling out of opposing forces, so that an object will remain at rest.

Force: A physical interaction (pushing or pulling) tending to change the state of motion (velocity) of an object.

Platform: The horizontal surface of a bridge on which traffic travels.

Resultant: A force that results from the combined action of two other forces.

Rigidity: The amount an object will deflect when supporting a weight. The less it deflects for a given amount of weight, the greater its rigidity.

been disrupted, and the cards will fall in the direction exerted by the stronger force.

The science of architecture and engineering is largely the analysis of force: how to distribute and direct the many forces acting on a structure to ensure that it remains in equilibrium.

A card house can stand because the forces acting on it add up to a resultant of zero.
CORBIS-BETTMANN.

THE CARD–CASTLE.

The arch redistributes forces to maintain equilibrium One early development in architecture that uses the principle of distribution of force is the arch. The arch directs the downward force of the supported weight around the arch and into the ground. In a stone arch, for example, each stone has slightly tapered sides. The weight on the top stone causes it to push out and down on the next stone, and so on around the curve of the arch until it reaches the ground. An arch can support greater weight than a straight beam across an opening, even when the beam and arch are built of the same materials. This is because the force in an arch squeezes, or compresses, the material in the arch, rather than bending it the way it does in a beam. Most materials are stronger in compression than they are in bending. The greatest bending force in a beam takes place in the center,

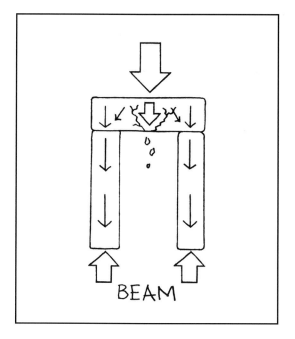

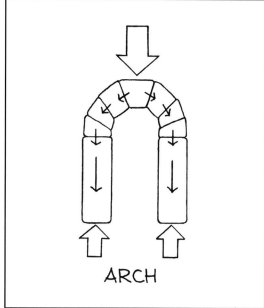

RIGHT: The arch is an effective design because it distributes the downward force around the arch and into the ground. GALE GROUP.

LEFT: The beam design is limited in the weight it can bear because the middle section is unsupported. GALE GROUP.

where it is unsupported. Over time, the bending force on the beam could cause it to crack.

The same principle applies to bridges. The platform of a bridge, the flat surface over which vehicles travel, can be supported either by a beam or by an arch. A simple beam bridge can extend only a limited distance before its weight and the weight of the traffic upon it would cause the beam to fail. An arch bridge more effectively transfers the force of this weight out to the ground. Many large bridges today use arches as part of their design.

In the first project, you will construct two bridges—one using a beam and one using an arch—and determine whether the arch can support more weight. In the second project, you will see if you can increase the strength of the beam design by increasing the vertical height of the beam.

PROJECT 1

Arches and Beams: Which is strongest?

Purpose/Hypothesis In this project, you will construct one bridge using an arch and one

How to Experiment Safely

Use only iron fishing sinkers for weights in this experiment. If only lead sinkers are available, substitute coins or some other easily measurable form of weights. Lead is toxic and should not be handled without proper protection.

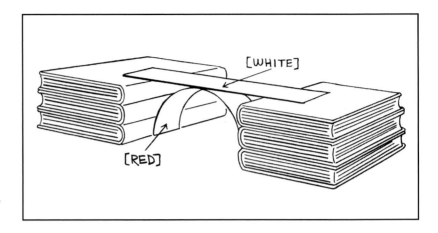

Steps 4 and 6: Set-up of arch bridge. GALE GROUP.

using a beam. The bridges will use the same vertical supports and platforms, and the arch and beam will be of identical thickness. You will test the bridges to determine how much weight each one can support.

Level of Difficulty Easy/moderate.

Materials Needed

- 1 sheet of red poster board, 14 x 22 inches (36 x 56 cm)
- 1 sheet of white poster board, 14 x 22 inches (36 x 56 cm)
- scissors
- ruler
- 10 iron fishing sinkers, 0.5-ounce (14-gram) each
- 4 stacks of textbooks, each approximately 5 inches (12 cm) tall

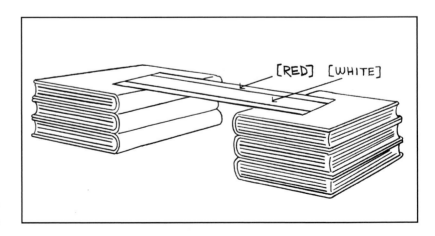

Steps 5 and 6: Set-up of beam bridge. GALE GROUP.

Approximate Budget $15 for poster board and sinkers.

Timetable Approximately 40 minutes.

Step-by-Step Instructions

1. Cut two pieces of white poster board, 14 x 4 inches (36 x 10 centimeters). These will be the platforms of your bridges.
2. Cut two pieces of red poster board, 14 x 5 inches (36 x 12 centimeters). These will be the support designs (beam and arch) of your bridges.
3. Place two stacks of textbooks about 8 inches (20 centimeters) apart. Do the same with the other two stacks. These will be the vertical supports of your bridges.
4. Bend one piece of red poster board into an arch and place it between one pair of vertical supports. This will be the arch of one bridge. The peak of the arch should be the same height as the vertical supports. Adjust the distance between the vertical supports until the peak of the arch is even with the top of the two stacks.
5. Lay the other red piece across the second pair of vertical supports. This will be the beam of the other bridge. Adjust the distance between the vertical supports until it is the same as the distance on the arch bridge.
6. Measure and mark the centers of the two pieces of white poster board. Lay each of the white pieces across a pair of vertical supports so that the center mark is halfway across the opening. These will be the platforms of your bridges. The weights must be placed on or near the centerpoints you marked on the platforms. Your bridges should look like the illustrations.
7. Measure the height of the platforms (at the center) and record this height on a data chart. Place one weight on the center point of each bridge. Measure any distance the center of the platform has dropped. Record this on your data chart. Add another weight as close to the first as possible and measure the height again.
8. Continue adding weights to the bridges. Measure and record the distance each platform drops after each new weight is added. Repeat this process until both of the bridges have collapsed.

Troubleshooter's Guide

Here is a problem you may encounter, some possible causes, and ways to solve the problem.

Problem: The accordion folds of the beams tend to flatten out, decreasing the vertical height of the beam.

Possible causes:

1. Your tape is not holding. Try folding the edges of the white platform around the beam and then taping the assembly.
2. Your poster board is not rigid enough. Use thicker poster board.

Summary of Results Examine your data and compare the results of the tests for the two designs. Did your predictions prove true? Which design proved to be the sturdier one? Summarize your results in writing.

Change the Project By altering the project, you can investigate other questions about bridges. How does doubling the thickness of the arch or the beam affect its strength? What if you construct the arch bridge with two arches instead of one? Also consider changing the materials. Is rigidity always a good thing? See which supports more weight, a slightly flexible design made of cardboard, or an identical design made of wooden hobby sticks.

PROJECT 2

Beams and Rigidity: How does the vertical height of a beam affect its rigidity?

Purpose/Hypothesis Rigidity is a measure of how much an object, such as a bridge, will deflect when supporting a weight. Bridges must not only be strong, but they must also be fairly rigid to keep the platform level without sagging. In this project, you will construct three beam-support bridges using beams of different vertical heights. You will test each one and compare the results to determine whether increasing the height of a beam can make this bridge design more rigid.

Level of Difficulty Moderate.

Materials Needed

- 1 sheet of red poster board, 14 x 27 inches (36 x 68 centimeters) or the equivalent with 2 sheets
- 1 sheet of white poster board, 14 x 22 inches (36 x 56 centimeters)
- scissors
- tape
- ruler
- 10 iron fishing sinkers, 0.5-ounce (14-gram) each
- 6 stacks of textbooks, each approximately 5 inches (12 centimeters) tall

How to Experiment Safely

Use only iron fishing sinkers for weights in this experiment. If only lead sinkers are available, substitute coins or some other easily measurable form of weights. Lead is toxic and should not be handled without proper protection.

Approximate Budget $15 for poster board and sinkers.

Timetable Approximately 40 minutes.

Step-by-Step Instructions

1. Cut three pieces of white poster board, all 14 x 4 inches (36 x 10 centimeters). These will be the platforms of your bridges.

2. Cut three pieces of red poster board, 14 x 6 inches (36 x 15 centimeters), 14 x 9 inches (36 x 23 centimeters), and 14 x 12 inches (36 x 30 centimeters). These will be used to make the beams of your bridges.

3. Place the stacks of textbooks in three pairs. The stacks should be about 10 inches (25 centimeters) apart. These will be the vertical supports of your bridges.

4. On the 14 x 6-inch piece of red poster board, measure and mark the board so the 6-inch (15-centimeter) width is divided into six 1-inch (2.5-centimeter) segments. Fold the board carefully along these marks so it looks like the illustration.

5. Divide the 14 x 9-inch poster board into six 1.5-inch- (3.8-centimeter-) wide segments and divide the 14 x 12-inch poster board into six 2-inch- (5-centimeter-) wide segments. Carefully fold each one into an accordion shape.

6. Lay the three folded red pieces across the three pairs of vertical supports. These will be the beams of the bridges.

7. Measure and mark the centers of the three pieces of white poster board. These will be the platforms of your bridges. The weights must be placed on or near the centerpoints you marked on the platforms.

8. Attach the platforms to the beams using tape. Place the beam/platform assemblies across the three pairs of vertical supports with the beam-side down. Your bridges should look like the illustration.

9. Measure the vertical height of each bridge, from the bottom of the folded beam to the

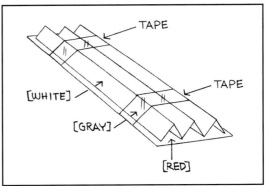

Step 4: Illustration of accordion-fold beam. GALE GROUP.

Steps 6 to 8: Set-up of beam bridge. GALE GROUP.

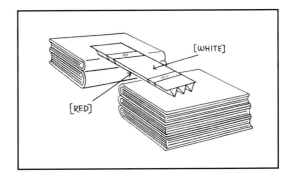

Troubleshooter's Guide

Here is a problem you may encounter during this project, some possible causes, and ways to solve the problem.

Problem: One of the bridges tends to twist and dump its weight before collapsing.

Possible causes:

1. Your weights are off center. Place your weights as close to the center mark as possible.
2. Your poster board is not rigid enough. Use thicker poster board.

top of the platform. Record this information on a data chart.

10. Measure the height of the platforms at the center and record this height on your data chart. Place one weight on the center point of each bridge. Measure the distance the center of the platform has dropped. Record this on your data chart. Add another weight as close to the first as possible and measure again.

11. Continue adding weight to the bridges. Measure and record the distance each platform drops after each new weight is added. Repeat this process until both of the bridges have collapsed.

Summary of Results Examine your data and compare the results of the tests for the three beams. Did your predictions prove true? How much does each increase in vertical beam height increase the beam's ability to support weight? Summarize your findings in writing.

Change the Project By altering the project, you can determine whether it is preferable to construct a wide bridge with a low vertical height or a narrow bridge with a greater vertical height. Which is stronger, a bridge 4 feet (1.2 meter) wide and 2 feet (0.6 meter) high, or a bridge 2 feet (0.6 meter) wide and 4 feet (1.2 meter) high? Also consider changing the materials. Is rigidity always a good thing? See which supports more weight, a slightly flexible design made of cardboard or an identical design made of wooden hobby sticks.

Design Your Own Experiment

How to Select a Topic Relating to this Concept Watching the way your bridge designs reacted to the weight placed on them may have already given you ideas for improving them. Architecture and design engineering encompasses a wide range of structures and products you see and use every day. Can you think of a way to make something work better or keep people safer? Testing ideas in miniature is a vital tool for trying out new ideas.

Think about combining the ideas and designs used in these projects. Can you think of a way to use the strongest beams in the second project to make a stronger arch? Can you build a bridge that uses both a beam and an arch? If you are doing a project as a group, try holding a competition for bridge designs.

If you want to do an experiment or a project, check the Further Readings section and talk with your science teacher or school or community media specialist to start gathering information on structure and shape questions that interest you.. As you consider possible experiments or projects, be sure to discuss them with your science teacher or another knowledgeable adult before trying them. Some of them might be dangerous.

Steps in the Scientific Method To do an original experiment, you need to plan carefully and think things through. Otherwise, you might not be sure which question you are answering, what you are or should be measuring, and what your findings prove or disprove.

This modern-day bridge combines the arch and the beam designs. GALE GROUP.

Here are the steps in designing an experiment:

- State the purpose of—and the underlying question behind—the experiment you propose to do.

- Recognize the variables involved, and select one that will help you answer the question at hand.

- State a testable hypothesis, an educated guess about the answer to your question.

- Decide how to change the variable you selected.

- Decide how to measure your results.

Recording Data and Summarizing the Results In the projects included here and in any experiments or projects you develop, you can look for ways to display your data in more accurate and interesting ways. For example, can you think of a better way to measure the weight sustained by the bridge? Should you test the structures by distributing the weight across the span?

Remember that those who view your results may not have seen the experiment performed, so you must present the information you have gathered in as clear a way as possible. Including photographs or illustrations of the steps in the experiment is a good way to show a viewer how you got from your hypothesis to your conclusion.

Related Projects To develop other experiments or projects on this topic, take a look at the structures and shapes of things you see around you every day. Take different design options and test them in miniature. Consider ways you could reinforce the bridges you built to enable them to hold more weight. Can you think of a better way to construct new models?

For More Information

Briscoe, Diane. *Bridge Building: Bridge Designs and How they Work.* Bloomington, MN: Red Brick Learning, 2004.

Gibson, Gary. *Making Shapes.* Brookfield, CT: Copper Beech Books, 1995. Demonstrates a variety of structural shapes and how they are applied in construction.

Hawkes, Nigel. *Structures: The Way Things are Built.* New York: MacMillan Publishing Company, 1990. Looks at ancient and modern structures and describes how they were built.

National Aeronautics and Space Administration (NASA). *Newton's Laws of Motion.* http://www.grc.nasa.gov/WWW/K-12/airplane/newton.html (accessed on February 6, 2008). Descriptions and graphics of Isaac Newton's three laws of motions.

Slafer, Anna, Keven Cahill, and the National Building Museum. *Why Design?: Activities and Projects from the National Building Museum.* Chicago: Chicago Review Press, 1995.

Stevenson, Neil. *Architecture: The World's Greatest Buildings Explored and Explained.* New York: DK Publishing, 1997. Examines in depth the history, design, and construction of fifty buildings and structures from around the world.

The Visual Dictionary of Buildings. New York: DK Publishing, 1992. Clearly illustrates and provides terminology for numerous architectural features from ancient to modern times.

WGBH Educational Foundation. *Building Big.* http://www.pbs.org/wgbh/buildingbig/index.html (accessed on February 6, 2008). Information and activities on bridges, domes, skyscrapers, dams, and tunnels.

88

Time

Anyone who has ever raced to finish an activity knows the importance of time. In modern day, people monitor time by the minute. Yet thousands of years ago, keeping track of time was not important. People went about their work and play when the Sun was in the sky and they slept when the Sun was down. Over the years, people began to notice patterns in the Sun's rising and falling. Eventually these patterns led to a system of keeping time that was accepted throughout the world.

The natural rhythms of the Sun and Moon established the time concepts of year, month, and day. Other timekeeping classifications—weeks, hours, minutes, and seconds—are manmade inventions. The concept of time has intrigued some of the most prominent scientists. It has also led to the development of several major discoveries.

Breaking up time Ancient Egyptians noticed that the Sun rose at different positions on the horizon depending on the season. In the warmer season when the crops grew, the Sun rose farther to the north. In the cooler season after the last harvest, the Sun rose farther to the south. They noted the position of the sunrise on a particular morning and tracked this position through the seasons. They found it took 365 sunrises before the Sun returned to the same position. Today people know that 365 days is the time it takes Earth to orbit around the Sun. We call that length of time a year. Technically, a year is 365 days, 5 hours, 48 minutes, and 46 seconds.

The ancient Egyptians also noticed a full moon occurred once every $29\frac{1}{2}$ days—which is what we now call a month, from the Greek and Latin words for moon. The Egyptians chose to split up a month into groups of seven days. Historians theorize they could have selected the number seven because ancient peoples believed (wrongly) that seven heavenly bodies revolved around Earth.

It takes 365 days—one year— for Earth to orbit around the Sun. NASA.

As Earth revolves around the Sun, the planet also rotates. A day is the amount of time it takes for Earth to complete one rotation. As it spins, half of Earth faces the Sun and has light; the other half faces away from the Sun and is dark. When a day exactly begins depends upon one's point of view. Ancient Egyptians began their day at dawn; Babylonians, Jews, and Muslims began at dusk; and Romans began their day at midnight. A solar day is the time it takes the Sun to return to its highest point in the sky. While the average day in a year measures twenty-four hours, lengths of individual days vary. After Earth has completed one rotation it must spin for about an extra four minutes around the Sun for the Sun to reach the same point in the sky. Astronomers measure a day by the length of time it takes for Earth to make a complete turn with respect to the stars, which is constant throughout the year. This is called a sidereal day and it lasts 23 hours 56 minutes and 4.1 seconds of average solar time.

Hours came about when Egyptians studied the movement of the stars at night. They noted a regular motion of the stars and divided the night into twelve equal parts, based on the rising of a particular star or stars in the night sky. They then decided to divide the day into the same number of parts, known as hours.

To measure daylight's hours, they used a sundial to track a shadow as the Sun moved across the sky (actually as Earth revolved beneath the Sun). A sundial has an upright part in the center called a gnomon. The gnomon casts a shadow across a surface that is divided into twelve equal parts. As the Sun moves across the sky, the tip of the gnomon's shadow creeps across the twelve sections. The sundials in Egypt were probably fairly accurate because this area is relatively close to the equator. Near the equator the position of the Sun is always high overhead throughout the year, and the length of time the sun is up each day is almost constant. Farther north or south from the equator, the time the sun is up can be very long or very short depending on the season. For example, in northern Alaska the Sun never sets in mid-summer and never rises during mid-winter. Under those conditions, sundials would not be of much value in keeping time.

The water clock was another type of time measurement that ancient people used. The water clock did not depend on an area's location or the changing rhythms of the Sun. In a water clock, a bowl with a small hole in the bottom was filled with water. Lines were marked on the inside of the bowl to symbolize the hours. As the water dripped slowly out the bottom, the water level sank, revealing the lines in the bowl. A water clock worked steadily at all times of the night and day, but someone had to refill the supply of water when it was empty.

Swing time A revolution in science that began in the sixteenth century had a significant impact on time. First, Polish mathematician

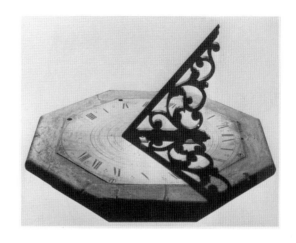

Sundials tell time by the position of the sun. CORBIS-BETTMANN.

The water clock was another type of time measurement that ancient peoples used. GALE GROUP.

In the late 1500s, Galileo Galilei was the first to begin experimenting with the concepts of a pendulum and oscillation. THE LIBRARY OF CONGRESS.

Nicolas Copernicus (1473–1543) found that Earth rotates around the Sun, not the other way around as was previously believed. His work caused a great deal of controversy because it was generally accepted at the time that Earth was the center of the universe. Eventually, the Copernican theory became accepted, and people could know Earth's location when they calculated time.

Then in 1581 Italian teenager Galileo Galilei (1564–1642) made a significant finding. The story goes that while Galileo was attending a church service, he began to watch a heavy lamp swinging from a chain attached to the ceiling. He used his pulse as a timepiece to note how long it took for each swing or oscillation. Whether the length of the swings was long or short, each swing always took the same amount of time.

Galileo began experimenting with a pendulum, a free-swinging weight, usually consisting of a heavy object attached to the end of a long rod or string, suspended from a fixed point. He found that the amount of time it takes a pendulum to complete one full swing had nothing to do with the weight of the pendulum or how far the pendulum swings. The length of time it takes for the pendulum to go back and forth depends only on the length of the pendulum. Galileo designed a simple pendulum timepiece, but he never built it.

In 1656 Dutch scientist Christian Huygens (1629–1695) used Galileo's ideas of oscillation to build the first pendulum clock. Inside this clock the regular movements of the pendulum turned wheels that controlled the hands of the clock. It was accurate to within one minute a day.

A mess of times Until the late 1800s, the world was a jumble of times. Countries, cities, and even neighboring towns were using their own local time, setting their clocks to noon when the Sun was directly overhead. Four o'clock in one city could be seven minutes past four in a town a short distance away. As travel, industry, and communication began to grow, it was decided there should be a standard time throughout the world.

In 1884 the world was officially divided into 24 time zones, like 24 segments of an orange. There was one zone for each hour of the day, and the time within each zone was the same. The starting point for the time zones was an imaginary north-south line that ran through Greenwich,

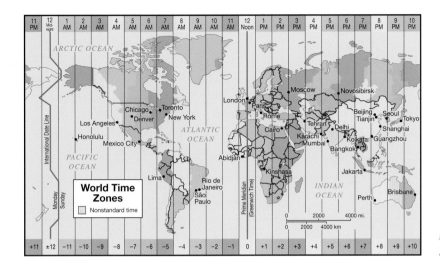

There are twenty-four time zones worldwide, one for each hour of the day. GALE GROUP.

England. The east–west distance around the world from this imaginary line determined each area's time zone. This system of time is called Greenwich Mean Time (GMT).

Space-time: It's all relative Moving into the past and future has long been a favorite theme of science fiction authors, but the subject of moving in time has also fascinated scientists. For years people thought that time was an absolute: It could not be stretched or condensed. In 1887 two scientists found that the speed of light—how fast light travels in a vacuum—appeared unchanged by the movement of its source or that of the observer. The speed of light is rounded off to 186,000 miles per second (297,600 kilometers per second).

Then in the early 1900s physicist Albert Einstein (1879–1955) changed people's view of time and space. Where something is located is its place in space. Einstein said that time combines with space to form space-time, and that it is not absolute: How fast time moves depends on how fast the person measuring time is moving in space. Einstein's theory showed that time is relative, and so his theory is called the Theory of Special Relativity. The faster an object travels, the more slowly time passes for that object. This would only be noticeable at speeds approaching the speed of light.

A simple theoretical example would be how you would perceive time if you were looking at a clock while moving away from it on a rocket traveling at the speed of light. When you first look back at the clock, you see that it reads 2 hours, 20 minutes, and 11 seconds. This image of the

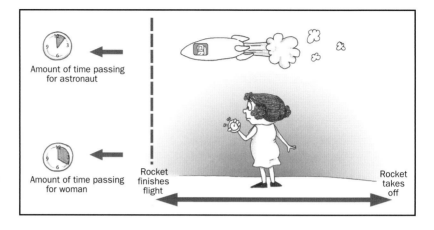

Amount of time passing for astronaut

Amount of time passing for woman

Rocket finishes flight

Rocket takes off

clock is being carried to you through space on a beam of light traveling at the speed of light—the same speed as your rocket. When you look back at the clock five seconds later, you discover that the clock still reads the same time as it did before because the beam of light is just barely able to keep up with your rocket, so the image you see does not change. Therefore time does not change for you either.

Atomic time Over the years scientists have broken up time into increasingly smaller bits. To divide time with such precision, researchers again turned to something found in nature—an atom. The negative charges in atoms vibrate at a regular rhythm. Atomic clocks tell time by measuring "ticks" inside a cesium atom. One second is defined as the time it takes a cesium atom to "tick" 9,192,631,770 times.

The first atomic clock was developed in the 1940s and scientists keep improving its accuracy. This clock is so accurate that it loses no more than one second about every 20 million years.

EXPERIMENT 1

Pendulums: How do the length, weight, and swing angle of a pendulum affect its oscillation time?

Purpose/Hypothesis The swing of a pendulum led to one of the first accurate timepieces ever developed. There are three main factors in a pendulum: the weight hanging on the pendulum, the length of the pendulum from the point of suspension to the weight, and the distance

WORDS TO KNOW

Control experiment: A setup that is identical to the experiment, but is not affected by the variable that acts on the experimental group.

Gnomon: The perpendicular piece of the sundial that casts the shadow.

Greenwich Mean Time (GMT): The time at an imaginary line that runs north and south through Greenwich, England, used as the standard for time throughout the world.

Hypothesis: An idea in the form of a statement that can be tested by observation and/or experiment.

Oscillation: A repeated back-and-forth movement.

Pendulum: A free-swinging weight, usually consisting of a heavy object attached to the end of a long rod or string, suspended from a fixed point.

Solar day: Called a day, the time between each arrival of the Sun at its highest point.

Sidereal day: The time it takes for a particular star to travel around and reach the same position in the sky; about four minutes shorter than the average solar day.

Sundial: A device that uses the position of the Sun to indicate time.

Theory of special relativity: Theory put forth by Albert Einstein that time is not absolute, but it is relative according to the speed of the observer's frame of reference.

Water clock: A device that uses the flow of water to measure time.

Variable: Something that can affect the results of an experiment.

---

or angle of the pendulum's swing. In this experiment, you will predict what factors affect the amount of time it takes a pendulum to complete one full back-and-forth motion, or oscillation.

Before you begin, make an educated guess about the outcome of this experiment based on your knowledge of pendulums. This educated guess, or prediction, is your hypothesis. A hypothesis should explain these things:

- the topic of the experiment
- the variable you will change
- the variable you will measure
- what you expect to happen

A hypothesis should be brief, specific, and measurable. It must be something you can test through further investigation. Your experiment will prove or disprove whether your hypothesis is correct. Here is one possible hypothesis for this experiment: "The time it takes a pendulum to complete an oscillation is only affected by the length of the pendulum: the shorter the length, the less time it takes."

What Are the Variables?

Variables are anything that might affect the results of an experiment. Here are the main variables in this experiment:

- the weight of the substance on the pendulum
- the length of the string or twine
- the angle of the pendulum's swing

In other words, the variables in this experiment are everything that might affect the pendulum's oscillation. If you change more than one variable at the same time, you will not be able to tell which variable had the most effect on the time it takes to make one oscillation.

In this case, the variables you will change, one at a time, are the weight you hang on the pendulum, the length of the pendulum, and the angle of its swing. The variable you will measure is the time it takes for the pendulum to complete an oscillation.

Conducting a control experiment will help you isolate each variable and measure the changes in the dependent variable. Only one variable will change between the control experiment and each of your pendulum trials. To change only one variable at a time, it is important to always begin the pendulum's swing at the same point, and to use the same weight and string length. Then you will change one variable. The pendulum in your control experiment will always have a length of 16 inches (40 centimeters), start at a 45-degree angle, and have a weight of two washers.

You will complete three tests in this experiment. You will measure how a pendulum's oscillation is affected by the pendulum's swing angle, weight, and length. For each variable you will use a stopwatch to note the exact time it takes for the pendulum to complete one back-and-forth swing, or oscillation. To lessen the effect of human error, you will conduct three trials of each test, then average the times.

Level of Difficulty Easy to Moderate (because of the number of trials needed).

Materials Needed

- stopwatch
- 6 metal washers
- a 16-inch (40-centimeter) piece of string or twine
- a 24-inch (60-centimeter) piece of string or twine
- a paperclip

Step 3: Data chart for Experiment 1. GALE GROUP.

Time	Trial 1	Trial 2	Trial 3	Average
Angle				
45°				
60°				
75°				
Weight				
2 washers				
4 washers				
6 washers				
Length				
8 inches				
16 inches				
24 inches				

- pendulum support: any stable object at least 3 feet (91 centimeters) high, such as a table
- pencil
- protractor
- masking tape

Approximate Budget $5 (not counting stopwatch. If you do not have a stopwatch, try using a precise timer that you can start and stop).

Timetable 45 minutes.

Step-by-Step Instructions

1. Tape the pencil onto the table so that half the pencil hangs over the edge of the table (or other pendulum support).
2. Pull a paperclip slightly apart to make a hook and tie the end of the 16-inch (40-centimeter) long piece of string tightly to the closed end of the paperclip. Tie the other end of the string to the pencil. Place two washers on the paperclip hook.
3. Create a chart with a column listing the control, the varying weights, angles, and lengths. List the time it takes for one oscillation across the top row for three trials and the average time.
4. Tape the protractor to the edge of the table, directly in back of the pendulum so that the 0° mark lines up with the string.
5. Control Swing: Pull the pendulum back to the 45° mark. Using your stopwatch, time how long it takes for the pendulum to complete one full swing. Repeat two more times, noting the times for each swing in the control row for each variable.
6. Swing Angle: Repeat Step 5, pulling the pendulum back to 60° and 75°. Write down the time it takes for each trial.
7. Weight: Add two more washers so there are a total of four washers on the paperclip. Pull the pendulum back to the 45° mark and time one complete swing. When you have completed the three trials, add another two washers and repeat.

Step 5: Pull the pendulum back to the 45° mark. GALE GROUP.

Troubleshooter's Guide

Below are some problems that may arise during this experiment, some possible causes, and some ways to remedy the problems.

Problem: One of my trials came out with a much different time than the other two trials.

Possible cause: This experiment requires careful attention to detail. This could be due to human error. Make sure you always reset the stopwatch after every trial. Redo the three trials again. If you have trouble accurately measuring the time of one swing, measure the time of two swings and divide the time you measured by 2 before recording it on your chart.

Problem: The pendulum is swinging erratically and not moving in a smooth, flat arc.

Possible cause: Make sure the pendulum stand is on a flat surface and the pencil is flat on that surface. There could also be outside factors effecting the swing, such as wind, the jostling of the pendulum stand, or brushing the string with your hand while swinging.

Problem: The washers are falling off the paperclip.

Possible cause: Try using either smaller, flatter washers or a larger paperclip. The washers should be of equal size and weight for all trials, but what they weigh will not affect the experiment.

8. Length: Remove the string from the pencil and cut the string in half. Tie the 8-inch (20-centimeter) string to the pencil. Return to the standard weight, two washers, and pull back to the standard 45° angle. Time one full swing for the three trials.

9. Construct the standard pendulum except with the 24-inch (60 centimeter) piece of string: Attach the paperclip with two washers and tie to the pencil. Pull the weight back to 45° and time one full swing. Repeat two more trials. Note the results in a chart.

Summary of Results Either with a calculator or by hand, average the three times for each trial and note them on your chart. (In this case, you add up the three times and divide the total by three to get the average.) Compare the data from the nine different tests. Determine which of the variables affected the time of the pendulum's swing—the swing angle, the weight, or the length. How did this variable affect the time? Check your findings against the predictions you made in your hypothesis. You can create three separate graphs of the data, each conveying the results of one variable, and compare them to each other. The y-axis can represent the change in the variable and the x-axis can represent the amount of time it takes to complete an oscillation.

Change the Variables Using the same materials and methods, you can change the variables by combining the different variables you tested. Does using a heavy weight and a short angle cause the time of a pendulum's swing to differ between a light weight and a long angle? Would an oscillation of a short cord and a heavy weight take more, less, or the same amount of time than an oscillation of a long chord and a light weight? Make sure you change only one variable at a time so that you can determine which variable is causing the change. For example, if you are looking at the heavy weight/short angle versus the light weight/long angle, conduct an experiment first timing the oscillation of a heavy weight/short angle, a heavy weight/long angle, a light weight/short angle, and a light weight/long angle.

EXPERIMENT 2

Water Clock: Does the amount of water in a water clock affect its accuracy?

Purpose/Hypothesis Unlike sundials, water clocks do not depend on the daylight hours or a sunny day. This fact made water clocks useful timekeeping devices among ancient cultures. There are many different versions of water clocks. Ancient water clocks used one container with markings on it. A later water clock design has water drip at a constant rate from one container into another container below it. The height of the water in the bottom container indicates the amount of time that has passed since the clock was started.

One challenge in designing an accurate water clock relates to the rate at which the water flows or drips out of the container. The quantity of water in a container is one factor that can affect the drip rate of the water. In a container of water, all the water pushes downwards, causing pressure on the water at the bottom. A greater quantity of water will cause a greater quantity of pressure pushing downwards; less water will result in less pressure.

In this experiment you will investigate how the amount of water can affect a water clock's accuracy. You will first make a simple water clock and measure a specific period of time with the water always remaining at a constant level. This will be your control. You will then use three different levels of water that will each drip into the container: a quarter, half, and three-quarters filled.

Before you begin, make an educated guess about the outcome of this experiment based on your knowledge of water clocks and timekeeping.

What Are the Variables?

Variables are anything that might affect the results of an experiment. Here are the main variables in this experiment:

- The temperature of the water
- The size of the containers
- The size of the hole in the container
- The number of containers the water flows through
- The amount of water used

In other words, the variables in this experiment are everything that might affect the drip rate of the water. If you change more than one variable at the same time, you will not be able to tell which variable had the most effect on the water clock's accuracy.

How to Experiment Safely

This project poses very few hazards. Be careful with the thumbtack. If you are concerned about spilling water, place old newspapers on the floor under the area where you are conducting the experiment.

This educated guess, or prediction, is your hypothesis. A hypothesis should explain these things:

- the topic of the experiment
- the variable you will change
- the variable you will measure
- what you expect to happen

A hypothesis should be brief, specific, and measurable. It must be something you can test through further investigation. Your experiment will prove or disprove whether your hypothesis is correct. Here is one possible hypothesis for this experiment: "As the amount of water in a water clock decreases, the accuracy of the water clock will also decrease."

In this case, the variable you will change is the amount of water in the water clock. The variable you will measure is the clock's ability to measure time. At the end of the experiment you will examine the water's ability to keep time compared to the control.

Having a control experiment will help you isolate each variable and measure the changes in the dependent variable. Only one variable will change between the control experiment and the experimental water clocks, and that is the amount of water in the container. For the control experiment you will use a full container that will have level water pressure and time one minute. At the end of the experiment you will compare the one-minute markings with the markings of the experimental clocks.

Level of Difficulty Moderate.

Materials Needed

- thumbtack or pin
- watch with second hand
- ruler
- water
- rectangular plastic container (roughly 1 gallon or 3.7 liters)
- cylindrical tall glass jar
- 2 chairs, with flat seats
- masking tape
- cup
- marking pen

Approximate Budget $10.

Timetable 45 minutes.

Step-by-Step Instructions

1. Measure the height of the rectangular plastic container and draw a mark at the one-quarter, one-half, and three-quarters points.

2. Use the thumbtack to punch a small hole in the bottom of the plastic container in the center. Position the container so that each side rests on a chair, with the middle open.

3. Place the cylindrical glass on the floor directly beneath the hole.

4. Hold your finger tightly over the hole in the plastic container and completely fill the container with water. Have a cup of water nearby to keep the container full as the water drips out.

5. Take your finger off the hole and let the water drip out into the glass on the floor for one minute. While the water is dripping, refill the container with water so that it remains completely full.

6. After one minute place your finger over the hole and empty the container in a sink. Place a piece of masking tape lengthwise along the cylindrical glass and draw a small line on the tape at the water level.

7. Use the ruler to precisely measure the height of the water in the glass. This measurement equals one minute. From the one-minute mark measure four more one-minute marks. You should have five evenly spaced lines along the masking tape, one for each minute.

8. Return the plastic container to its position on the chairs. Hold your finger over the hole and fill the water level to the one-quarter mark. Remove your finger and time how long the water takes to reach each of the marks on the tape. Do not put more water in the container. Note your results in a chart.

Troubleshooter's Guide

Below is a problem that may arise during this experiment, a possible cause, and a way to remedy the problem.

Problem: The water ran out before it completes the five minutes.

Possible cause: The pinhole may be too large or your plastic container may not be large enough. Repeat the experiment, using a smaller pin or thumbtack. You could also shorten your time measurement, but the experiment works best if timed for at least three minutes.

Setup of Experiment 2: Making a water clock. GALE GROUP.

9. Repeat the process with the starting water level at the one-half point and the three-quarters point. Note your results.

Summary of Results Examine your chart of the times. Was your hypothesis correct? How did the starting water level at the one-quarter mark compare to the control minute? How did the times change as a result of the water level? Plot your results with the time on one axis and the starting water level on the other axis. Can you think of ways to make your water clock remain accurate? Write a summary of your results and conclusions.

Design Your Own Experiment

How to Select a Topic Relating to this Concept The topic of time has many angles that you can explore. You could examine areas related to the mechanical property of time, such as in a watch or grandfather clock. Other topics you could explore include cultural differences in keeping time, the inventions of keeping time and how they have impacted everyday life; and the theory of time travel.

Check the Further Readings section and talk with your science or physics teacher to learn more about time. If you want to build something for an experiment, such as a timekeeping device, make sure to check with an adult before using any tools.

Steps in the Scientific Method To do an original experiment, you need to plan carefully and think things through. Otherwise you might not be sure what question you are answering, what you are or should be measuring, or what your findings prove or disprove.

Here are the steps in designing an experiment:

- State the purpose of—and the underlying question behind—the experiment you propose to do.
- Recognize the variables involved and select one that will help you answer the question at hand.
- State your hypothesis, an educated guess about the answer to your question.
- Decide how to change the variable you selected.
- Decide how to measure your results.

Recording Data and Summarizing the Results In any experiment you conduct, you should look for ways to clearly convey your data. You can do this by including charts and graphs for the experiments. They should be clearly labeled and easy to read. You may also want to include photographs and drawings of your experimental setup and results, which will help others visualize the steps in the experiment. You might decide to conduct an experiment that lasts several months. In this case, include pictures or drawings of the results taken at regular intervals.

If you are preparing an exhibit, you may want to display your results, such as any experimental setup you designed. If you have completed a nonexperimental project, explain clearly what your research question was and illustrate your findings.

Related Projects The subject of time is a broad one and can include many projects. You could examine how different timekeeping devices work, such as a watch and a solar watch, by carefully taking them apart. You could also investigate solar time by building a sundial. There are many different types of sundials. You can build a sundial with the goal to tell time to within minutes or build a sundial to examine how keeping time with it changes over the seasons. Other timekeeping devices you could explore include a shadow clock, a sand clock, and different types of water clocks.

You could also examine the idea of time and relativity. There are scientists who hypothesize that moving backwards or forwards in time is theoretically possible, and there are other scientists who disagree. You could explore this debate and make your own conclusions.

For More Information

"Albert Einstein: Person of the Century." *Time.com.* http://www.time.com/time/time100/poc/home.html (accessed February 3, 2008). Albert Einstein was named *Time* magazine's Person of the Century; site includes articles, links, and the runners up.

Ganeri, Anita. *The Story of Time and Clocks.* New York: Oxford University Press, 1996. Explores the development of recording and measuring time.

MacRobert, Alan M. "Time and the Amateur Astronomer." *Sky & Telescope.* http://skyandtelescope.com/howto/basics/article_259_1.asp (accessed February 3, 2008). Summary of the different time systems used from ancient to modern day.

National Institute of Standards and Technology. "A Walk Through Time." http://physics.nist.gov/GenInt/Time/ (accessed February 3. 2008]. A look at time from ancient calendars to modern day.

Skurzynski, Gloria. *From Seasons to Split Seconds.* Washington D.C.: National Geographic Society, 2000. The history and science of time and timekeeping.

Snedden, Robert. *Time.* New York: Chelsea House, 1996. Looks at scientists involved with time and time's role in the universe.

89

Tropisms

W hy do plants grow toward light? How far will plants stretch to reach light? These questions fascinated the famous British biologist Charles Darwin (1809–1882), who is best known for formulating the theory of natural selection. Also called survival of the fittest, natural selection is the process by which plants and animals best adapted to their environment to survive and pass their traits on to their offspring. Darwin studied tropism, which includes the bending of plants toward light, because he believed that this trait helped plants reach the light they needed to survive.

Charles Darwin, who helped us understand evolution, also studied plant growth. LIBRARY OF CONGRESS.

In 1880, Darwin performed experiments showing how the growing tip of a plant bends toward a light source. This behavior is called phototropism. *Photo* means "light," and *tropism* means "the growth or movement of a plant toward or away from a stimulus." Thus, *phototropism* means "the tendency of a plant to grow toward a source of light." At the same time, Darwin noticed that some shade-loving plants turn away from light, a behavior called negative phototropism.

Darwin also discovered another kind of tropism: geotropism, meaning "a bending toward Earth." He found that the roots of plants are sensitive to gravity, the attraction of Earth's mass on objects, and grow toward the center of gravity, which is the planet's core.

Auxins hold the key In 1926, Dutch botanist Fritz W. Went discovered that a group of plant hormones called auxins strongly affect plant growth. Hormones are chemicals produced in the

Auxins have caused the shady side of the plant stems to grow more quickly than the sunny side, turning the plant toward the light. PHOTO RESEARCH-ERS INC.

cells of plants and animals that control bodily functions. Stem cells with a large supply of auxins grow faster than stem cells with just a little of these hormones. Auxins are repelled (turned away) by sunlight, so when light shines on one side of a stem, the auxin moves toward the shady side. Thus, growth slows or stops on the side facing the light. While the shady side of the stem grows more quickly, the sunny side remains nearly the same. In time, the longer side of the stem arcs over the shorter side, bending the plant toward the light.

Roots' reaction to gravity is also controlled by the hormone auxin. However, although auxin speeds the growth of cells in plant stems, it slows the growth of cells in roots. For example, if a plant in a pot is turned on its side, gravity pulls the auxin to the underside of the root, where it slows growth. Then the top side of the root grows more quickly. As the top side grows longer than the underside, the root is forced downward toward Earth. This behavior makes sure that the roots grow deep into the soil, anchoring the plant. At the same time, the stem of the plant grows away from gravity, a negative geotropism. This behavior exposes the leaves to sunlight, which the plant needs for photosynthesis.

Reaching out—to water and fence posts Two growing behaviors do not seem to be controlled by auxins. A behavior called hydrotropism causes roots to grow toward a water source. This behavior is controlled by cells in the growing areas of the roots that are sensitive to the presence of water. The root cells grow at different rates, bending the root in the direction of the water. Growing toward water increases the plant's chances of survival.

The second behavior occurs in vines and climbing plants and is called thigmotropism. *Thigmo-* means "touch"; thigmotropism is the tendency for a plant to grow toward a surface it touches. Vines and climbing plants have delicate stems called tendrils. When a tendril touches a solid object, such as a fence post, plant cells on the side away from the post grow very quickly, pushing the tendril toward the post and making it curl around it. That is how plants such as sweet peas, beans, and morning glories climb fences.

Why are scientists interested in tropisms? Researchers have created chemical growth substances based on auxins that offer many benefits. These artificial auxins can be sprayed or dusted on stored potatoes to slow the growth of eyes or on fruit and flower petals to stop them from falling too soon. They can also be used as herbicides to kill broad-leaved weeds. In addition, these "fake" auxins encourage root growth in plant cuttings.

Food webs, interconnected sets of food chains, depend on plants. People are part of food webs, so the world's population also depends on plants. For this reason, we need to learn as much as possible about plant growth to feed our expanding population. Your own experiments can interest and educate others about this vital topic.

Auxins cause roots to grow longer on their top side, pushing the root toward the ground.
GALE GROUP.

EXPERIMENT 1

Phototropism: Will plants follow a maze to reach light?

Purpose/Hypothesis In this experiment, you will find out whether plants will grow sideways through a maze to reach light. Before you begin, make an educated guess about the outcome of this experiment based on your knowledge of plant growth. This educated guess, or prediction, is your hypothesis. A hypothesis should explain these things:

- the topic of the experiment
- the variable you will change
- the variable you will measure
- what you expect to happen

A hypothesis must be brief, specific, and measurable. It must be something you can test through observation. Your experiment will prove or disprove whether your hypothesis is correct. Here is one possible hypothesis for this

What Are the Variables?

Variables are anything that might affect the results of an experiment. The main variables in this experiment are:

- the type and health of the plants
- the position and strength of the light
- the distance from the plant to the light
- the temperature where the plants are placed
- the amount of water they receive

In other words, the variables in this experiment are everything that might affect plant growth. If you change more than one variable during the experiment, you will not be able to tell which variable had the most effect on plant growth.

WORDS TO KNOW

Auxins: Plant hormones that strongly affect plant growth.

Control experiment: A set-up that is identical to the experiment but is not affected by the variable that affects the experimental group.

Food webs: Interconnected sets of food chains, which are a sequence of organisms directly dependent on one another for food.

Geotropism: The tendency of roots to bend toward Earth.

Gravity: The attraction of Earth's mass on objects.

Heliotropism: The tendency of plants to turn towards the Sun throughout the day.

Hormones: Chemicals produced in the cells of plants and animals that control bodily functions.

Hydrotropism: The tendency of roots to grow toward a water source.

Hypothesis: An idea in the form of a statement that can be tested by observation and/or experiment.

Photosynthesis: The process by which plants use sunlight to convert carbon dioxide and water into food and oxygen.

Phototropism: The tendency of a plant to grow toward a source of light.

Thigmotropism: The tendency for a plant to grow toward a surface it touches.

Tropism: The growth or movement of a plant toward or away from a stimulus.

Variable: Anything that might affect the results of an experiment.

experiment: "A plant will grow sideways through a maze to reach a light that is about 10 inches (25 centimeters) away."

In this case, the variable you will change is the position of the light, and the variable you will measure is the plant's growth toward the light. You expect the plant to grow sideways through the maze toward the light positioned at the other end of the maze.

Setting up a control experiment will help you isolate one variable. Only one variable will change between the control plant, which is not being "experimented on," and the experimental plant. That variable is the position of the light. The light will continue to be overhead for the control plant, as usual. It will be coming from the side for the experimental plant.

You will measure the direction of growth for the experimental plant and the control plant. If the experimental plant grows sideways while the control plant continues to grow upright, you will know your hypothesis is correct.

Level of Difficulty Moderate, because of the time involved.

Materials Needed

- 2 small potatoes with eyes (buds)
- 2 small planting pots with saucers
- potting soil
- scissors
- an empty shoe box with a top
- 3 strips of cardboard, each about 5 inches (12.5 centimeters) long and as wide as the height of the shoe box
- masking tape
- ruler
- water
- a warm, sunny spot

Approximate Budget $2 for the potatoes and planting materials.

Timetable 1 to 2 weeks for the potato plants to sprout; plus 1 to 2 weeks for the experiment once the plants have sprouted.

Step-by-Step Instructions

1. Allow the potatoes to sit in a warm, sunny place for a week or two until their buds (eyes) start to grow.

2. Plant each potato in a pot with the eye or eyes just above soil level. Water both pots.

3. Take the cover off the shoe box. Cut a section about 2 inches (5 centimeters) square out of one end. (See illustration.)

4. Follow these steps to form a maze inside the box:

   a. Tape one cardboard strip to the right side and bottom of the box about 2 inches (5 centimeters) from end. (It should end about 2 inches [5 centimeters] from the left side of the box.)

   b. Tape another strip to the left side and bottom of the box about 2 inches (5 centimeters) from the first strip. (It should end about 2 inches [5 centimeters] from the right side of the box.)

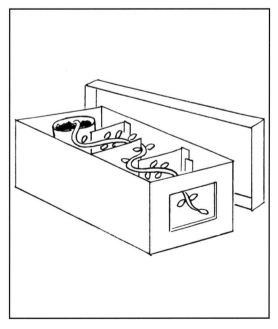

Steps 3 to 5: Set-up of shoe box maze. GALE GROUP.

		Sun.	Mon.	Tues.	Wed.	Thurs.	Fri.	Sat.
Experiment plant	Growth in cm.							
	Sketch							
Control plant	Growth in cm.							
	Sketch							

Step 7: Recording chart for Experiment 1. GALE GROUP.

c. Repeat for the third strip, taping it to the right side and bottom of the box, as shown in illustration.

d. Leave space at the far end of the box for a potato plant.

5. Place one potato plant in the far end of the box. This is your experimental plant. Place the other potato plant outside of—but near—the box, where it will get the same amount of sun as the box. This second plant is your control experiment.

6. Water both plants, if needed, and put the lid on the shoe box.

7. Every day, take the lid off the shoe box. Use the ruler to measure the growth and direction of growth of both plants. Record this information on a chart (see illustration). Also make sketches of the growth. Keep the lid on the box the rest of the time. Water both plants whenever the soil feels dry.

Summary of Results Create a chart like the one shown to record your findings. Be sure to record your observations every day. Make the chart easy to read, as it will become part of your display.

After the plant has been growing in the box for a week or two, study your chart and sketches and decide whether your hypothesis is correct. Did the experimental plant grow through the maze to reach the light? Did the control plant grow upward toward the light, as plants usually do?

Write a paragraph summarizing your findings and explaining whether your hypothesis was correct and how you know.

Change the Variables You can vary this experiment by changing the variables. For example, use rooted avocado pits or sunflower or bean seedlings. Just make sure the experimental and control plants are identical and healthy. You can also move the position of the light. Construct identical mazes in two shoe boxes. Then place one box flat, as in this experiment, and one on end with the light hole at the top. Put a plant at the far end of the first box and at the bottom of the second box. See whether plants move faster through the maze when they are growing up or growing sideways. Finally, you can change the distance of the light from the plants. Construct more elaborate mazes to test the limits of a plant's efforts to reach the light.

EXPERIMENT 2

Geotropism: Will plant roots turn toward the pull of gravity?

Purpose/Hypothesis In this experiment, you will find out whether plant roots change the direction they are growing as their position is changed in relation to the pull of gravity. Before you begin, make an educated guess about the outcome of this experiment based on your knowledge of plant growth. This educated guess, or prediction, is your hypothesis. A hypothesis should explain these things:

- the topic of the experiment
- the variable you will change
- the variable you will measure
- what you expect to happen

Troubleshooter's Guide

Problem: One or both plants are not growing at all.

Possible cause: The plant may have been diseased or infested with insects. Repeat the experiment with different plants.

Problem: The control plant is growing sideways, too.

Possible cause: The light might have been coming from a low position, perhaps blocked by a window blind. Remove any obstructions and make sure the light comes from overhead. The control plant should begin growing upright.

Problem: The experimental plant is growing straight up and pushing against the top of the box.

Possible causes:

1. Light might have been seeping in through cracks in the box, drawing the plant upward. Cover the box with a towel, making sure not to cover the light hole at the end. Also, make sure to replace the box lid immediately after making your daily growth measurements.

2. The light source might not have been strong enough. Place both plants in a sunnier spot or remove one cardboard strip to let in more light.

Problem: By the end of a week, the experimental plant has barely started to grow through the maze.

Possible causes: You might not have allowed enough time, or the plant may be growing slowly because of cool temperatures or too little light. If you remedy these problems, the plant should continue to grow or grow faster.

What Are the Variables?

Variables are anything that might affect the results of an experiment. Here are the main variables in this experiment:

- the type of seeds and their germination rate
- the amount of light and water the seeds receive
- the temperature where the seeds are placed
- the direction of the pull of gravity

In other words, the variables in this experiment are everything that might affect the direction of root growth. If you change more than one variable during the experiment, you will not be able to tell which variable had the most effect on the roots.

A hypothesis must be brief, specific, and measurable. It must be something you can test through observation. Your experiment will prove or disprove whether your hypothesis is correct. Here is one possible hypothesis for this experiment: "Roots will change the direction they grow as their position is changed in relation to the pull of gravity."

In this case, the variable you will change is the direction of the pull of gravity, and the variable you will measure is the direction of root growth. You expect the roots to grow toward the pull of gravity.

Setting up a control experiment will help you isolate one variable. Only one variable will change between the control seeds, which are not being "experimented on," and the experimental seeds. That variable is the direction of the pull of gravity, the attraction of Earth's mass on objects. Gravity will continue to pull from the bottom for the control seeds as they remain with their roots pointing down. Gravity will seem to pull from different directions as you turn the experimental seeds so their roots point in various directions.

You will record the direction of root growth for the experimental seeds and the control seeds. If the roots of the experimental seeds grow in different directions as you turn them, while the control seeds' roots continue to grow straight down, you will know your hypothesis is correct. The experimental roots will be turning toward the direction of the pull of gravity.

Level of Difficulty Moderate, because of the time involved.

Materials Needed You can complete this experiment using small panes of glass held together with rubber bands and set in cake pans. As an alternative, you can use large glass jars with lids. The panes are easier to turn to encourage roots to grow in a circle. However, glass panes are more

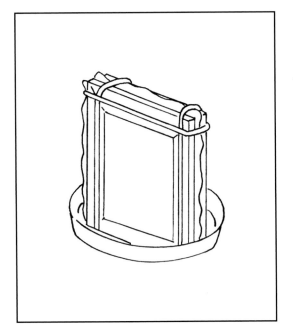

Steps 4 to 7: Set-up of control and experimental glass pane "sandwiches." GALE GROUP.

expensive and require careful handling to avoid accidents.

- four 10-inch (25-centimeter) squares of glass with the edges taped for safety
- 8 large rubber bands
- 2 cake pans or other flat containers, large enough to hold the squares of glass standing on an edge
- bean or sunflower seeds
- paper towels
- water
- eyedropper
- warm, sunny spot
- optional: camera and film

Approximate Budget $16 for four 10-inch (25-centimeter) squares of double-strength glass (or $8 for the same amount of single-strength glass); about $1 for seeds.

Timetable 2 to 3 weeks for the roots to complete a circle.

Step-by-Step Instructions

1. Cut five or six layers of paper towels to form a 10-inch (25-centimeter) square pad.
2. Place the pad on one glass square and cover the pad with enough water to moisten it.
3. Arrange six to eight seeds in a circle on the pad.
4. Carefully place another square of glass on top, so the pad and seeds are like the filling in a sandwich.
5. Place four rubber bands around the "sandwich," at the top, bottom, and both sides, to hold it together.

Alternative method: Fill a jar with damp, crumpled paper towels. Then carefully place the seeds in a row around the inside of the jar between the towels and the glass.

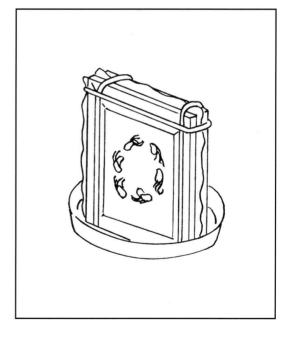

Step 10: Experimental "sandwich" with roots formed into a circle. GALE GROUP.

6. Repeat Steps 1 through 5 to create a control experiment.

7. Place the cake pans side by side in a warm, sunny spot. Stand each "sandwich" vertically in a cake pan, propping it up with books or other supports, if necessary. If you are using the alternative method, place the jars side by side in a warm, sunny spot.

8. Leave the control sandwich (or control jar) in this position throughout the experiment.

9. Use the eyedropper to moisten the towels if they dry out.

10. After the roots have grown about 1 inch (2.5 centimeters), turn the experimental sandwich (or jar) once, resting it on its side. Now the roots should point to the side. In a few days, the roots should bend downward toward the pull of gravity again. Then turn the sandwich once again, so the top is the bottom. When the roots point down again, turn the sandwich again. Continue until the roots form a circle.

11. Every day, record the root growth you see in both experimental and control seeds on a chart (see illustration). If possible, take photographs of the two sandwiches (or jars) together each time you turn the experimental one.

	Sun.	Mon.	Tues.	Wed.	Thurs.	Fri.	Sat.
Experiment seeds							
Control seeds							

Step 11: Recording chart for Experiment 2. GALE GROUP.

Summary of Results Create a chart like the one illustrated to record your findings. Be sure to record your observations every day. Make the chart easy to read, as it will become part of your display.

Study your chart and decide whether your hypothesis was correct. Did the roots of the experimental seeds change direction as you changed the position of the roots in relation to the pull of gravity? Did the roots of the control seeds continue to grow downward, as they usually do? Write a paragraph summarizing your findings and explaining whether your hypothesis was correct and how your measurements and observations support it.

Change the Variables There are several ways you can vary this experiment. For example, try different seeds like mustard, radish, or other seeds. You can also change the light. Light one seed sandwich from the top and one from the bottom to see if the position of the light affects how the roots grow. Finally, you can change the amount of water the seeds receive. Set up two seed sandwiches, as in this experiment, then use the eyedropper to water only one section of the paper towels for the experimental seeds. The moisture will spread somewhat, but the farthest, driest roots should turn toward the moisture. This demonstrates hydrotropism, growing toward water.

EXPERIMENT 3

Heliotropism: How does the Sun affect the movement of certain plants?

Purpose/Hypothesis Heliotropism is the tendency of plants to follow the movement of the Sun throughout a day. "Tropism" means turning and "helio" comes from the Greek meaning

Troubleshooter's Guide

Experiments do not always work out as planned. However, figuring out what went wrong can definitely be a learning experience. Here are some problems that may arise during this experiment, some possible causes, and ways to remedy the problems.

Problem: One or both sets of seeds did not sprout and/or grow roots.

Possible causes:

1. The seeds may have been diseased or exposed to freezing temperatures or other adverse conditions. Dispose of them, clean the glass panes or jars thoroughly, and repeat the experiment with different seeds.

2. The seeds might have dried out or they might be too cold. Try adding more water or putting the seeds in a warmer spot. Or start again with new seeds.

Problem: The roots of the experimental plant did not form a circle.

Possible cause: They needed more time to grow between turns. Try again, allowing more time.

Problem: The stems of the new plants became tangled in the roots.

Possible cause: As roots grow toward gravity, stems grow away from it. Every time you turned the sandwich or jar, the stem also responded to the change in the pull of gravity. You might try seeds that grow less vigorous plants, such as mustard or radish seeds (which are also smaller and harder to handle). You can point out the stems' response to gravity as part of your experiment as well.

What Are the Variables?

Variables are anything that might affect the results of an experiment. Here are the main variables in this experiment:

- the type of sunflower
- the amount of water
- the placement of the sunflowers
- the age of the sunflowers

In other words, the variables in this experiment are everything that might affect the sunflower reacting to the Sun. If you change more than one variable at the same time, you will not be able to tell which variable had the most effect on plant movement.

sun. In heliotropic plants, flowers, leaves, and stems can all move in the direction of the Sun.

Sunflowers are a heliotropic species. In this experiment you will observe and measure how sunflowers move in relation to the Sun. You will need to grow the sunflower plants because generally sunflowers have more of a tendency to be heliotropic when they are young. By comparing the movement of sunflowers left alone in the Sun to sunflowers moved away and blocked from the Sun, you can measure how the Sun's movement affects the plants throughout the day.

Before you begin, make an educated guess about the outcome of this experiment based on your knowledge of sunflowers and heliotropism. This educated guess, or prediction, is your hypothesis. A hypothesis should explain these things:

- the topic of the experiment
- the variable you will change
- the variable you will measure
- what you expect to happen

Step 3: In the morning, note or draw the plants direction in relation to the sun. Look at the leaves, stem, and any flower buds. ILLUSTRATION BY TEMAH NELSON.

A hypothesis should be brief, specific, and measurable. It must be something you can test through further investigation. Your experiment will prove or disprove whether your hypothesis is correct. Here is one possible hypothesis for this experiment: "The sunflowers moved away from the Sun will either stop moving or move towards the Sun while the plants left alone will move towards the Sun throughout the day."

In this case, the variable you will change is the availability of the Sun to the sunflower. The variable you will measure is the movement of the sunflowers.

Level of Difficulty Easy to Moderate, due to the time involved.

Materials Needed

- sunflower seeds, at least eight (avoid giant or tall sunflowers)
- potting soil
- 3 pots or dishes to grow flowers
- large tree or other object outside that can block sun
- open sunny area
- several warm, sunny days

Approximate Budget $5.

Timetable 20 minutes setup time; several minutes every day to care for the plants, and approximately 45 minutes every day for the last several days to week.

Step-by-Step Instructions

1. Plant two seeds (in case one does not grow) in each pot and water. Follow the directions on the packet. Sunflowers need sun, so you will likely need to find a sunny spot for the pots.

2. When the young plants begin to sprout leaves and are about to bud, set the pots outside near one another in an open, sunny area. A good time to do this is when you have at least two days you can

How to Experiment Safely

There are no safety hazards in this experiment.

Step 4: At midday, turn one of the pots sitting in the sunny area around in a half-circle. Place one pot in the shade.
ILLUSTRATION BY TEMAH NELSON.

Troubleshooter's Guide

Below is a problem that may arise during this experiment, a possible cause, and a way to remedy the problem.

Problem: None of the sunflowers are moving towards the Sun.

Possible cause: The sunflowers may be too young for you to notice. If they have only just germinated, allow them to grow until you see some leaf shoots and the beginnings of a flower bud, and then begin your observations.

Problem: The sunflowers are not growing.

Possible cause: Sunflowers need a lot of sun and water. Make sure your soil is rich in nutrients. Purchase another bag of sunflower seeds, or you can buy young sunflowers and continue the experiment.

observe the plants at three different times throughout the day.

3. In the morning, note or draw the plants direction in relation to the Sun. Look at the leaves, stem, and any flower buds.

4. At midday, turn one of the pots sitting in the sunny area around in a half-circle. Again note or draw how the plants in each of the pots face in relation to the Sun.

5. In the late afternoon, before the Sun sets, note the direction each of the plants face in relation to the Sun.

6. For the next week, continue the experiment by repeating Steps 3–5. You may want to shorten or lengthen the experiment depending upon your schedule and observations.

Summary of Results Examine your drawings and notes. How did the direction of the leaves, stems, and buds that only had afternoon shade differ from the plants in the pot you turned around. Did the sunflowers you left alone move with the Sun? Was your hypothesis correct. Consider some advantages for plants to always face the Sun. What would be some disadvantages for some plant types, such as desert plants. Write a summary of your findings. You may want to include drawings or pictures.

Change the Variables One of the ways you can vary this experiment is to test heliotropism in different types of plants. You can ask at a gardening store or nursery what plants you could test. You can also investigate if certain desert plants would move to avoid the Sun. Another variable you can change is the free movement of the plants. What would happen if you prevented the sunflowers from moving for part of the day? How would it affect growth or direction?

Design Your Own Experiment

How to Select a Topic Relating to this Concept Whether your interest in plants is old or new, plants offer fascinating questions to explore through science experiments. Consider what puzzles you about plants. What have you wondered about? For example, if you cut the growing tip off a plant, will the remaining stem still turn toward the light? What if you turn a potted plant upside down and put the light source underneath the plant? Will the stem grow downward, toward the light?

Do roots grow differently if the seeds are planted upside down? What happens if you cut the tip off roots? Will they still turn toward the pull of gravity? Which way would roots grow in a zero-gravity environment? How might tropisms affect plants growing in a space station?

Check the Further Readings section and talk with your science teacher or school or community media specialist to start gathering information on tropism questions that interest you.

Steps in the Scientific Method To do an original experiment, you need to plan carefully and think things through. Otherwise, you might not be sure what question you are answering, what you are or should be measuring, or what your findings prove or disprove.

Here are the steps in designing an experiment:

Thigmotropism is the behavior that causes this green bean vine to grow up and around the wire support. PHOTO RESEARCH-ERS INC.

- State the purpose of—and the underlying question behind—the experiment you propose to do.
- Recognize the variables involved, and select one that will help you answer the question at hand.
- State a testable hypothesis, an educated guess about the answer to your question.
- Decide how to change the variable you selected.
- Decide how to measure your results.

Recording Data and Summarizing the Results In the two tropism experiments, your raw data might include not only charts of measurements of plant or root growth, but also drawings or photographs of these changes.

If you display your experiment, you need to limit the amount of information you offer, so viewers will not be overwhelmed by detail. Make clear your beginning question, the variable you changed, the variable you measured, the results, and your conclusions about plant growth. Viewers—and judges at science fairs—will want to see how each experiment was set up, including the shoe-box maze or seed sandwiches you created. The plants or seeds or a photograph or drawing of the plant or root growth at several stages during the experiment would be valuable and interesting. Be sure to label everything you include clearly to show how it fits together. Viewers will want to know what kinds of plants or seeds you used, how long each step took, and other basic information.

Related Projects There are a variety of projects relating to plants and plant growth that you can undertake. You can make a paper or clay model of the reproductive parts of flowers, or you can collect and display different kinds of plants that have been equally exposed to acid rain. Or you can demonstrate how a process works, such as showing how water circulates through a plant from the roots up the stem and out through the leaves.

For More Information

Alvin, Virginia, and Robert Silverstein. *Plants.* New York: Henry Holt, 1996. Explains the plant kingdom classifications and specific kinds of plants, from the first seed plants to edible plants.

Capon, Brian. *Plant Survival: Adapting to a Hostile World.* Portland, OR: Timber Press, 1994. Covers ways that plants have adapted to adverse conditions, such as cold or hot temperature and too much or too little precipitation.

Catherall, Ed. *Exploring Plants.* Austin, TX: Steck-Vaughn, 1992. Provides information and projects relating to plant structures, functions, reproduction, and growth.

Cochrane, Jennifer. *Nature.* New York: Warwick Press, 1991. Examines how plants have invaded seemingly inhospitable land and managed to thrive there.

Hangarter, Roger P. "Plant Tropic Responses." *Plants-In-Motion.* http://plantsinmotion.bio.indiana.edu/plantmotion/movements/tropism/tropisms.html (accessed February 25, 2008). Brief movies of different plants showing tropics responses.

Kerrod, Robin. *Plant Life.* New York: Marshall Cavendish, 1994. Information about plant biology, groups, and habitats.

Parker, Steve. *Science Project Book of Plants.* New York: Marshall Cavendish, 1989. Features more experiments and explanations about plants and their growth.

Tesar, Jenny. *Green Plants.* Woodbridge, CT: Blackbirch Press, 1993. Includes information on the metabolism, reproduction, and growth of plants, plus their reactions to the environment and role in the food web.

Van Cleave, Janice. *Plants: Mind-Boggling Experiments You Can Turn into Science Fair Projects.* New York: Wiley, 1997. Illustrates possible projects, along with lots of information about plants and plant processes.

90

Vegetative Propagation

Your grandmother proudly shows you an African violet she has grown from seed. Its flower is really unusual: pink with tiny red dots. She grew this plant by pollinating a pink African violet with a red one and planting the seeds that resulted. You remember that pollination is the transfer of pollen from the male reproductive organs to the female reproductive organs of plants. It is a form of sexual reproduction.

Only one of your grandmother's seedlings produced dotted flowers. She knows that if she pollinates this special plant with pollen from a different violet, she might not get any more plants with dotted flowers. Pollinated seeds, like the fertilized eggs of animals, contain the characteristics of both parents. The flower-color characteristics of the other violet may be stronger than the ones in the special plant. If so, none of the seedlings from this pollination will have dotted flowers.

Still, your grandmother is smiling. She knows how to grow more of these special plants without using pollen or seeds. She will use vegetative propagation.

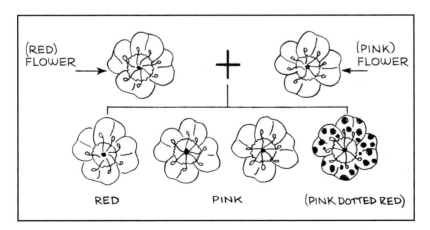

Pollination mixes the characteristics of two parent plants. GALE GROUP.

Pollination has produced African violets of many colors in this greenhouse. PETER ARNOLD INC.

Auxins can speed up plant growth or slow it down. GALE GROUP.

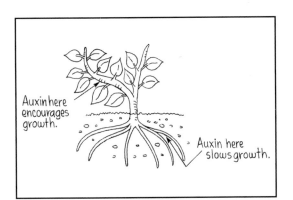

Auxin here encourages growth.

Auxin here slows growth.

What is vegetative propagation? Vegetative propagation is a form of asexual reproduction, a reproductive process that does not involve the union of two individuals in the exchange of genetic material. In sexual reproduction, genetic material transfers characteristics from both parents to their offspring. But plants produced by vegetative propagation, or asexual reproduction, have only one parent, so they have the genetic material of only that parent. They are identical to that parent.

Grandma does not want any new characteristics in her seedlings, just the ones from her special parent plant, so she will grow new violets from that plant's leaf cuttings. Growing plants from leaf cuttings is one form of vegetative propagation. In Experiment 1, you will grow new plants from leaf and stem cuttings.

How can a plant grow from a leaf or stem? In many plants, cells in the stem tips, root tips, leaves, and certain other areas of the plant are capable of becoming different kinds of plant tissue. These cells allow the stem of a plant to produce roots. They allow the eye, or bud, of a potato to produce both roots that grow downward and shoots that grow upward and become the stems and leaves of a new potato plant. You will explore the growth of potato eyes during Experiment 2.

Plant hormones help control this growth. A hormone is a chemical produced in living cells that regulates the functions of the organism. Auxins are a group of plant hormones responsible for patterns of plant growth.

When a stem begins to grow horizontally, gravity causes auxin to accumulate on the lower side of the stem. This hormone makes the cells on that side grow longer. This forces the growing tip of the stem to turn upward. Auxin has the opposite effect on roots. A concentration of auxin on the lower side of roots stops growth there. As the top side of the root continues to grow, the root tip turns downward.

Whether you are a strict vegetarian or live from hamburger to hamburger, you need plants! PETER ARNOLD INC.

English scientist Charles Darwin (1809–1882) noticed that plants' tendency to bend toward light increased the chances of their survival. He figured out that the growing tip of the plant controlled this bending, but it was not until 1926 that the Dutch botanist (one who studies plants) Fritz W. Went isolated the hormone auxin in the growing tip.

Since then, scientists have produced artificial auxins. They are used to improve root growth and produce seedless fruits by stimulating the growth of fruit without pollination. These hormones can also stop fruit from falling from trees before it is ripe. In addition, the hormones slow the ripening of fruit that will be shipped long distances and help preserve potatoes, onions, and other vegetables that will be stored for an extended period. Auxins can also kill weeds by speeding up their growth cycle.

Learning about plant growth can help you increase your plant collection. More importantly, it can enable you to better understand the plants that we depend on for our existence. Without plants, also called producers, the plant-eaters or herbivores starve. Without herbivores, the meat-eaters or carnivores go hungry, too.

EXPERIMENT 1

Auxins: How do auxins affect plant growth?

Purpose/Hypothesis In this experiment, you will try to produce new plants from stem and leaf cuttings. You will treat half of the cuttings with the plant hormone auxin, while the other half will not be treated. The difference between the two groups of cuttings in root, leaf, and stem

WORDS TO KNOW

Asexual reproduction: A reproductive process that does not involve the union of two individuals in the exchange of genetic material.

Auxins: A group of plant hormones responsible for patterns of plant growth.

Carnivore: A meat-eating organism.

Control experiment: A setup that is identical to the experiment but is not affected by the variable that will be changed during the experiment.

Genetic material: Material that transfers characteristics from a parent to its offspring.

Herbivore: A plant-eating organism.

Hormone: A chemical produced in living cells that regulates the functions of the organism.

Humidity: The amount of water vapor (moisture) contained in the air.

Hypothesis: An idea in the form of a statement that can be tested by observation and/or experiment.

Pollination: The transfer of pollen from the male reproductive organs to the female reproductive organs of plants.

Producer: An organism that can manufacture its own food from nonliving materials and an external energy source, usually by photosynthesis.

Sexual reproduction: A reproductive process that involves the union of two individuals in the exchange of genetic material.

Tuber: An underground, starch-storing stem, such as a potato.

Variable: Something that can affect the results of an experiment.

Vegetative propagation: A form of asexual reproduction in which plants are produced that are genetically identical to the parent.

growth will tell you whether auxin makes any difference. Before you begin, make an educated guess about the outcome of this experiment based on your knowledge of plant propagation. This educated guess, or prediction, is your hypothesis. A hypothesis should explain these things:

- the topic of the experiment
- the variable you will change
- the variable you will measure
- what you expect to happen

A hypothesis should be brief, specific, and measurable. It must be something you can test through observation. Your experiment will prove or disprove whether your hypothesis is correct. Here is one possible hypothesis for this experiment: "Stem cuttings treated with auxin will grow more roots, taller stems, and more leaves, and treated leaf cuttings will grow more new plants than will untreated stem and leaf cuttings."

In this case, the variable you will change is the auxin treatment, and the variable you will measure is root, stem, and leaf growth for the stem cuttings and the number of new plants grown by the leaf cuttings. Your untreated cuttings will serve as a control experiment to allow you to measure any difference in growth. If the treated cuttings grow more than the untreated ones, you will know your hypothesis is correct.

Level of Difficulty Moderate, because of the time and materials involved.

Materials Needed

- stem cuttings from several plants, including geranium, coleus, petunia, fuchsia, dieffenbachia, dracena, philodendron, and ivy
- leaf cuttings from several plants, including African violet, gloxinia, rex begonia, piggyback plant, peperomia, sansevieria, and succulents (such as a jade plant)
- rooting hormone powder, such as Rootone or Hormodin
- pruning shears or scissors
- two 4-inch-diameter (10-centimeter-diameter) pots with saucers for each kind of cutting you plan to make (one pot for the treated cuttings and one for the untreated cuttings)
- potting soil (if possible, mix vermiculite or perlite, two kinds of soil conditioners, into the soil)
- pot labels and a marker
- pencil
- water
- clear plastic bags big enough to fit over each pot
- ruler

What Are the Variables?

Variables are anything that might affect the results of an experiment. Here are the main variables in this experiment:

- the types and health of the plants from which the cuttings are taken
- the size of the plant cuttings and the locations from which they are taken on the parent plants
- the light, water, soil, and temperature conditions under which the cuttings are grown
- treatment with the hormone auxin

In other words, the variables in this experiment are everything that might affect the growth of the cuttings. If you change more than one variable, you will not be able to tell which variable had the most effect on growth.

How to Experiment Safely

Be very careful in using the shears or scissors to make the cuttings. You might ask an adult to help you. Also try not to get the rooting hormone on your skin or especially in your eyes. Wash your hands after setting up the experiment.

Approximate Budget Costs will depend on whether you need to buy plants or can take cuttings from available plants. Pots cost about $1 each. Potting soil is $3 to $4 for a large bag. A container of Rootone will be $4 to $5.

Timetable 3 weeks for the cuttings to sprout and grow.

Step-by-Step Instructions

1. Label each pair of pots "Experimental" and "Control," along with the name of the plant.

2. Fill each pot with soil, leaving 1 inch (2.5 centimeters) or so at the top of pot.

3. Take the cuttings. Make at least two cuttings of each plant for the experimental pot and two identical cuttings of the same plant for the control pot. (You will need extra cuttings in case some die.) For stem cuttings from each plant you selected:

 a. Take four 3- to 4-inch (7.5 to 10 centimeter) cuttings from the plant. Slice at an angle to expose as many special growing cells in the stem as possible. Cut just below where a leaf is attached.

 b. Pull off any leaves close to the bottom of the cuttings.

 c. Use the pencil to make two holes 2 inches (5 centimeters) deep in each pot.

 d. Dip about 1 inch (2.5 centimeters) of the end of two cuttings into the container of rooting hormone. Tap the stem to remove excess powder.

 e. Gently put the stem of each treated cutting into a hole in the experimental pot without rubbing off the powder. Pat the soil around the cutting.

 f. Put the two untreated cuttings into holes in the control pot, and pat the soil around them.

4. For leaf cuttings from each plant you selected:

 a. Cut four healthy leaves from the plant. The leaves might have stems attached or not, but make the cuttings identical.

 b. Use the pencil to make two shallow grooves in the potting soil of each pot.

c. Dip the bottom edge (and any stem) of two leaves into the container of rooting hormone. Tap the leaves to remove excess powder.

d. Gently place each treated leaf into the soil in the experimental pot without rubbing off the powder. Pat the soil around it.

e. Put the two untreated leaves into the control pot, and pat the soil around them.

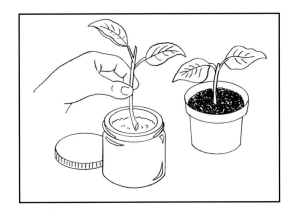

Steps 3d and 3e: Dip cuttings into root hormone and then gently plant them in experimental pot. GALE GROUP.

5. Water all the cuttings and place the pots in a warm, light spot, but not in direct sunlight.

6. Place a plastic bag loosely over each pot to keep the humidity level high around the cuttings. Humidity is the amount of water vapor (moisture) contained in the air. The cuttings will all have a better chance of taking root and growing if the air around them is moist.

7. Observe and record any visible growth on a chart similar to the one illustrated. Stem cuttings may grow taller and grow more leaves. Leaf cuttings may sprout tiny leaves at their base.

8. Check the soil in each pot twice a week and water any pots that feel dry.

9. At the end of Week 3, gently pull each cutting out of its pot, shake off the soil, and record the number and length of any roots that have grown.

Summary of Results Use the data on your chart to create some or all of these graphs:

- a line graph comparing the height of the experimental and control stem cuttings at the end of each week
- a line or bar graph comparing the leaf growth of the two groups of stem cuttings at the end of each week
- a bar graph comparing the number of new plants growing on the leaf cuttings at the end of each week
- a chart comparing the final root growth of all cuttings, carefully labeling the stem and leaf cuttings

Then study the graphs and your growth chart and decide whether your hypothesis was correct. Did the experimental stem cuttings show more stem, leaf, and root growth than the control cuttings? Did the experimental leaf cuttings grow more tiny new plants than the control

Record of Growth

Stem Cuttings	End of Week 1	End of Week 2	End of Week 3
Experimental cuttings, (plant name) Beginning height: Beginning number of leaves:	Height: Number of leaves: Other growth:	Height: Number of leaves: Other growth:	Height: Number of leaves: Other growth: Root growth:
Control cuttings, (same plant) Beginning height: Beginning number of leaves:	Height: Number of leaves: Other growth:	Height: Number of leaves: Other growth:	Height: Number of leaves: Other growth: Root growth:

Leaf Cuttings	End of Week 1	End of Week 2	End of Week 3
Experimental cuttings, (plant name)	Growth observed:	Growth observed:	Growth observed: Root growth:
Control cuttings, (same plant)	Growth observed:	Growth observed:	Growth observed: Root growth:

Step 7: Recording chart for Experiment 1. GALE GROUP.

cuttings? Write a paragraph summarizing your findings and explaining whether they support your hypothesis.

Change the Variables Here are some ways to vary this experiment:

- Use cuttings from plants that are harder to root, such as woody stem cuttings from a rose bush.

- Try a variation on leaf cuttings: cut rex begonia leaves into wedge-shaped pieces or cut sansevieria leaves horizontally into short lengths. Dip the bottom edges of some pieces into rooting hormone, and plant in potting soil.
- Treat all cuttings with rooting hormone and experiment with the amount of humidity around the cuttings to see how that affects their growth.
- Root the cuttings in water instead of soil. Cover the top of the water containers with clear plastic wrap or aluminum foil and make a hole for each cutting. Stir rooting hormone into the water of some cuttings to see if it improves root growth under these conditions.
- Sprinkle seeds with rooting hormone before planting them. Compare their growth with that of untreated seeds.

Modify the Experiment In this experiment you looked at how auxins effect plant growth. Researchers now know that auxin activity is affected by the time of day. Like people, plants go through a natural cycle every 24 hours. Plants may produce more auxins at night, for example, because that is when water is most available and the plants are preparing for daylight.

You can modify this experiment and increase the level of difficulty by experimenting with auxins and the day-night cycle. By using lights, you will not let the plants experience a nighttime. Make a hypothesis about how depriving plants of nighttime will effect growth.

You will need two more pots and two grow lights. (If you only have one light you could conduct the two experimental cuttings one after another.) For each of your trial experiments, set up one more pot and label it "Experimental/Daylight." You should have three pots for each of the cuttings. Prepare the Experimental/Daylight cuttings at the same time and the same way as the "Control" setup.

Troubleshooter's Guide

Here are some problems that may arise during this experiment, some possible causes, and ways to remedy the problems.

Problem: All or most of the cuttings rotted.

Possible cause: The humidity was too high. Try again, watering the cuttings less or not using the plastic bags.

Problem: All or most of the cuttings dried up.

Possible causes:

1. The cuttings needed more water. Try again, checking every other day to see if the soil has dried out.
2. The cuttings received too much direct sun. Place them where they will receive light but not direct sun.

Problem: The control cuttings from one kind of plant grew more than the experimental cuttings from another kind of plant.

Possible cause: Different types of plants have different growth rates. Focus on whether cuttings from the same plant grew better when they were treated with the rooting hormone.

During the day, place all the pots in an area where they receive light. Every night, turn a grow light on over the "Experimental/Daylight" pots. Make sure the pots are far away from the Experimental and Control pots so these plants can experience darkness. In the morning, you can turn off the lights and turn them back on in the evening. Over the next three weeks observe and record any visible growth. How do the cuttings of the daylight trials compare to the Control and Experimental cuttings? Was your hypothesis correct? What can you learn from this experiment about when plants may produce auxins and how that affects plant growth?

EXPERIMENT 2

Potatoes from Pieces: How do potatoes reproduce vegetatively?

Purpose/Hypothesis In this experiment, you will cut up potatoes and plant different parts of them to determine which parts can be used for vegetative propagation. The potatoes we eat are actually tubers, which are underground, starch-storing stems. The eyes, or buds, on one potato can develop into several identical new plants through vegetative propagation. The starch stored in the potato or tuber provides food for the new plant until it develops its own root system.

Here are the questions to investigate: Do only the eyes of potatoes develop into new plants? What about chunks of potato without eyes? And will eyes grow without any potato attached? To find out, you will plant some chunks of potato with eyes, some chunks without eyes, and some eyes without potatoes attached.

Before you begin, make an educated guess about the outcome of this experiment based on your knowledge of plant propagation. This educated guess, or prediction, is your hypothesis. A hypothesis should explain these things:

- the topic of the experiment
- the variable you will change
- the variable you will measure
- what you expect to happen

A hypothesis should be brief, specific, and measurable. It must be something you can test through observation. Your experiment will prove or disprove whether your hypothesis is correct. Here is one possible hypothesis for this experiment: "Only chunks of potatoes with eyes will develop into new potato plants."

In this case, the variable you will change is whether the potato has an eye, and the variable you will measure is the presence or absence of new growth. Your control experiment will consist of planting potato chunks without eyes and planting eyes without potato chunks attached to them. If only the chunks with eyes sprout, you will know that your hypothesis is correct. This result will prove that the special cells in plant stems and leaves that can develop into different kinds of plant tissue are also present in potato eyes. However, the eyes require the starch food in potatoes in order to reproduce successfully.

Level of Difficulty Moderate, because of the time involved.

Materials Needed

- 2 or 3 seed potatoes (available at garden supply stores or farmers' markets) or other potatoes that have not been treated to stop the growth of eyes
- three 5- or 6-inch- (12- or 15-centimeter) diameter pots and saucers
- pot labels and a marker
- potting soil (if possible, mix vermiculite or perlite into the soil)
- sharp knife and cutting board
- water
- ruler

Approximate Budget $6 for potatoes, pots, and potting soil.

Timetable 3 weeks.

Step-by-Step Instructions

1. Locate the green or white eyes on the potatoes. If there are no eyes yet, place the potatoes in a shallow dish that contains about 1 inch

What Are the Variables?

Variables are anything that might affect the results of an experiment. Here are the main variables in this experiment:

- the kind of potatoes used
- the light, water, soil, and temperature conditions under which the potato parts are grown
- the presence of eyes in the potato chunks
- whether the eyes have potato attached

In other words, the variables in this experiment are everything that might affect the growth of new potato plants. If you change more than one variable, you will not be able to tell which variable had the most effect on the new plant growth.

How to Experiment Safely

Take care in cutting the potatoes into chunks. You might ask an adult to help you.

Steps 4 and 5: Set-up of three pots with soil and potato chunks. GALE GROUP.

(2.5 centimeters) of water. Leave the dish in a sunny place for several days, and eyes should appear.

2. Carefully cut up the potatoes, creating two or three chunks with eyes attached. Also create two or three chunks that do not have eyes. One surface of these chunks should be covered with potato skin.

3. Use your fingernail to gently separate two or three eyes from a potato.

4. Mark the three pots *Chunks with eyes, Chunks without eyes,* and *Eyes only.*

Growth Record

	End of Week 1	End of Week 2	End of Week 3
Potato chunks without eyes	Growth observed:	Growth observed:	Growth observed:
Potato chunks without eyes	Growth observed:	Growth observed:	Growth observed:
Eyes with no potato attached	Growth observed:	Growth observed:	Growth observed:

Step 7: Recording chart for Experiment 2. GALE GROUP.

5. Fill each pot about half full of soil and place the appropriate chunks or eyes on the soil. Cover with more soil.

6. Water all pots and place them in a warm, sunny location.

7. Observe and record any growth you see, using a chart like the one illustrated. Feel the soil every other day and add water when it seems dry.

Summary of Results Study the findings on your chart and decide whether your hypothesis was correct. Did only the potato chunks with eyes sprout? Did the eyes without potato attached sprout and then die? Write a paragraph summarizing your findings and explaining whether they support your hypothesis.

Change the Variables Here are ways to vary this experiment:

- Use a different type of potato, such as baking, red, or sweet potatoes, to see if the experiment results change.

- Leave different amounts of potato attached to the eyes to determine how much potato results in the best growth.

- Sprinkle a rooting hormone on potato chunks, with and without eyes, to see if it changes the results of the experiment. (Versions of the growth hormone auxin are often sprayed on potatoes to slow the growth of eyes. Auxin can both promote and discourage plant growth, depending on how much is used and when it is applied.)

Troubleshooter's Guide

Here are some problems that may arise during this experiment, some possible causes, and ways to remedy the problems.

Problem: Nothing in any of the pots sprouted.

Possible causes:

1. The pots might have been too cold or the soil too dry. Try again, providing good growing conditions for all the pots.

2. The potatoes might have been old or diseased. Try again with new potatoes.

Problem: Some of the chunks without eyes sprouted.

Possible cause: Perhaps they contained eyes that had not yet broken through the potato's skin. Take the chunks out of the soil and see if eyes have developed. If so, eliminate them from your experiment.

Problem: Some of the eyes without potato attached are growing.

Possible cause: A small amount of potato might be attached, providing a temporary source of food. Continue the experiment to see if the eyes keep growing. (They might, if they develop roots quickly enough.)

Design Your Own Experiment

How to Select a Topic Relating to this Concept You can explore many other aspects of vegetative propagation. Consider what you would like to know about this topic. For example, you might investigate growing new plants by using runners (strawberries and spider plants), suckers (succulents such as aloe), or air-layering (dieffenbachia and dracena).

Check the Further Readings section and talk with your science teacher or school or community media specialist to start gathering information on plant growth questions that interest you. As you consider possible experiments, be sure to discuss them with your science teacher or another knowledgeable adult before trying them. Some of the chemicals or procedures might be dangerous.

Steps in the Scientific Method To do an original experiment, you need to plan carefully and think things through. Otherwise, you might not be sure which question you are answering, what you are or should be measuring, or what your findings prove or disprove.

Here are the steps in designing an experiment:

- State the purpose of—and the underlying question behind—the experiment you propose to do.
- Recognize the variables involved, and select one that will help you answer the question at hand.
- State a testable hypothesis, an educated guess about the answer to your question.
- Decide how to change the variable you selected.
- Decide how to measure your results.

Recording Data and Summarizing the Results In the plant growth experiments, your raw data might include charts, graphs, drawings, and photographs of the changes you observed. If you display your experiment, make clear the question you were answering, the variable you changed, the variable you measured, the results, and your conclusions. Explain what materials you used, how long each step took, and other basic information.

Related Projects You can undertake a variety of projects related to vegetative propagation. For example, how small a piece of a leaf will produce new plants? Will all parts of a leaf produce new plants equally well? Will a bulb (an underground stem, like a potato) produce two identical plants if it is cut in half and both parts are planted? Which will bloom first, a plant grown from seed or a plant reproduced vegetatively?

For More Information

Alvin, Virginia, and Robert Silverstein. *Plants.* New York: Twenty-First Century Books, 1996. Offers a general description of the plant kingdom and its classification system, along with discussion of specific kinds of plants, such as poisonous ones.

Bleifeld, Maurice. *Botany Projects for Young Scientists.* New York: Franklin Watts, 1992. Contains a collection of activities and experiments, exploring photosynthesis, plant structures, and growth.

Hershey, David. *Plant Biology Science Projects.* New York: Wiley, 1995. Outlines plant-related science projects that will interest young adults.

Missouri Botanical Garden. *Biology of Plants.* http://www.mbgnet.net/ bioplants/ (accessed on February 6, 2008). Basic information about plant biology and life.

Tocci, Salvatore. *Experiments with Plants.* New York: Children's Press, 2001.

Van Cleave, Janice. *Spectacular Science Projects with Plants.* New York: Wiley, 1997. Presents facts and experiments relating to plants.

91

Vitamins and Minerals

Vitamins and minerals are substances that are essential for people to grow, develop, and remain healthy. Vitamins are organic, meaning that they contain carbon and come from living organisms. Minerals are inorganic, meaning that they do not contain carbon or come from living organisms. Except for two vitamins, humans cannot make any of their own vitamins and minerals. People must get these nutrients from foods. Diseases characterized by lack of nutrients are called deficiency diseases.

There are hundreds of vital functions that require proper vitamins and minerals. Maintaining strong bones and muscles, ensuring good vision, healing wounds, providing energy, and fighting infections are a few examples of how the body uses these substances. For years researchers focused their work on determining the amount of each vitamin and mineral needed to avoid any health problems. The Recommended Daily Allowance (RDA) are guidelines formulated by the U.S. government for the amount of each substance a person needs every day. Researchers also are exploring how vitamins and minerals can prevent and treat disease.

An alphabet of vitamins The discovery of vitamins is a story of many people working to understand disease symptoms. In England during the 1700s, it was common for sailors traveling on long voyages to develop bleeding gums, loose teeth, and bruised skin. Some symptoms were more severe and caused many sailors to die. A Scottish naval doctor found that citrus fruits cured the sick sailors, and prevented others from getting ill. The substance in these fruits was unknown at the time. The disease, called scurvy, is now known to be caused by a lack of vitamin C, also called ascorbic acid.

Other physicians around the world were recognizing how the changes in a person's—or animal's—diet affected health. For the deadly disease beriberi, it was a study of chickens that furthered vitamin research. When

Vitamin A for healthy vision

Fluorine gives strong enamel, which prevents cavities

Vitamin K clots blood when cut

A combination of vitamins and minerals gives strong bones and muscles

Vitamins and minerals perform many functions in the body and are essential for good health. GALE GROUP.

Vitamins are categorized into two types: water soluble and fat soluble. GALE GROUP.

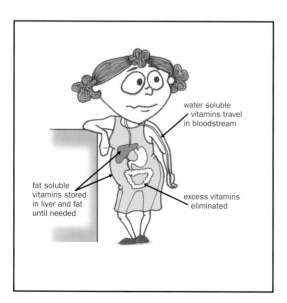

water soluble vitamins travel in bloodstream

fat soluble vitamins stored in liver and fat until needed

excess vitamins eliminated

a group of chickens started coming down with beriberi-like symptoms, it was discovered they had been fed white rice instead of their usual brown rice. Upon switching them back to the brown rice, the chickens recovered. This led to the theory that patients were not falling ill from something they took in, but from something they were missing from their diet.

In 1913, scientists isolated the first vitamin, vitamin A, and named it after the first letter of the alphabet. Vitamin B1, or thiamine, was the first B vitamin found and is the vitamin in brown rice that prevents beriberi, a deficiency disease involving the nervous system. As more vitamins were isolated, scientists continued to name them with letters.

The human body needs thirteen different vitamins. These vitamins serve many functions vital to good health. For example, one of vitamin A's main roles is in the production of retinal. Eyes need retinal to sense light, and it is manufactured with the help of vitamin A. Even today, vitamin A deficiency causes blindness in millions around the world, and is a major cause of childhood blindness. Vitamin B12 maintains healthy nerve cells and red blood cells, and is also needed to make DNA, the genetic material in all cells.

People's bodies can only make two vitamins—vitamin K and vitamin D. The sunlight reacts with a chemical in the skin to produce vitamin D, which is necessary for hard bones. About half of the vitamin K a person needs is made in the intestines, from the bacteria that live there. Vitamin K helps make blood clot when there is a cut, preventing too much blood from flowing out of the body. People need to get the rest of the required vitamin K, and all the other vitamins, through foods.

Fats and water Vitamins are also divided into two categories: fat-soluble and water-soluble. The fat-soluble vitamins dissolve in fats. These vitamins are stored in the body's fat

Vitamins	Major functions	Major sources
A (fat soluble)	helps night vision and color vision, growth, healthy skin, fights sickness	apricots, nectarines, carrots, liver, eggs, milk, broccoli, pumpkin
B$_1$ - thiamine (water soluble)	strong muscles, growth	brown breads, beans, grain, cereals, nuts, peas
B$_2$ - riboflavin (water soluble)	helps eyesight; heals cuts, bruises; involved in making red blood cells	milk, cheese, eggs, leafy vegetables, meat, brown breads
C - absorbic acid (water soluble)	repairs broken bones, strong gums and teeth, fights infections	green vegetables, berries, tomatoes, oranges, lemons, grapefruit, and citrus juices
D (fat soluble)	strong bones, teeth	body makes this with sun; tunafish, eggs; added to milk
E (fat soluble)	protects eyes, skin, liver; protects lungs from pollution; helps store Vitamin A	vegetable oils, leafy green vegetables, peanuts
K (fat soluble)	clots blood when wounded	leafy green vegetables, cabbage, cheese, broccoli
Minerals		
Calcium	strong teeth, bone; crucial roles in nerve and muscle cells	milk, yogurt, cheeses, fortified in some juices
Iron (trace mineral)	transports oxygen in red blood cells	red meat, poultry, fish, dried beans, apricots, raisins
Zinc (trace mineral)	heals cuts, helps body grow	seafood, liver, eggs, peanuts, grain food, dark meat of chicken
Fluorine (trace mineral)	strong tooth enamel	sardines, salmon, apples, eggs; added to water
Magnesium (macromineral)	strong bones, controls body temperature	milk, eggs, cheese, yogurt, meats, seafood, molasses
Potassium (macromineral)	keeps the heart strong	bananas, potatoes, raisins, melons, broccoli, beef

A selection of the roles some vitamins and minerals play and their sources. GALE GROUP.

tissues and liver until the body needs them. Fat-soluble vitamins can remain in storage from a few days to a year. Vitamins A, D, E, and K are all fat-soluble vitamins.

Water-soluble vitamins dissolve in water and travel through the bloodstream. They move quickly through the blood and need to be replenished often. As the vitamins stream through the body, organs and tissues pick up the vitamins they need. Whatever the body does not use comes out in urine. Water-soluble vitamins include Vitamin C and the B vitamins.

Mind your minerals Minerals originate in the ground and are taken in by plants and animals. Water in the ground soaks up such minerals as calcium (Ca), magnesium (Mg), and iron (Fe). This natural, mineral-rich

Brown rice and other grains are a good source of vitamin B1, which helps build muscle.
COPYRIGHT © KELLY A. QUIN.

water is called hard water. Animals get their minerals when they eat the plants. Plants absorb minerals from the water in the soil. People ingest the majority of minerals directly from foods. They either eat plants directly or consume the animals that have eaten the plants.

People need a smaller amount of minerals than vitamins. These minerals play a number of crucial roles. They help build strong bones and teeth, transmit nerve signals, maintain a regular heartbeat, metabolize food, and many other functions.

Minerals are categorized into two types based on how much of the mineral a person needs for good health. The two groups are macrominerals and trace minerals. The body needs a larger amount of macrominerals than trace minerals, although both types are essential. The macromineral group is made up of calcium, phosphorous, magnesium, sodium, potassium, and chloride. Trace minerals include iron, manganese, copper, iodine, zinc, chromium, fluoride, and selenium.

Food sources Vitamins and minerals are found in a variety of foods. Each type of food contains a certain amount of vitamins and minerals. Some foods are a rich source of these nutrients, such as broccoli, and others, such as soda, are not a significant source. For most people, eating a well-balanced diet with a wide variety of foods supplies the necessary amounts of vitamins and minerals. People who are ill or do not get their nutrients through food take supplements, or additional vitamins and minerals.

Many foods are fortified or enriched with essential vitamins and minerals. Water, for example, is fortified with additional mineral fluorine. Vitamin D is added to milk after it is heated to kill germs, which causes it to lose Vitamin D in the process. Many cereals and juices are also fortified with vitamins and minerals.

Packages list the RDA for the vitamins and minerals they contain. There are RDAs provided for children, teenagers, and adults. The RDA listed on food packaging is the amount that an average, healthy adult should consume each day.

EXPERIMENT 1

Vitamin C: What juices are the best sources of vitamin C?

Purpose/Hypothesis Vitamin C is a water-soluble vitamin that is essential for human growth and health. In this experiment, you will explore the relative quantity of vitamin C in different juices. To measure the amount of vitamin C you will observe the chemical reaction of vitamin C with iodine.

Iodine mixed with water forms ions, which are charged particles. When ions mix with starch they produce a compound that has a blue color. Ascorbic acid, or vitamin C, breaks up the bond between the ions and the starch, reversing the color change. The more vitamin C in a substance, the quicker the bonds will be broken, and the faster the liquid will turn clear.

You will test the vitamin C content of orange, grapefruit, and apple juice. Make sure all the juices are fresh—not from concentrate. You can use your imagination and test a variety of other juices also, such as tomato, grape, and carrot. You will first create a bond between a starch solution and iodine. You will then slowly add juice to the solution to determine the amount it takes for the juice to break the bond, turning the solution clear.

Before you begin, make an educated guess about the outcome of this experiment based on your knowledge of vitamin C. This educated guess, or prediction, is your hypothesis. A hypothesis should explain these things:

- the topic of the experiment
- the variable you will change
- the variable you will measure
- what you expect to happen

A hypothesis should be brief, specific, and measurable. It must be something you can test through further investigation. Your experiment will prove or disprove whether your hypothesis is correct. Here is one possible hypothesis for this experiment: "The orange juice will contain more vitamin C than the other two juices."

In this case, the variable you will change is the type of juice. The variable you will

What Are the Variables?

Variables are anything that might affect the results of an experiment. Here are the main variables in this experiment:

- the type of juice
- the freshness of the juice
- the temperature of the juice

In other words, the variables in this experiment are anything that might affect the speed at which the vitamin C breaks up the bond. If you change more than one variable at the same time, you will not be able to tell which variable has the highest concentration of vitamin C.

Minerals in the earth are taken in by plants, which are then ingested by animals. Humans can get their required minerals by eating plants and animals. GALE GROUP.

WORDS TO KNOW

Control experiment: A setup that is identical to the experiment, but is not affected by the variable that acts on the experimental group.

Deficiency disease: A disease marked by a lack of an essential nutrient in the diet.

Fat-soluble vitamins: Vitamins such as A, D, E, and K that can be dissolved in the fatof plants and animals.

Fortified: The addition of nutrients, such as vitamins or minerals, to food.

Hypothesis: An idea in the form of a statement that can be tested by observation and/or experiment.

Inorganic: Made of or coming from nonliving matter.

Macrominerals: Minerals needed in relatively large quantities.

Minerals: Inorganic substances that originate in the ground; many are essential nutrients.

Organic: Made of, or coming from, living matter.

Scurvy: A disease caused by a deficiency of vitamin C, which causes a weakening of connective tissue in bone and muscle.

Supplements: A substance intended to enhance the diet.

Trace minerals: Minerals needed in relatively small quantities.

Variable: Something that can affect the results of an experiment.

Vitamins: Organic substances that are essential for people's good health; most of them are not manufactured in the body.

Water-soluble vitamins: Vitamins such as C and the B-complex vitamins that dissolve in the watery parts of plant and animal tissues.

measure is the relative amount of juice it takes to make the solution clear.

Conducting a control experiment will help you isolate each variable and measure the changes in the dependent variable. Only one variable will change between the control and your experiment. For your control in this experiment you will use a solution of pure vitamin C. At the end of the experiment you can compare the results of the control with the experimental results.

Level of Difficulty Moderate.

Materials Needed

- paper towel

- spoon

- 500-milligram vitamin C tablet
- cornstarch
- 4 small clear glasses or jars, such as baby food jars
- iodine (available at drug stores)
- apple juice
- orange juice
- grapefruit juice
- other juices: tomato, carrot, or grape (optional)
- dropper
- measuring cup
- measuring spoons
- paper towel
- marking pen
- 2 mixing cups

How to Experiment Safely

Be careful when handling iodine: It is a poison and can stain your skin, clothing, and countertops.

Approximate Budget $10.

Timetable 1 hour.

Step-by-Step Instructions

1. Write the name of the juice to be tested on each of the jars. Label one jar "Vitamin C."

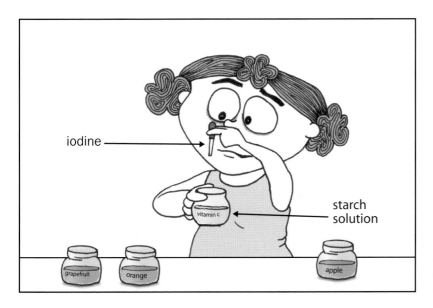

Step 6: Add one drop of iodine to each jar. Cap the jar and swirl. GALE GROUP.

Troubleshooter's Guide

Below is a problem that may arise during this experiment, a possible cause, and a way to remedy the problem.

Problem: The pure vitamin C took as many drops as a juice to turn clear.

Possible cause: You may not have crushed and dissolved the vitamin C thoroughly. Make sure the tablet is in a fine powder before you pour it in the water, then mix briskly and repeat the experiment.

2. To prepare the starch solution, mix ½ teaspoon (2.5 milliliters) of cornstarch in 1 cup (0.25 liters) warm water. Stir thoroughly until the cornstarch dissolves.

3. Crush the vitamin C tablet in a folded paper towel.

4. Dissolve the crushed tablet in 2 cups (0.5 liters) of warm water. The vitamin C solution is now 500 milligrams/milliliters, or 1 milligram/milliliter. Allow to cool to room temperature.

5. Put 2 tablespoons (30 milliliters) of the starch solution into each jar.

6. Add one drop of iodine to each jar. Cap the jar and swirl. The solution should turn blue-black.

7. Test the control solution: Add 1 drop of the vitamin C solution to its jar and swirl. Add another drop, if needed, until the blue-black color has disappeared. Note the results in a chart.

8. Test each juice: Add 1 drop of the orange juice to its jar and swirl. Continue to add drops, swirling after each drop, until the blue color clears completely. Note the number of drops in the chart.

9. Repeat with the apple and the grapefruit juices. Note your results.

Summary of Results Examine how many drops it took for each juice to dissolve the bond and clear the color. Graph the results of your experiment. Which juice had the highest concentration of vitamin C? How did this juice compare to the test standard, pure vitamin C? Hypothesize how the vitamin C content of other types of beverages—vegetable juice, carrot juice, soda, and sports drinks—would compare the juices you tested.

Change the Variables In this experiment you can change the variables in several ways. You can use the same type of juice, such as orange juice, and vary the brands. You could also test the vitamin C content in different solid foods by blending a set quantity of each food with a set amount of water. Length of storage, heat, light, and oxygen can all affect the amount of vitamin C in beverages and food. You could change each of these variables for one kind of food or beverage. With one type of juice you could also vary the freshness. For example, you could test one frozen concentrate orange juice, one store-bought refrigerated orange juice, and one freshly squeezed orange juice.

EXPERIMENT 2

Hard Water: Do different water sources have varying mineral content?

Purpose/Hypothesis Water that contains minerals in it is called hard water. The hardness or level of the mineral content varies from location to location. In this experiment, you will examine the mineral content of various waters by mixing the water with soap.

Two common elements in hard water are magnesium and calcium. These minerals can lessen the cleaning ability of soap by preventing the lathering action. Hard-water minerals readily bind to the soap molecules, forming a large and heavy compound that sinks. The result is a soap scum that does not dissolve in water. (Water softeners remove the hard minerals.)

To determine the hardness of varying water sources, you will mix water with soap. You will use tap water, rainwater, and chalk-water. Chalk is a form of limestone, which is composed of calcium.

Before you begin, make an educated guess about the outcome of this experiment based on your knowledge of minerals and hard water. This educated guess, or prediction, is your hypothesis. A hypothesis should explain these things:

- the topic of the experiment
- the variable you will change
- the variable you will measure
- what you expect to happen

A hypothesis should be brief, specific, and measurable. It must be something you can test through further investigation. Your experiment will prove or disprove whether your hypothesis is correct. Here is one possible hypothesis for this experiment: "The water highest in minerals will be the chalk water; the water least high in minerals will be the rainwater."

What Are the Variables?

Variables are anything that might affect the results of an experiment. Here are the main variables in this experiment:

- the water source
- the amount of soap
- the type of soap
- the mineral added

In other words, the variables in this experiment are everything that might affect the amount of soap scum the water produces. If you change more than one variable at the same time, you will not be able to tell which variable had the most effect on the soap scum.

How to Experiment Safely

If you are not using a disposable eyedropper, make sure to wash the dropper thoroughly to remove all traces of the soap. Be careful when handing the hot water.

In this case, the variable you will change is the water source. The variable you will measure is the hardness of the water.

Conducting a control experiment will help you isolate each variable and measure the changes in the dependent variable. Only one variable will change between the control and your experiment. For your control you will use distilled water, water that has no minerals in it. At the end of the experiment you can compare the control and the experimental results.

Level of Difficulty Easy to Moderate.

Materials Needed

- eyedropper
- liquid soap
- 4 small plastic bottles with caps
- measuring cup (with spout preferably)
- funnel (optional)
- piece of chalk (calcium)
- tap water
- rain water
- distilled water
- spoon
- cup or bowl to collect rain water
- marking pen

Approximate Budget $5.

Timetable 45 minutes (not counting the time it takes to wait for rain).

Step-by-Step Instructions

1. On a day when rain is forecast, place a bowl outside to collect at least 1 cup of rainwater.

Step 8: After placing two drops of liquid soap in each of the bottles, shake each bottle and examine the amount of soap scum. GALE GROUP.

2. Over a measuring cup, scrape about 1 teaspoon (5 milliliters) of chalk into powder using the edge of a spoon.

3. Measure 1 cup (240 milliliters) of hot distilled water into the cup. Stir the ground chalk and water thoroughly. Cool to room temperature.

4. Label the bottles: "Calcium," "Tap," "Control," and "Rain."

5. Pour the chalk water into its designated bottle. (There may be some chunks left over on the bottom so pour slowly.) You may need to use a funnel for this. Rinse out the measuring cup.

6. Measure out 1 cup (240 milliliters) of tap water and carefully pour into its bottle. Rinse the cup and repeat with the distilled and rain water.

7. Using the eyedropper, place two drops of the liquid soap into each of the bottles.

8. Shake each of the bottles and examine the amount of soap scum. Note a description of the results.

9. Allow the bottles to sit for 15 minutes and, again, note the results.

Troubleshooter's Guide

Below are some problems that may arise during this experiment, some possible causes, and some ways to remedy the problems.

Problem: The chalk did not dissolve in the water.

Possible cause: You may not have scraped the chalk into a fine enough powder. Chalk will dissolve better in warmer water than cooler water. Repeat the experiment, making sure to use hot water and a fine powder.

Problem: There was no difference in the amount of scum between the calcium water and the tap water.

Possible cause: Try allowing the bottles to sit for another 15 minutes to determine if there is a difference as the soap bubbles disappear.

Summary of Results Examine the results of your experiment. Was your hypothesis correct? How does the rainwater compare to the control? The ability of soap and detergent to lather directly affects their ability to clean. Hypothesize why water softeners are popular in some areas of the country more than others. What would be the result of simply adding more soap or detergent? Write an analysis of the experiment, including an explanation of your results for each type of water.

Change the Variables In this experiment you can change the variable by altering the water source. You can focus on one type of water, such as tap water or mineral water. Different geographic locales will have varying amounts of mineral in the water. You can also try the experiment on different brands of mineral water.

In order to keep in top physical shape, athletes require the proper balance of vitamins and minerals. AP/WIDE WORLD.

Modify the Experiment

You can modify this experiment by increasing the level of difficulty and experimenting with water softeners. Water softeners inactivate the minerals in water. Adding water softener to hard water can lead to less soap scum and more lather.

You will need to gather three cups, three bottles, and a laundry water softener. Follow the experiment procedures, making sure to save the soapy water in the bottles. After you have determined which water is highest in minerals, make three more cups of this hard water. Pour one cup of hard water into each of the three bottles. Place two drops of liquid soap into each of the bottles. In two of the bottles, drop in a different amount of water softener. You could add two drops in one bottle and four drops in the second bottle. The third bottle will be the control. Make sure you label each of the bottles.

Shake each of the bottles and note the results. How much lather or soap scum did each bottle make? How do the results compare to the natural rain water? Try using different amounts of water softener. Is there an amount you can use that will give results similar to the rainwater? You might want to graph your findings and summarize your results.

Design Your Own Experiment

How to Select a Topic Relating to this Concept There are many possible projects related to vitamins and minerals. As almost all foods contain some amounts of vitamins and minerals, you can work with food and beverages. You can also focus on where vitamins and minerals are derived from, and their effect on various life forms.

Check the Further Readings section and talk with your science or nutrition teacher to learn more about vitamins and minerals. You can also gather ideas from examining the vitamin and mineral contents listed on the packaging of the foods you eat.

For most people, eating a well-balanced diet with a wide variety of foods supplies the necessary amounts of vitamins and minerals. COPYRIGHT © KELLY A. QUIN.

Steps in the Scientific Method To conduct an original experiment, you need to plan carefully and think things through. Otherwise, you might not be sure what question you are answering, what you are or should be measuring, or what your findings prove or disprove.

Here are the steps in designing an experiment:

- State the purpose of—and the underlying question behind—the experiment you propose to do.
- Recognize the variables involved and select one that will help you answer the question at hand.
- State your hypothesis, an educated guess about the answer to your question.
- Decide how to change the variable you selected.
- Decide how to measure your results.

Recording Data and Summarizing the Results Your data could include charts and drawings, such as the one you did for these experiments. They should be clearly labeled and easy to read. You may also want to include photographs and drawings of your experimental setup and results, which will help others visualize the steps in the experiment.

If you are preparing an exhibit, you may want to display your results, such as any experimental setup you designed. If you have completed a nonexperimental project, explain clearly what your research question was and illustrate your findings.

Related Projects There are many possible project ideas related to vitamins and minerals. You can examine the vitamins and minerals that you and people you know take in by adding up the foods you eat and charting the results. Compare the numbers to the Recommended Daily Allowances (RDA). You can also experiment with removing the minerals from certain types of food.

You could also examine how other species, besides humans, use vitamins and minerals. Different animals produce certain vitamins that humans do not. You could look at what elements these animals produce and how vitamins and minerals impact an animal's health. Vitamin and mineral deficiency is also a serious health problem in many parts of the world. A project on deficiency diseases could include examining several of these diseases and possible foods people of that area could easily attain to stop or prevent the disease. You could also conduct a research project on the history of the discovery of vitamins and minerals, and the work of finding more of these elements.

For More Information

"All About What Vitamins and Minerals Do." *KidsHealth.* http://kidshealth. org/kid/stay_healthy/food/vitamin.html (accessed on February 19, 2008). Easy-to-read explanation of vitamins and minerals.

Centers for Disease Control and Prevention. *Fruits & Veggies More Matters.* http://www.fruitsandveggiesmatter.gov/ (accessed on February 19, 2008). Provides benefits and recommended amounts of fruits and vegetables.

Food Standards Agency. "Vitamins and Minerals." *eatwell.* http://www.eatwell. gov.uk/healthydiet/nutritionessentials/vitaminsandminerals (accessed on February 19, 2008). Information about vitamins, minerals, and where they are found.

Kalbacken, Joan. *Vitamins and Minerals.* San Francisco, CA: Children's Press, 1998. Simple, basic information about vitamins and minerals.

United States Department of Agriculture. *Search the USDA National Nutrient Database for Standard Reference.* http://www.nal.usda.gov/fnic/foodcomp/ search (accessed on February 19, 2008). Search for the vitamin and mineral content of specific foods.

92

Volcanoes

On August 24, in 79 A.D., the citizens of Pompeii, in what is now Italy, woke up to a warm, sunny day. Some probably went to sit outside their beautiful villas to sit and admire the fruit trees, ornamental wall paintings, and statues in their enclosed gardens. Many of the villas overlooked the sparkling Bay of Naples. Businesses were opening and some were already bustling with activity. But life in Pompeii ended abruptly that morning when nearby Mount Vesuvius erupted. Pompeii and the neighboring town of Herculaneum were destroyed. More than 2,000 people were suffocated by the gas and ash that spewed from Vesuvius and covered Pompeii or by the lava flow of molten rock that leveled Herculaneum. Pliny the Younger, a Roman historian, saw the terrible event from the nearby town of Miseneum and wrote the first written, eyewitness account of a volcano's eruption.

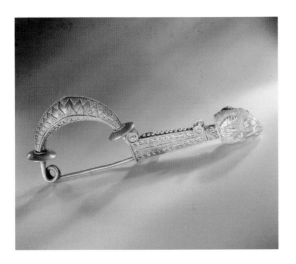

This gold pin, with the head of a ram at the tip, was found in Pompeii. CORBIS.

Today Vesuvius is still an active volcano, a conical or domelike mountain of lava, ash, and cinders that forms around a vent leading to molten rock deep within Earth. When volcanoes erupt, they literally blow their top, ejecting tons of rock and debris into the air, as well as sending clouds of toxic gases and steam and rivers of lava down the sides of the mountain.

Get the drift? After the Americas were discovered, scientists observed that Earth's continents fit together like the pieces of a jigsaw puzzle. The scientists believed that the continents had once been joined together in one land mass and then violently separated. In 1912, German meteorologist Alfred Wegener (1880–1930) proposed that the continents were moving apart slowly at a predictable rate.

Alfred Wegener's theory about continental drift was a first step in discovering the dynamics of a volcano. CORBIS CORP.

He coined the term continental drift and conducted much research to support his theory. Many thought Wegener's idea was radical, but his suggestion that some force caused the continents to move eventually became the key to unlocking the dynamics of a volcano.

After Wegener died, the geologists who agreed with his theory took it a step further. They proposed that the radioactive decay of naturally occuring elements deep within Earth produced tremendous heat. The heat was so intense that it melted rock, forming a vast caldron of liquid that boiled and swirled in vast amounts. This bubbling mass generated convection currents, currents of molten rock. The scientists suggested that these molten rock currents pushed up under ridges in the ocean and through active volcanoes—moving the continents.

How does a volcano blow its top? Deep under a volcano is Earth's mantle, a layer that lies between the the Earth's crust or outermost layer, which extends 25 miles (40 kilometers) down, and Earth's core. The further down, the hotter the temperature gets. Earth's inner core can reach 13,000°F (7,000°C). At the top of the mantle, around 30 miles (45 kilometers) down, magma can be found. Magma is liquid rock that consists of gases and silica; this substance collects and forms pools known as a magma chambers,—which are the volcano's furnace. The gases bubble through the magma, making the liquid hotter and lighter than surrounding rocks, and this helps push this volatile liquid mixture up through a volcano's vent.

Even the slight strain of tides can affect the inner pressure of a volcano and cause it to blow. Most often, though, the cause is the movement of tectonic plates, large flat pieces of rocks that form Earth's outer crust and fit together like pieces of a cracked eggshell. Grinding or overlapping can melt some of the plate rock, which pushes it up into the magma chamber, where it causes a magma surge. If the dome over a volcano's vent is obstructed with rock or dirt, pressure builds up even more, causing a more violent eruption. The same basic principles that govern tectonic plate movement can cause both earthquakes and volcanic

WORDS TO KNOW

Continental drift: The theory that continents move apart slowly at a predictable rate.

Convection currents: Circular movement of a fluid in response to alternating heating and cooling.

Crust: The hard outer shell of Earth that floats upon the softer, denser mantle.

Lava: Molten rock that occurs at the surface of Earth, usually through volcanic eruptions.

Magma: Molten rock deep within Earth that consists of liquids, gases, and particles of rocks and crystals. Magma underlies areas of volcanic activity and at Earth's surface is called lava.

Magma chambers: Pools of bubbling liquid rock that are the source of energy causing volcanoes to be active.

Magma surge: A swell or rising wave of magma caused by the movement and friction of tectonic plates, which heats and melts rock, adding to the magma and its force.

Mantle: Thick dense layer of rock that underlies Earth's crust and overlies the core.

Seismograph: A device that records vibrations of the ground and within Earth.

Seismometer: A seismograph that measures the movement of the ground.

Tectonic plates: Huge flat rocks that form Earth's crust.

Volcano: A conical mountain or dome of lava, ash, and cinders that forms around a vent leading to molten rock deep within Earth.

---

eruptions, so it is not surprising that both can be detected by the same instrument. While seismographs are used mostly for detecting earthquakes, they can also detect vibrations deep within Earth that indicate the gradual rise of magma.

Sometimes there's a good side to a down side The citizens of Pompeii and others who died because of volcanic eruptions would certainly disagree that there is any positive side to this natural disaster; but volcanic eruptions do have some good effects. If an eruption produces a layer of ash less than 8 inches (20 centimeters) thick, farmers get a free, nutritient-rich natural fertilizer blanketing their land. For example, the ash from Mount Vesuvius helps the grapes grow in that area's wine region. Although the 20 feet (6 meters) of ash that covered Pompeii smothered every living thing, the ash also preserved the city, its artifacts, and its inhabitants. Archeological findings have shown us in detail the civilization of an ancient people who were lively, cultured, and gifted.

In the following projects you will be able to learn more about volcanoes.

How to Experiment Safely

Do not activate the volcano's eruption without adult supervision. Wear goggles to do it. Always handle scissors carefully.

PROJECT 1

Model of a Volcano: Will it blow its top?

Purpose/Hypothesis In this activity you will construct a working model of a volcano. This model will demonstrate the dynamics of magma flow and the gaseous buildup that causes a volcano to blow.

Level of Difficulty Moderate.

Materials Needed

- glue
- 8-inch (20-centimeter) long plastic tube, 1.5 inches (3.8 centimeter) in diameter
- 4 plastic straws
- newspaper
- masking tape
- scissors
- 4 rolls plaster of Paris gauze (or papier-maché mix and newspaper)
- empty film container
- effervescent antacid tablets
- water
- goggles or other eye protection
- brown and red water-based or acrylic paint
- cornstarch
- baking soda
- vinegar
- red food coloring

Approximate Budget $10 to $15.

Timetable 2 to 3 hours.

Step-by-Step Instructions

1. Place about six sheets of newspaper over the surface you will be working on.

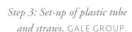
Step 3: Set-up of plastic tube and straws. GALE GROUP.

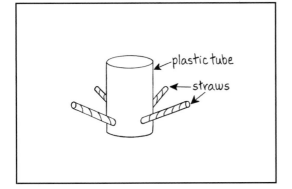

2. Poke four holes in the plastic tube between 1 and 2 inches (2.5 to 5 centimeters) from the bottom. Make sure the straws can fit through the holes.

3. Glue the straws into the tube's holes, making sure the glue does not clog the straws' openings.

4. Twist a sheet of newspaper into a stick shape. Repeat with several sheets.

5. Wrap the sticks around the tube, making sure the straws stick out, and tape into place. The bottom should be wide and the top narrower, just like a volcano.

6. Gently moisten the plaster of Paris strips and wrap them around the volcano. Make sure you cover all the newspaper.

7. Allow to dry for 30 minutes. Trim the straws that are protruding out of the volcano.

8. Paint the surface with brown and red water-based or acrylic paint and allow to dry.

9. Using leftover material, create a cap that covers the top of the plastic tube. Make sure it's removable but snug.

10. Remove the volcano cap.

11. Place one to five antacid tablets inside the plastic film container.

12. Pour 1 tablespoon of water into the container. Snap the top on and drop into the plastic tube opening at the top of the volcano.

13. Place the volcano cap back on quickly, stand back, and watch it blow!

14. Remove the volcano cap.

15. Mix 1 cup (224 grams) of cornstarch with 0.75 cup (178 milliliters) of water. Add ten drops of red food coloring. Add 0.25 cup (56 grams) baking soda mix and add 0.25 cup (56 grams) of vinegar.

16. Pour the mixture into the plastic tube and observe. The magma mixture will swell inside the volcano and cause a bubbling eruption. Slowly the magma will creep

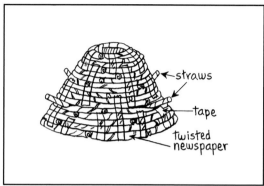

Steps 4 and 5: Wrap newspaper sticks around the tube, making sure the straws stick out, and tape into place. GALE GROUP.

Step 16: The magma mixture will swell inside the volcano and cause a bubbling eruption. Slowly the magma will creep out of the volcano and become lava. GALE GROUP.

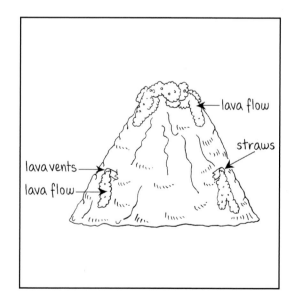

Troubleshooter's Guide

Here are some problems that may arise during this project, possible causes, and ways to remedy the problems.

Problem: The magma/lava flow did not come out of the straws.

Possible cause: The tubes are clogged. Stick a pipe cleaner through the straws to make sure the tubes are open. Add more vinegar and baking soda to the mix and try again.

Problem: The film container did not blow the top off the volcano.

Possible cause: You need more antacid. Try adding more to the container and do not forget to wear your goggles.

out of the volcano and become lava. Lava should also slowly come out of the straw vents on the side.

Summary of Results Write a paragraph explaining what you witnessed when the volcano erupted and the magama/lava flowed. Research how Mount Vesuvius blew and compare your volcano with how that volcano erupted. Make a diagram of the internal structure of the volcano.

PROJECT 2

Looking at a Seismograph: Can a volcanic eruption be detected?

Purpose/Hypothesis Seismometers are instruments that detect disturbances in Earth's crust. Used mostly for earthquake detection, they can also measure the turbulence of a volcano's magma activity. The disturbance or activity is recorded on a seismograph, a sheet of paper that shows the intensity of the activity. For this project you will construct a seismograph that will simulate the types of disturbances that indicate volcanic activity.

Level of Difficulty Easy.

Steps 1 to 3: Set-up of shoe box and coil toy. GALE GROUP.

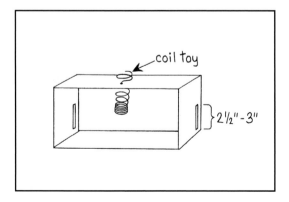

Materials Needed

- shoe box
- metal coil toy (like a Slinky)
- metal block (or a stone), 2 by 2 inches (5 x 5 centimeters)
- pencil
- roll of adding machine tape
- scissors
- tape

Approximate Budget $2 to $5 for purchase of coil toy and adding machine tape.

Timetable Less than 30 minutes.

Step-by-Step Instructions

1. Cut a 2.5 to 3-inch (6 to 7-centimeter) slit on each side of a shoe box.
2. With scissors cut the coil toy in half.
3. Poke a hole in the top of the box and pull a few coils of the toy through.
4. Tape the metal block to the spring.
5. Tape the pencil to the block. Face the tip toward the back and make sure the tip touches the back wall.
6. Carefully feed the paper through both slits cut in the side walls. Do not tear the paper. You have now built the seismograph.
7. Place your seismograph on a table.
8. Place any heavy object on top of the seismograph to hold it in place.
9. Ask a friend to help by gently shaking the table or lifting it off the ground a half inch.
10. As your friend is causing the disturbance, slowly and gently pull the paper through the hole.

Summary of Results Examine your seismic data. The tape records the magnitude of seismic disturbances in Earth's crust that can lead to a magma surge. Mark your tape with observations of what may have happened if a volcano really erupted. Refer to the illustration of the sample seismograph paper for ideas.

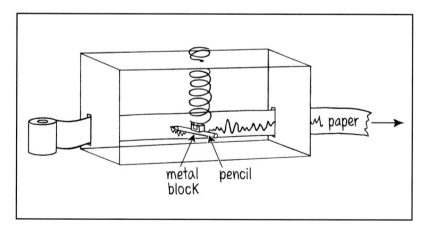

metal block   pencil

Steps 4 to 6: Set-up of the seismograph. GALE GROUP.

Troubleshooter's Guide

Here are some problems that may arise during this experiment, some possible causes, and ways to remedy the problems.

Problem: The pencil does not move up and down.

Possible cause: The coil toy is too tight. Either try a heavier coil toy or gently stretch the coil toy until the coils no longer touch each other.

Problem: The pencil is not making clear marks on the seismograph paper.

Possible cause: The pencil is not touching the paper. Adjust it or try using a marker with a fine tip.

Design Your Own Experiment

How to Select a Topic Relating to this Concept These projects are simple models that will familiarize you with some of the important dynamics of a volcano. If you wish to investigate further, research the type, sizes, and places of volcanoes. Or lava flows, properties of lava, or the effects of volcanic ash may interest you.

Check the Further Readings section and talk with your science teacher or school or community media specialist to start gathering information on volcano questions that interest you.

Steps in the Scientific Method To do an original experiment, you need to plan carefully and think things through. Otherwise, you might not be sure what question you are answering, what you are or should be measuring, or what your findings prove or disprove.

Here are the steps in designing an experiment:

- State the purpose of—and the underlying question behind—the experiment you propose to do.
- Recognize the variables involved, and select one that will help you answer the question at hand.
- State a testable hypothesis, an educated guess about the answer to your question.

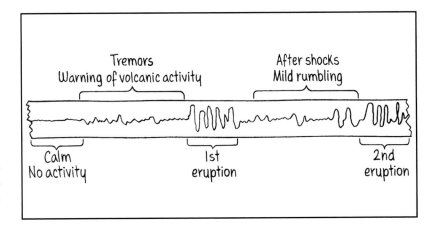

Sample seismograph paper with observations recorded. How does your paper compare? GALE GROUP.

- Decide how to change the variable you selected.
- Decide how to measure your results.

Recording Data and Summarizing the Results
In any experiment, you should keep notes and data organized so that others can utilize and understand it. Charts, graphs, and pictures are excellent ways to share and summarize your results.

Related Projects Besides constructing a model of a volcano and simulating its eruption, you could investigate the environmental effects of eruptions or past climate changes due to eruptions. Start by asking a question you want answered. Then construct an investigation around that question.

For More Information

North Dakota and Oregon Space Grant Consortia. *Volcano World.* http://volcano.und.edu (accessed on January 12, 2008).

Rubin, Ken. *Volcano & Earthquakes.* New York: Simon & Schuster Books for Young Readers, 2007.

Van Rose, Susanna. *Volcano & Earthquake.* New York: Knopf, 1992. Photographs and text explain the causes and effects of volcanoes and earthquakes and examine specific occurrences throughout history.

Mount Tolbachik in Russia's Kamchatka Peninsula erupted on July 6, 1975, spewing lava that gushed at a speed of 550 feet (168 meters) per second.
AP/WIDE WORLD PHOTOS.

93

Water Cycle

Water is found not only in oceans, rivers, streams, ponds, swamps, puddles, and similar places. It is also stored in the soil, in polar ice caps, and in underground areas called aquifers. Some water is actually in the air as water vapor. The water cycle, sometimes called the hydrologic cycle, is the continuous movement of water between the atmosphere, land, and bodies of water. Rainstorms are the major way that water gets from the atmosphere to Earth. Then the rain seeps into the soil or runs over land into streams, rivers, and oceans.

Over time, water evaporates from lakes, ponds, swamps, rivers, oceans, and even soil, changing from a liquid to a gas called water vapor. This water vapor rises into the atmosphere again, where it cools and condenses around dust or salt particles in the air, turning back into droplets of liquid. When the droplets get too heavy to remain in the air, they fall as precipitation: rain, snow, sleet, or hail.

Water vapor is often invisible, but on a warm summer day, you can feel water vapor. The air often feels damp because it contains a lot of water vapor.

How much water can the air hold? There is a limit to how much water vapor air can hold. When the air becomes saturated with water vapor, the excess water vapor condenses into droplets of water. Water vapor high in the atmosphere forms clouds, large masses of droplets. When these clouds are close to the ground, we call them fog. You have probably also seen water vapor condense on windows or on cold drink glasses.

Is the water cycle a new idea? The water cycle is driven by the Sun and gravity and affects climate, soils, erosion, habitat, transportation, and so on. This cycle has been recognized and studied by scientists for thousands of years. Leonardo da Vinci wrote about it in the 1400s. The founders of modern hydrologic study were Pierre Perroult (1608–1680),

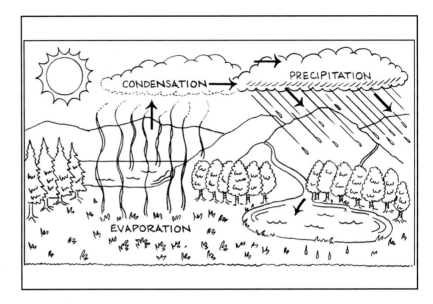

Illustration of global water cycle. GALE GROUP.

Edme Mariotte (1620–1684), and Edmund Halley (1656–1742). Today, people who study the water cycle are called hydrologists.

People can affect the water cycle. For example, paving land with concrete decreases the amount of water that can enter the soil. Using dams to create artificial lakes or reservoirs increases evaporation. What other factors affect the water cycle? How do temperature and surface area affect the rate at which water changes into water vapor? You will have an opportunity to explore these questions in the following two experiments.

EXPERIMENT 1

When it is really cold outside you can see your breath. What you see is water vapor. GRANT HEILMAN.

Temperature: How does temperature affect the rate of evaporation?

Purpose/Hypothesis Evaporation occurs when liquid water turns into water vapor, a gas. The more water that evaporates and then condenses back into water droplets in the atmosphere, the more rain that falls.

In this experiment, you will determine how water temperature affects the rate of evaporation. Before you begin, make an educated guess about the outcome of this experiment based on your

1248

WORDS TO KNOW

Aquifer: Underground layer of sand, gravel, or spongy rock that collects water.

Condense/condensation: The process by which a gas changes into a liquid.

Control experiment: A set-up that is identical to the experiment but is not affected by the variable that affects the experimental group. Results from the control experiment are compared to results from the actual experiment.

Evaporate/evaporation: The process by which liquid changes into a gas.

Hydrologists: Scientists who study water and its cycle.

Hydrology: The study of water and its cycle.

Hypothesis: An idea in the form of a statement that can be tested by observation and/or experiment.

Precipitation: Water in its liquid or frozen form when it falls from clouds in the atmosphere as rain, snow, sleet, or hail.

Saturated: Containing the maximum amount of a solute for a given amount of solvent at a certain temperature.

Surface area: The area of a body of water that is exposed to the air.

Variable: Something that can affect the results of an experiment.

Water (hydrologic) cycle: The constant movement of water molecules on Earth as they rise into the atmosphere as water vapor, condense into droplets and fall to land or bodies of water, evaporate, and rise again.

Water vapor: Water in its gaseous state.

---

knowledge of evaporation. This educated guess, or prediction, is your hypothesis. A hypothesis should explain these things:

- the topic of the experiment
- the variable you will change
- the variable you will measure
- what you expect to happen

A hypothesis should be brief, specific, and measurable. It must be something you can test through observation. Your experiment will prove or disprove whether your hypothesis is correct. Here is one possible hypothesis for this experiment: "The warmer the water temperature, the more evaporation will occur."

In this case, the variable you will change will be the temperature of the water, and the variable

The water cycle is important to all life forms because it brings water continuously to land and removes many impurities along the way. AP IMAGES.

What Are the Variables?

Variables are anything that might affect the results of an experiment. Here are the main variables in this experiment:

- the temperature of the water
- the temperature of the surrounding air
- the amount of water in each container at the beginning and end of the experiment
- the surface area of the water
- the amount of humidity or water vapor in the air

In other words, the variables in this experiment are everything that might affect the rate of evaporation of the water. If you change more than one variable, you will not be able to tell which variable had the most effect on the evaporation.

you will measure will be the amount of water left in your containers at the end of the experiment. You expect the container with the warmer water will have less water left because more has evaporated into the air.

Setting up a control experiment will help you isolate one variable. Only one variable will change between the control and your experimental containers, and that is the water temperature. The control container will remain at room temperature. You will make the water in the experimental containers cooler or warmer than room temperature.

You will record the amount of water you put into your containers and the amount of water left after the containers spend a day at different temperatures. If the container with the hotter water has less water left in it, your hypothesis is correct.

Level of Difficulty Easy.

Materials Needed

- 3 containers of the same size, shape, and material
- 6 cups (3 pints or 1.4 liter) water
- ice cubes

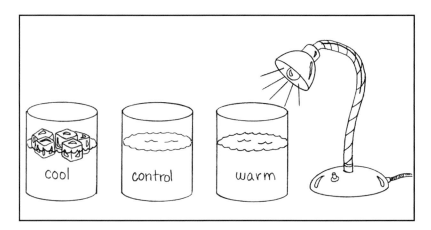

Step 2: Set-up of three containers. GALE GROUP.

- an insulated container large enough to hold one of the three containers above (an ice chest would work)
- thermometer
- measuring cup
- graduated cylinder
- flexible lamp

How to Experiment Safely

If your containers are made of glass, handle them carefully. Also be careful not to touch the light bulb in the lamp.

Approximate Budget Less than $15. (Most of these materials should be available in the average household.)

Timetable 1 to 2 hours to set up and take the initial data, plus another 24 hours to take the final data.

Step-by-Step Instructions

1. Measure 2 cups (1 pint or 0.4 liters) of water into two containers. Fill the third container to the same level with a mixture of water and as many ice cubes as will fit. Mark the water level on the side of each container.
2. Label one container "control," the second one "warm," and the third one with the ice "cool."
3. Place all three containers in a room where the temperature is about 70 to 72°F (21 to 22°C). Use the thermometer to take the temperature, and record it on your data sheet.
4. Leave the control container as is. Place the cool container inside the insulated container. Take the water temperature and record it.

Jar	Air temperature	Water temperature	Amount of water left
cool			
control			
warm			

Data sheet for Experiment 1.
GALE GROUP.

Troubleshooter's Guide

Experiments do not always work out as planned. However, figuring out what went wrong can definitely be a learning experience. Here is a problem that may arise during this experiment, a possible cause, and ways to remedy the problem.

Problem: The containers all lost about the same amount of water.

Possible cause: The water temperatures were not different enough. Use more ice in the cool one, and place the light bulb closer to the warm one.

5. Place the flexible light so it shines directly on the warm container but does not warm the other two containers. After an hour or so, take the water temperature and record it.

6. Leave your containers in place for 24 hours.

7. The next day, use the graduated cylinder to measure the amount of water remaining in each container. Record your findings.

Summary of Results Study your results. How did the air temperature affect the amount of evaporation from each container? Was your hypothesis correct? Summarize what you found.

Change the Variables You can change the variables and repeat this experiment to learn more. Try controlling the temperature more closely so you can measure the change in evaporation rate that occurs with a smaller temperature difference. You can also see if any changes in the results occur when you change the size or shape of your containers. What do you notice?

Modify the Experiment This experiment examines how the temperature of water affects its evaporation rate. Wind speed also can have a significant affect on evaporation. You can make this experiment more challenging by measuring how wind speed compares to temperature in affecting the rate of evaporation.

In order to measure wind speed, you will need two small fans that are the same size. You can use the same three containers you used to test temperature differences. Again, fill each of the containers with two cups of water. Set one fan to a low speed and place it near the first container. Set the second fan on a high speed and place it near the second container. The third container will be your control. Leave the containers alone for 24 hours, and then use the graduated cylinder to measure the remaining water in each container.

Compare your data for wind speed and temperature variations. The results only measure how two specific wind speeds compare to specific temperatures. In actuality, wind and temperature would vary and they would play a role together. You can experiment with different wind speeds and temperatures to find the highest or lowest evaporation rate. You can also look at humidity, another key weather

event that affects evaporation rate. Humidity is the amount of water vapor in the air. You can experiment with humidity by using a humidifier, and placing a container of water in an enclosed area, such as a closet.

EXPERIMENT 2

Surface Area: How does surface area affect the rate of evaporation?

Purpose/Hypothesis In this experiment, you will fill containers of different sizes with the same amount of water to explore how their surface area affects the rate of evaporation. For example, if you poured a certain amount of water in a tall, thin test tube with a small surface area, and the same amount in a short, broad cake pan with a large surface area, which container would have the greater rate of evaporation?

Before you begin, make an educated guess about the outcome of this experiment based on your knowledge of evaporation. This educated guess, or prediction, is your hypothesis. A hypothesis should explain these things:

Which body of water do you think experiences the most evaporation? PETER ARNOLD INC.

- the topic of the experiment
- the variable you will change
- the variable you will measure
- what you expect to happen

A hypothesis should be brief, specific, and measurable. It must be something you can test through observation. Your experiment will prove or disprove whether your hypothesis is correct. Here is one possible hypothesis for this experiment: "A greater surface area will lead to faster evaporation."

In this case, the variable you will change will be the surface area of your trays. The variable

What Are the Variables?

Variables are anything that might affect the results of an experiment. Here are the main variables in this experiment:

- surface area of the water
- amount of water
- length of the experiment
- temperature of the water
- the temperature of the surrounding air
- the amount of humidity or water vapor in the air

In other words, the variables in this experiment are everything that might affect the rate of evaporation of the water. If you change more than one variable, you will not be able to tell which variable had the most effect on the evaporation.

you will measure is amount of evaporation that occurs.

For the control experiment, you will use a medium-sized tray. For the experimental containers, you will use larger and smaller trays. You will measure how much evaporation occurs by monitoring the water level in the trays over time and measuring the amount of water left. If the tray with the largest surface area shows the fastest rate of evaporation, then your hypothesis is correct.

Level of Difficulty Easy.

Materials Needed

- 3 metal or plastic square or rectangular watertight trays or containers of different sizes
- ruler or tape measure
- water
- graduated cylinder

Approximate Budget Less than $5. (Most of these materials should be available in the average household; try to borrow the graduated cylinder.)

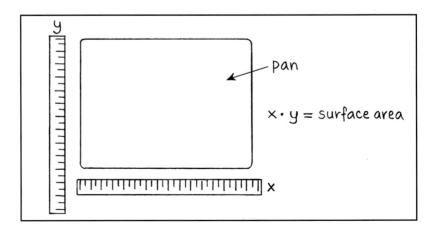

Step 1: Figuring the surface area of the tray. GALE GROUP.

	Pan #	Surface area	Water left
Day #1			
Day #2			
Day #3			
Day #4			
Day #5			

Data sheet for Experiment 2.
GALE GROUP.

Timetable About 5 days.

Step-by-Step Instructions

1. With your ruler, measure both sides of each tray. Multiply the two sides together to get the surface area of the tray. Record these numbers on your data sheet (see illustration).

2. Measure exactly the same volume of water into each tray. The amount is not important, as long as you know how much it is and put the same amount in each tray.

3. Place the trays side by side under the same conditions. They should either all be exposed to sunlight or all be in the dark, for example.

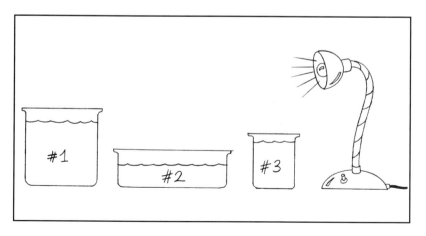

Steps 2 and 3: Set-up of the three trays. Place the trays side by side under the same conditions. GALE GROUP.

Troubleshooter's Guide

Here are some problems that may arise during this experiment, some possible causes, and ways to remedy the problems.

Problem: No evaporation occurred.

Possible cause: Your containers did not receive enough light or heat for measurable water to evaporate. Try putting all of them in direct sunlight.

Problem: Evaporation seemed the same in all the containers.

Possible cause: There is not enough difference in the surface areas of your containers. Try using larger trays and smaller trays.

4. After the trays sit for a day, pour the water from each tray into the graduated cylinder and measure it. Record this information on your data sheet, and pour the water back into the same tray. Be careful not to lose any water as you pour.

5. Repeat Step 4 every day for five days.

Summary of Results To find out how much water evaporated each day, subtract the amount of water left each day from the amount from the previous day. Compare your findings. What have you discovered? Did the tray with the largest surface area lose the most water to evaporation? Did the tray with the smallest surface area lose water to evaporation at the slowest rate? Was your hypothesis correct? Summarize what you have found.

Change the Variables You can vary this experiment in several ways. For example, you can use pans that are really big and really small. Compare the evaporation rates. What does this tell you about evaporation from lakes, ponds, and oceans?

You can also experiment with the effect of temperature. Try moving all your pans to a very warm or very cool place, such as a refrigerator. What happens then? Be sure to record the temperature in the places you put the pans.

Finally, you can use containers with similar surface area but different depths. Determine the effect of depth on the evaporation rate.

Design Your Own Experiment

How to Select a Topic Relating to this Concept If you are interested in the water cycle, you could study the evaporation rate when water is moving and still, investigate the evaporation differences between saltwater and fresh water, or compare how concrete and soil affect the rate of evaporation.

If you are more interested in condensation, you could try making your own clouds and studying the effects of water temperature, air temperature, and sizes of water bodies. Or you may want to study the surfaces on which rain falls on and measure how long it takes to evaporate or seep into the soil.

Check the Further Readings section and talk with your science teacher or school or community media specialist to start gathering information on water cycle questions that interest you.

Steps in the Scientific Method To do an original experiment, you need to plan carefully and think things through. Otherwise you might not be sure what question you are answering, what your are or should be measuring, or what your findings prove or disprove.

Here are the steps in designing an experiment:

- State the purpose of—and the underlying question behind—the experiment you propose to do.
- Recognize the variables involved, and select one that will help you answer the question at hand.
- State a testable hypothesis, an educated guess about the answer to your question.
- Decide how to change the variable you selected.
- Decide how to measure your results.

Recording Data and Summarizing the Results Your data should include charts, such as the one you did for these experiments. They should be clearly labeled and easy to read. You may also want to include photos, graphs, or drawings of your experimental setup and results.

If you are preparing an exhibit, draw diagrams of your procedure and display your containers. If you have done a nonexperimental project, explain clearly what your research question was and illustrate your findings.

Related Projects In addition to completing experiments, you could prepare models that demonstrate the water cycle or you could research how the water cycle is being affected by human actions, globally or locally. You might study the amounts of rainfall in different parts of the country and how landforms affect rainfall. You might go in many directions with your interests.

For More Information

Hooper, Meredith, and Christopher Coady. *The Drop in My Drink: The Story of Water on Our Planet.* New York: Viking Children's Books, 1998. Detailed information on the water cycle, interesting facts about water, and important environmental information.

"Hydrologic Cycle." *Earthscape.* http://www.und.edu/instruct/eng/fkarner/pages/cycle.htm (accessed on March 2, 2008). Explanation of the water cycle process along with activities.

National Aeronautics and Space Administration. *Droplet and the Water Cycle.* http://kids.earth.nasa.gov/droplet.html(accessed on March 2, 2008). A game were users follow the cycle of a water droplet.

U.S. Geological Survey. "The Water Cycle." *Water Science for Schools.* http://ga.water.usgs.gov/edu/watercycle.html (accessed on March 2, 2008). Information and illustrations on the water cycle.

Walker, Sally M. *Water Up, Water Down: The Hydrologic Cycle.* Minneapolis, MN: Carolrhoda Earth Watch Book, 1992. Descriptions of the water cycle, historically important experiments, and the water cycle's importance to all life on Earth.

94

Water Properties

Without water, the life forms we see on Earth could not possibly exist. This simple combination of three atoms—one oxygen, two hydrogen—acts in complex ways that can turn a barren, dusty planet into a thriving biological community. What are the properties of water that make it so versatile and vital? How can we measure and compare water's properties to those of other liquids?

A number of observable properties of water result from its molecular structure, meaning not only the atoms that make up water, but also the shape of the water molecule. The bonds between the one oxygen and two hydrogen atoms do not form a straight line but form an angle like a wide *V*. This shape gives the molecule a positive electric charge on one side and a negative electric charge on the other. This charge gives water the properties of adhesion, the tendency to stick to certain other substances and cohesion, the tendency to stick to itself.

Adhesion and cohesion in everyday life The properties of adhesion and cohesion can be easily observed by watching raindrops on a windowpane. Adhesion holds the drops to the glass. Even if the window is tilted forward, some drops will cling to the underside of the pane. Cohesion can be seen if you trace the path of drops down the pane. Drops close to one another will be drawn together by cohesion, forming larger drops. Observe carefully and you will see that drops will far more readily join together than split apart. Splitting a water drop requires some energy or change to loosen the bonds that hold the molecules together.

Cohesion, as you might predict, results from the attraction of one water molecule's positive side to another water molecule's negative side.

The molecular structure of water. GALE GROUP.

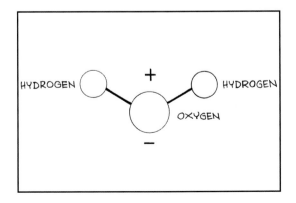

Water's adhesive force causes its meniscus to rise up the walls of the straw. Mercury's cohesive force causes it to bow away from the walls of the straw and toward itself. PHOTO RESEARCHERS INC.

Cohesion creates surface tension, which enables water bugs to "skate" along the water's surface without sinking. The first experiment will demonstrate that surface tension can keep afloat an object that is denser than water. You will then compare the surface tension of two other liquids to that of water.

Forces affecting adhesion Adhesion, water's tendency to cling to certain substances, creates capillary action. In extremely narrow spaces, such as inside water vessels in the stem of a plant, water will actually rise against gravity by the force of adhesion. This capillary action helps plants pull water up from the soil.

Observe the surface of water in a straw: the water can be seen "climbing" the wall of the straw. This bowing of the water's surface is called the meniscus, and it is caused by the strength of the water's adhesion to the solid around it. In liquids that have much stronger cohesion than adhesion, such as mercury, the meniscus bows upward at the middle and down at the edges.

Adhesion in water depends upon the structure of the second substance's molecules. Some substances are hydrophilic, attracted to water, and some are hydrophobic, not attracted to water. This explains why water will easily clean a salty film off your hands, but will not efficiently remove grease without using detergent. Salt is hydrophilic, but grease is normally hydrophobic. Detergent acts as a link between the water molecules and the grease. The molecules of the detergent possess one end that bonds with the grease and another end that bonds with water. When these detergent molecules coat the grease, they change it from hydrophobic to hydrophilic (see illustration).

In the first experiment, you will demonstrate the strength of the cohesive force of water by floating a metal object (one that ordinarily would not float) on its surface. In the second experiment, you will measure the adhesive force between water and a solid by determining how much weight is required to break the strength of adhesion. You will

WORDS TO KNOW

Adhesion: Attraction between two different substances.

Buoyancy: The tendency of a liquid to exert a lifting effect on a body immersed in it.

Capillary action: The tendency of water to rise through a narrow tube by the force of adhesion between the water and the walls of the tube.

Cohesion: Attraction between like substances.

Density: The mass of a substance compared to its volume.

Hydrophilic: A substance that is attracted to and readily mixes with water.

Hydrophobic: A substance that is repelled by and does not mix with water.

Hypothesis: An idea in the form of a statement that can be tested by observation and/or experiment.

Meniscus: The curved surface of a column of liquid.

Variable: Anything that might affect the results of an experiment.

then predict how coating the solid with a hydrophobic substance such as grease or petroleum jelly will affect the strength of adhesion.

EXPERIMENT 1

Cohesion: Can the cohesive force of surface tension in water support an object denser than water?

Purpose/Hypothesis In this experiment, you will first demonstrate the strength of the cohesive force of water by floating a metal object on its surface. Then you will test the relative cohesive force of two other liquids by attempting to float the same object and others on them. Before you begin, make an educated guess about the outcome of this experiment based on your knowledge of the properties of water. This educated guess, or prediction, is your hypothesis. A hypothesis should explain these things:

- the topic of the experiment
- the variable you will change
- the variable you will measure
- what you expect to happen

A hypothesis should be brief, specific, and measurable. It must be something you can test

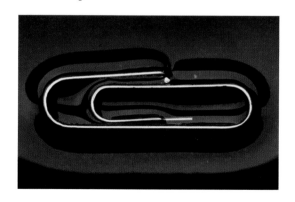

Surface tension of a paper clip floating on water. PHOTO RESEARCHERS INC.

What Are the Variables?

Variables are anything that might affect the results of an experiment. Here are the main variables in this experiment:

- the composition of the liquids
- the purity of the liquids
- the type of objects used to test surface tension
- the method by which the objects are placed on the liquids

In other words, the variables in this experiment are everything that might affect the surface tension of the liquid. If you change more than one variable, you will not be able to tell which variable had the most effect on surface tension.

How to Experiment Safely

Do not substitute any other liquids in this experiment without checking with your teacher first. Always wear goggles when experimenting with alcohol and work in a well-ventilated room. Keep the alcohol away from your nose and mouth.

through observation. Your experiment will prove or disprove whether your hypothesis is correct. Here is one possible hypothesis for this experiment: "We can determine from observation of surface tension whether other liquids have greater or lesser cohesion than water."

In this case, the variable you will change is the liquid, and the variable you will measure is whether the object floats or sinks. You expect that you will be able to observe the differences in surface tension between liquids.

Level of Difficulty Easy/moderate.

Materials Needed

- 3 wide-mouth glass jars or drinking glasses
- corn oil
- isopropyl alcohol
- distilled water
- 3 unused staples (make sure they are clean of any adhesive)
- 3 small sewing needles
- 3 small steel paper clips
- 3 large steel paper clips
- tweezers
- safety goggles

Approximate Budget $1 to $10. (Most materials may be found in the average household.)

Timetable 10 to 20 minutes.

Step-by-Step Instructions

1. Pour 2 inches (5 centimeters) of water into jar 1. Fill jar 2 to the same level with alcohol, and fill jar 3 to the same level with oil.
2. If you are using objects other that those in the materials list, make sure none of them is less dense than the liquid, which would make them float due to buoyancy and not due to

cohesion and surface tension. To find out, push each object to the bottom of the liquid. If it floats to the top, then you must replace it with something denser.

3. Using the tweezers, carefully place a staple flat on the surface of the water. You should have little difficulty floating the staple on the water.

4. Remove the staple and try the needle and the paper clips. Do not put two objects in the cup at the same time, and let any ripples settle before trying the next object.

5. On your chart, describe what each object does. Your chart should look something like the illustration.

6. Repeat Steps 3, 4, and 5 with jar 2 and jar 3.

Summary of Results Examine your chart and compare the results of the tests for each liquid. Did your predictions prove true? Were you able to get meaningful results for each liquid? Which liquid had the strongest cohesion? The weakest? How did the cohesive force of alcohol and oil compare to the cohesion of water?

Troubleshooter's Guide

When doing experiments in adhesion and cohesion, be aware that unintended impurities can greatly affect your results. Natural oil from your fingers can alter the behavior of a small object on water, and an invisible soap film on the inside of a glass can easily spoil your results. Here is a problem that may arise during this experiment, some possible causes, and ways to remedy the problem.

Problem: When any object is placed on the surface of the water, it sinks.

Possible causes:

1. None of your objects is light enough. Try using a staple and a sewing needle.

2. Your water has been contaminated. Dump it out, clean the glass, and make sure the glass is rinsed clean of any soap residue.

	staple	needle	sm. paper clip	lg. paper clip
cup one	floats	floats	sinks	sinks
cup two				
cup three				

Step 5: Sample data chart for Experiment 1. GALE GROUP.

What Are the Variables?

Variables are anything that might affect the results of an experiment. Here are the main variables in this experiment:

- the purity of the water
- the shape of the object used to test adhesion
- the type of substance applied to the object
- the amount of substance applied to the object

In other words, the variables in this experiment are everything that might affect the surface tension of the liquid. If you change more than one variable, you will not be able to tell which variable had the most effect on surface tension.

The materials pictured will serve to test your hypothesis, but you might wish to construct a sturdier set-up for demonstrations or repeated tests. GALE GROUP.

Change the Variables You can change the variables and conduct similar experiments. For example, what happens to the surface tension if you dissolve salt in the water? That is, does salty seawater have a different surface tension than fresh water? You can also change the temperature of the water—either cooling or heating it—to determine the effect on surface tension. Warning: Do not try heating the alcohol, as it may burn with an almost-invisible flame and cause injury or damage.

EXPERIMENT 2

Adhesion: How much weight is required to break the adhesive force between an object and water?

Purpose/Hypothesis In this experiment, you will first determine the strength of the adhesive force between a flat piece of wood and the surface of water. Then you will measure the effect of altering the adhesion between the two by adding a hydrophobic substance. Before you begin, make an educated guess about the outcome of this experiment based on your knowledge of the properties of water. This educated guess, or prediction, is your hypothesis. A hypothesis should explain these things:

- the topic of the experiment
- the variable you will change
  - the variable you will measure
  - what you expect to happen

A hypothesis should be brief, specific, and measurable. It must be something you can test through observation. Your experiment will prove or disprove whether your hypothesis is correct. Here is one possible hypothesis for this experiment: "A coating of a hydrophobic substance on an object will measurably reduce the adhesive force between that object and water."

In this case, the variable you will change is the coating on the object, and the variable you will measure is amount of weight (force) it takes to overcome the surface tension. You expect that a hydrophobic coating on an object will reduce the weight required to overcome surface tension.

Level of Difficulty Easy/moderate.

Materials Needed

- 9 x 12-inch (23 x 30-centimeter) pan
- block of balsa wood, approximately 6 inches (15 centimeters) square and less than 1 inch (2.5 centimeters) thick, available in most hobby stores)
- 12-inch (30-centimeter) or longer wooden dowel
- wooden ruler with three holes (to fit a three-ring binder)
- plastic container with two holes punched near the lip
- thumb tacks
- string
- pencil
- distilled water
- ¼-cup of a hydrophobic substance such as cooking oil, grease, or petroleum jelly
- 5 rolls of pennies (or enough to fill the container)

Approximate Budget $10 to $15. (Most materials may be found in the average household.)

Timetable 1 to 2 hours.

Step-by-Step Instructions

1. Assemble your balance.
   a. Measure and mark the exact center of the block of wood (draw two diagonals from corner to corner). Cut a 30-inch (76-centimeter) length of string and tie a small loop in one end. Push a thumb tack partway into the center mark. Twist the loop of string around the

Steps 1 to 3: The assembled balance should look like this.
GALE GROUP.

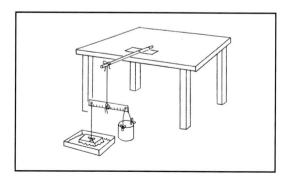

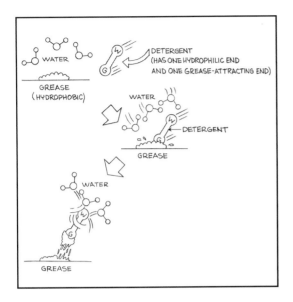

The action of detergent between water and grease. GALE GROUP.

tack, and push the tack as far into the wood as possible, securing the string.

b. Cut a 24-inch (60-centimeter) length of string and loop the end through the two holes in the lip of the plastic container. Then tie the end onto the length of string about 4 inches (10 centimeters) up from the container.

c. Cut a 6-inch (15-centimeter) length of string and tie it firmly around the dowel, 2 inches (5 centimeters) from the end. If necessary, put a tack next to the loop of string to keep it from slipping off. Tie the other end of the string through the center hole of the ruler.

d. Place the dowel on a desk so the ruler is suspended at least 6 inches (15 centimeters) out over the floor. Attach the wooden block's string to one of the outside holes on the ruler. Make sure that when the ruler is held level, the block is suspended 1 inch (2.5 centimeters) from the floor.

2. Attach the plastic container to the other end of the ruler and begin filling it with pennies until the weight is balanced. Record how many pennies equals the weight of the wood block.

3. Place the pan on the floor beneath the wood block. Fill the pan with water until the block is resting on the water's surface. The ruler should remain at or close to level. (You may need someone

	Trial #1	Trial #2	Trial #3
uncoated block	112 pennies	105 pennies	
block w/ hydrophobic substance			

Step 4: Sample data chart for Experiment 2. GALE GROUP.

Experiment Central, 2nd edition

to steady the ruler so it does not shift from side to side during this step.)

4. Begin adding pennies to the plastic container until the downward force of the weight overcomes the force of adhesion and lifts the block off the surface of the water. Record the number of pennies added on a chart like the one illustrated.

5. Wipe the block and let it sit in a warm place for several hours until it is dry. Coat the underside of the block with your hydrophobic substance. (Note: Once you have coated the block, you will not be able to repeat Step 4. Some of the substance may remain permanently on the wood, changing the adhesive force. If you wish to do repeated tests, you must use two blocks.)

6. Remove enough pennies so the block is balanced once more, and place the block back on the water's surface. Repeat Step 4. Record the number of pennies necessary to lift the block clear of the water.

Troubleshooter's Guide

When doing experiments in adhesion and cohesion, be aware that unintended impurities can greatly affect your results. Natural oil from your fingers can alter the behavior of a small object on water, and an invisible soap film on the inside of a container can easily spoil your results. Here are some problems that may arise during this experiment, some possible causes, and ways to remedy the problems.

Problem: The block breaks free of the adhesive force after the addition of very little or no weight.

Possible cause: The tack in the block is not properly centered. Pulling upward on one side of the block will overcome the adhesive force more easily. Center the tack.

Problem: The plastic container is full and the block still has not been balanced or lifted.

Possible causes:

1. Your container is too small.
2. Your block is too heavy. Use balsa wood (and not a hardwood).

Summary of Results Examine your data and compare the results of the tests with your hypothesis. Did your hypothesis prove true? Compare the number of pennies necessary to balance the block in Step 2 to the number necessary to break the surface tension in Step 4. The difference between these two numbers shows the strength of the surface tension. Note on your chart the exact number of pennies.

Change the Variables You can vary this experiment to investigate different aspects of adhesion and cohesion. Try altering the test materials to determine whether different solids have different levels of adhesion to water. Repeat the experiment using a block wrapped in plastic and another wrapped in aluminum foil. Hypothesize whether the two will

Cohesion, the bonding of water molecules to one another, enables this water bug to "skate" over the water's surface without sinking. PETER ARNOLD INC.

show different levels of adhesion and test your hypothesis. Be sure to check with your teacher before testing with new materials.

Modify the Experiment Hydrophobic substances, such as soap and oil, affect the surface tension of water. You can conduct a simple experiment with adhesion and surface tension with liquid soap and a small object, such as a staple. Take four or five small plastic wide-mouth glasses or bowls. Fill all the glasses about half way with water. Use the results of Experiment 1 to find an object that floats, such as a staple or small paperclip. With tweezers, carefully place the staple (or other object) in the first glass so that it floats. You should have at least five of the same object.

In the second glass, add a drop of liquid soap and stir. Wait for the water to settle and then slowly place a clean staple (or other object) into the glass. Does it float? Write down the number of soap droplets and the results on a chart. Now add two drops of soap to the third glass and stir. Again, place a clean staple carefully on top of the water and note the results. Continue add one more drop to each glass until the object no longer floats. If you reuse the glasses or objects, make sure you wash and dry them thoroughly. How does breaking the cohesive forces of water depend upon the amount of a hydrophobic substance? You can repeat this experiment with different size and shape objects.

Design Your Own Experiment

How to Select a Topic Relating to this Concept The simple experiments described here touch on only a few aspects of adhesion and cohesion. Many experiments on the nature of hydrophilic and hydrophobic substances can be performed with inexpensive, readily available materials.

Check the Further Readings section and talk with your science teacher or school or community media specialist to start gathering information on water property questions that interest you.

Steps in the Scientific Method To do an original experiment, you need to plan carefully and think things through. Otherwise, you might not be sure what question you are answering, what you are or should be measuring, or what your findings prove or disprove.

Here are the steps in designing an experiment:

- State the purpose of—and the underlying question behind—the experiment you propose to do.

- Recognize the variables involved, and select one that will help you answer the question at hand.

- State a testable hypothesis, an educated guess about the answer to your question.

- Decide how to change the variable you selected.

- Decide how to measure your results.

Recording Data and Summarizing the Results In the experiments included here and in any experiments you develop, you can look for ways to display your data in more accurate and interesting ways. Diagrams would be especially useful in Experiment 2.

Remember that those who view your results may not have seen the experiment performed, so you must present the information you have gathered in as clear a way as possible. Including photographs or illustrations of the steps in the experiment is a good way to show a viewer how you got from your hypothesis to your conclusion.

Related Projects To develop other experiments on this topic, think about adhesion and cohesion in everyday life. Why does a coaster stick to the bottom of a wet glass? Investigate the function of capillary action in plants. Think of ways you could demonstrate the reason oil spills are so damaging to our ecosystem. Investigate how oil spills are cleaned up without polluting the water with detergents.

For More Information

Environment Canada. "Properties of Water." *The Nature of Water.* http://www.ec.gc.ca/WATER/en/nature/prop/e_prop.htm (accessed on March 2, 2008). Lots of brief explanations about the different properties of water.

Kyrk, John. "Animated Essentials of Water and pH." http://www.johnkyrk.com/H2O.html (accessed on March 2, 2008). Animations of the chemical properties of water.

Ray, C. Claibourne. *The New York Times Book of Science Questions and Answers.* New York: Doubleday, 1997. Addresses both everyday observations and advanced scientific concepts on a wide variety of subjects.

U.S. Geological Survey. "Water Properties." *Water Science for Schools.* http://ga.water.usgs.gov/edu/waterproperties.html (accessed on March 2, 2008). Information and illustrations about the properties of water.

Van Cleave, Janice. *Chemistry For Every Kid.* New York: John Wiley and Sons, Inc., 1989. Contains a number of simple and informative demonstrations and investigations into properties of water, including cohesion, the meniscus, and capillary action.

95

Weather

Weather is the state of the troposphere at a particular time and place. The troposphere is the lowest layer of Earth's atmosphere, ranging to an altitude of about 9 miles (15 kilometers) above Earth's surface.

Weather differs from climate. Climate is the average weather that a region experiences over a long period. A change in the weather can mean a rain shower. A change in climate might consist of a year-round warming trend that affects how crops grow in a region.

All weather starts with the Sun's heat, but the Sun does not heat Earth's surface evenly. The Sun's direct rays make the equator regions much warmer than other areas, while the tilt of Earth's axis causes the hemisphere that is tilted toward the Sun to be warmer than the hemisphere that is tilted away from the Sun.

The elements of weather include temperature, humidity, cloudiness, precipitation (rain, snow, hail), wind, and air pressure. These elements interact to spread the Sun's heat more evenly around Earth. Without them, the equator region would get much hotter than it does, while the pole regions would get colder.

The Sun's rays shine directly on the equator, so that region gets very warm. The rays hit the North and South Poles at an angle, so the same amount of heat spreads over a wider area, thus these regions stay cool.
GALE GROUP.

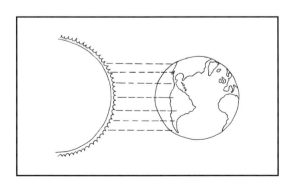

Air moves because of differences in both temperature and air pressure, also called atmospheric pressure. Atmospheric pressure is the pressure exerted by the atmosphere at Earth's surface due to the weight of the air.

As the Sun heats Earth's surface, the surface heats the air above it. As the air molecules warm up, they move farther apart. This reduces the density or heaviness of the air and creates an area of low air pressure. On the other hand, molecules in cool air are closer together, making that air denser and heavier. Cool air creates an area of high air pressure.

Recognizing different types of clouds can help you predict the weather. FIELD MARK PUBLICATIONS.

Air moves from areas of high pressure to areas of low pressure, creating wind. During Project 1, you will build an anemometer (pronounced an-eh-MOM-eter), a device that measures the speed of wind.

As warm air rises into the atmosphere, it carries with it water vapor, which is water in its gas form. As the air cools, the gas molecules move closer together and condense around very small particles of dust or salt in the air. The water vapor turns into its liquid form, water droplets. Clouds are huge masses of condensed water vapor.

As the droplets bump into each other, they join to form larger drops. In time, they are large and heavy enough to fall as rain. One rain drop can contain a million cloud droplets!

An English naturalist named Luke Howard gave cloud groups these Latin names in 1803: Cirrus (pronounced SEAR-us, from the Latin word for "curl of hair"); Stratus (from the Latin word for "layer"); Cumulus (pronounced CUME-u-lus, from the Latin word for "heap"); and Nimbus (from the Latin word for "rain").

Since then, meteorologists have used Howard's names to describe 10 types of clouds at three levels.

As warm, light air rises, cooler, heavier air rushes in to take its place, creating windy conditions. CORBIS.

High-level clouds about 20,000 feet (6.0 kilometers) above Earth include Cirrus, wispy clouds that precede bad weather; Cirrostratus, layers of clouds that signal rain; and Cirrocumulus, rippled clouds that signal unsettled weather

Middle-level clouds about 7,000 to 17,000 feet (2.1 to 5.2 kilometers) above Earth include Altocumulus, flat gray-white clouds that precede a summer storm; Altostratus, layers of gray clouds that indicate it will rain soon; and Nimbostratus, thick dark-gray clouds that signal rain or snow.

Low-level clouds less than 7,000 feet (2.1 kilometers) above Earth include Stratocumulus, gray or white rolls that indicate dry weather; Stratus, layers of gray clouds that often bring precipitation; Cumulus, fluffy white puffs seen on hot summer days; and Cumulonimbus, dark, towering clouds that bring storms.

Weather affects what we wear, what we eat, the kinds of work we do, how we have fun, and, most importantly, the ecosystem in which we live. Learning more about the weather helps us better understand the world in which we live.

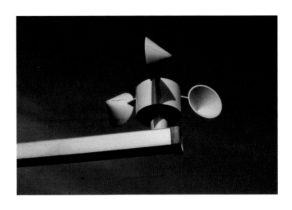

This cup anemometer is connected to instruments inside the weather station that record how many times the cups spin in a certain period of time. The spinning rate indicates the wind speed. PHOTO RESEARCHERS INC.

PROJECT 1

Wind: Measuring wind speed with a homemade anemometer

Purpose/Hypothesis In this project, you will make a simple anemometer and compare the wind speed measured by your anemometer with the wind speed measured in your region by the National Weather Service. The National Weather Service gathers wind speed and other weather information every one to six hours from about 1,000 land stations throughout the United States and its possessions. Meteorologists at the Weather Service use this information to make weather predictions, which are then broadcast over radio and television. The Service's weather stations use cup anemometers to measure wind speed.

Some television stations provide a live broadcast of the current wind speed; you might even see the speed change during the forecast. If you can tune in to one of these broadcasts, you can make your wind speed measurements simultaneously, thus eliminating the time variable.

WORDS TO KNOW

Anemometer: A device that measures wind speed.

Atmospheric pressure: The pressure exerted by the atmosphere at Earth's surface due to the weight of the air.

Climate: The average weather that a region experiences over a long period.

Control experiment: A set-up that is identical to the experiment but is not affected by the variable that will be changed during the experiment.

Density: The mass of a substance compared to its volume.

Ecosystem: An ecological community, including plants, animals, and microorganisms, considered together with their environment.

Hypothesis: An idea in the form of a statement that can be tested by observation and/or experiment.

Humidity: The amount of water vapor (moisture) contained in the air.

Meteorologists: Scientists who study weather and weather forecasting.

Troposphere: The lowest layer of Earth's atmosphere, ranging to an altitude of about 9 miles (15 kilometers) above Earth's surface.

Variable: Something that can affect the results of an experiment.

Water vapor: Water in its gas form.

Weather: The state of the troposphere at a particular time and place.

Level of Difficulty Easy/moderate.

Materials Needed

- metal or plastic protractor
- Ping-Pong ball
- 8 inches (20 centimeters) of strong thread
- transparent tape

Approximate Budget Less than $5. (Most or all of these materials should be available in the average household.)

Timetable 15 to 20 minutes.

Step-by-Step Instructions

1. Tape one end of the thread firmly to the Ping-Pong ball.
2. Tie the other end of the thread to the middle of the flat side of the protractor, as illustrated. The ball should hang down so the thread

crosses the rounded side of the protractor. The numbers (angles) marked on the rounded side will indicate wind speed.

3. Determine when the weather will be broadcast over a local radio or television station and whether it includes a live broadcast of wind speed.

4. At the same time as a live weather broadcast or about two hours before a taped broadcast, take your anemometer outside. Stand in an open area, away from trees, buildings, and traffic.

5. Hold the anemometer by one corner, with the flat side parallel to the ground.

6. As the wind blows, note the angle of the farthest movement of the thread. Record it on a chart similar to the one illustrated.

7. Use the scale provided to convert the angle to miles per hour (mph) and record it on your chart:

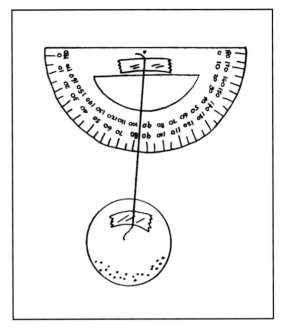

Steps 1 and 2: Set-up of Ping-Pong ball and protractor. GALE GROUP.

Angle= mph

    90° angle= 0 mph
    80° angle= 15 mph
    70° angle= 20 mph
    60° angle= 25 mph
    50° angle= 30 mph
    40° angle= 35 mph
    30° angle= 40 mph
    20° angle= 50 mph

8. Take a second wind-speed measurement and record it on the chart.

9. Add the wind speed from the radio or television broadcast to your chart.

10. Repeat Steps 4 to 9 on two more days and record the results.

Summary of Results Use the data on your chart to create a triple-bar graph comparing the three

Step 6: Data chart for Project 1. GALE GROUP.

Day 1 : ____	Day 2 : ____	Day 3 : ____
(date)	(date)	(date)

readings on each day. Then study your graph and chart and how accurately your anemometer measured wind speed. Were your own measurements on any day within 5 miles per hour (8 kilometers per hour) of those given in the radio or television broadcast? Write a paragraph summarizing your findings.

Modify the Project In this project you built an anemometer to measure wind speed. You can add to this project by also measuring wind direction. Using both an anemometer and a wind vane will give you two key measurements used to forecast the weather.

There are many materials you can use to build a simple wind vane. The finished wind vane will look similar to a "T" shape, with an arrowhead on one end and a tail on the other (see illustration). The top of the "T," the rod, is parallel to the ground and able to spin freely on a rod. The arrow points in the direction of the wind.

One way to build a wind vane is to attach a straw to a dowel or pencil. You can use a long tack to attach the straw in the middle point. Spin the straw around several times to make sure it spins freely. Cut out an arrow and tail from card stock. Ask an adult to help you cut slits into the straw and slip the paper into the straw. You may need tape. You will need a compass to determine north and south. Attach the dowel to a solid, wide base, such as a large plastic container that is weighted down. Tape a compass or write the direction points on the base. For a sturdier rod, you could use a dowel in place of a straw. You will need an adult to help you attach the rod into the larger dowel using a drill and screw. The adult helper can also cut small slits in both sides of the rod where you can slide the arrow and tail.

Place the wind vane in an open area with the anemometer. When you measure the wind speed, note the wind direction. Why is knowing both wind direction and speed important? Follow the weather reports and compare your measurements and weather predictions to the reports.

EXPERIMENT 2

Clouds: Will a drop in air temperature cause a cloud to form?

Purpose/Hypothesis In this experiment, you will create a cloud in a bottle by making water vapor condense around tiny smoke particles in the air. To make the vapor condense, you will suddenly reduce the air pressure, allowing the water vapor molecules to move farther apart and cool off.

But is it the drop in temperature that causes the cloud to form? And will a cloud form without tiny particles in the air? To find out, you will also try the experiment without a drop in temperature and without smoke particles in the air. (You might need a helper to complete these experiments.)

Before you begin, make an educated guess about the outcome of this experiment based on your knowledge of clouds. This educated guess, or prediction, is your hypothesis. A hypothesis should explain these things:

- the topic of the experiment
- the variable you will change
- the variable you will measure
- what you expect to happen

A hypothesis should be brief, specific, and measurable. It must be something you can test through observation. Here is one possible hypothesis for this experiment: "A cloud will form only after a drop in temperature and only when particles are present in the air."

In this case, the variable you will change in the first part of the experiment is the air pressure (and hence the air temperature), and the variable you will change in the second part of the experiment is the presence of smoke particles in the bottle. The variable you will measure in both parts of the experiment is the presence of a cloud. You expect the cloud will form only when the temperature drops and particles are present.

What Are the Variables?

Variables are anything that might affect the results of an experiment. Here are the main variables in this experiment:

- how much the air pressure increases and then drops inside the bottle
- whether the bottle contains smoke particles and how many particles are present
- whether the bottle is tightly sealed
- the amount of water in the bottom of the bottle
- the air temperature outside the bottle

In other words, the variables in this experiment are everything that might affect the formation of a cloud. If you change more than one variable, you will not be able to tell which variable had the most effect on the cloud formation.

How to Experiment Safely

Ask an adult to help you light and handle the matches.

Steps 3 to 7: Set-up of cloud experiment. GALE GROUP.

You will complete two control experiments. In one, you will determine whether a cloud will form without a drop in temperature. In the other control experiment, you will see if a cloud will form without smoke particles in the air. If a cloud forms only when the temperature drops and when particles are present, you will know that your hypothesis is correct.

Level of Difficulty Easy/moderate—but you may need someone to help you manipulate the materials.

Materials Needed

- three 1-quart (1-liter) plastic soda bottles, empty and clean, with caps
- matches
- flashlight
- labels and a marker
- measuring cup
- water

Approximate Budget Less than $5. (Most materials should be available in the average household.)

Timetable 1 hour.

Step-by-Step Instructions

Step 9: Data chart for Experiment 2. GALE GROUP.

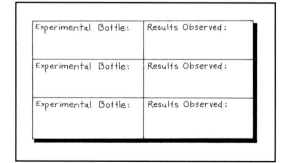

1. Label one bottle "Experimental" and two bottles "Control."
2. Pour 1 cup of water into each bottle.
3. Drop two lighted matches into the Experimental bottle and quickly screw on the cap.
4. Let the matches burn until the water puts them out.
5. Shake the bottle to make the air inside moist.
6. With the bottle upright, squeeze the bottle to increase the air pressure inside.

7. Place the flashlight so it shines into the bottle (or have your helper hold the flashlight).

8. Quickly unscrew the cap to lower the pressure inside the bottle and cool off the water vapor.

9. Check to see if a cloud forms. If it does, it will last only a few seconds. Record your observations on a chart similar to the one illustrated.

10. Using one of the Control bottles, repeat Steps 3 through 9, omitting Step 8. (Do not unscrew the cap, so the air pressure and temperature of the water vapor inside the bottle do not change.)

11. Observe this Control bottle for at least three minutes to see whether a cloud forms. Record your observations.

12. Using the other Control bottle, repeat Steps 5 through 9. (This time, you do not perform Steps 3 and 4 so the bottle contains no smoke particles.)

13. Observe the second Control bottle for at least three minutes to see whether a cloud forms. Record your observations.

Summary of Results Study the findings on your chart and decide whether your hypothesis was correct. In which bottles did a cloud form? Write a paragraph summarizing your findings and explaining whether they support your hypothesis.

Change the Variables Here are some ways you can vary this experiment:

- Try increasing or reducing the amount of smoke particles, or try adding dust to the air inside the bottle instead of smoke particles.

- Experiment with the amount of water in the bottle. Try the experiment with no water at all.

Troubleshooter's Guide

Here are some problems that may arise during this experiment, some possible causes, and ways to remedy the problems.

Problem: A cloud did not seem to form inside the Experimental bottle.

Possible causes:

1. The air pressure did not get high enough inside the bottle. Try again, squeezing the bottle harder.

2. You unscrewed the cap too slowly, allowing the air to cool so slowly that the water vapor did not condense. Try again, unscrewing it as quickly as possible.

3. The bottle did not contain enough smoke particles. Try again, dropping in three or four lighted matches.

4. You did not look into the bottle quickly enough and missed the cloud. Try again, and have a helper unscrew the cap so you can observe what is happening.

Problem: A cloud formed in the Control bottle that contained no smoke particles.

Possible cause: The air in the bottle already contained other tiny particles. Rinse the bottle and try again.

A weather vane can determine wind direction. ILLUSTRATION BY TEMAH NELSON.

- Complete the experiment using saltwater and no smoke particles. Shake the bottle vigorously to release salt from the water into the air. (Most cloud particles actually form around salt released into the air from ocean waves.)
- Try doing the experiment outside on a chilly day. Instead of unscrewing the cap, see if the air outside the bottle chills the air inside enough to form a cloud.

Design Your Own Experiment

How to Select a Topic Relating to this Concept You can explore many other aspects of weather. Consider what you would like to know about this topic. For example, you might want to find out how Earth's rotation affects wind direction. Or you might try your hand at predicting the weather by observing clouds.

Check the Further Readings section and talk with your science teacher or school or community media specialist to start gathering information on weather questions that interest you. As you consider possible experiments, be sure to discuss them with your science teacher or another knowledgeable adult before trying them. Some of the materials or procedures might be dangerous.

Steps in the Scientific Method To do an original experiment, you need to plan carefully and think things through. Otherwise, you might not be sure which question you are answering, what you are or should be measuring, or what your findings prove or disprove.

Here are the steps in designing an experiment:

- State the purpose of—and the underlying question behind—the experiment you propose to do.
- Recognize the variables involved, and select one that will help you answer the question at hand.
- State a testable hypothesis, an educated guess about the answer to your question.
- Decide how to change the variable you selected.
- Decide how to measure your results.

Recording Data and Summarizing the Results In your wind speed and cloud-making experiments, your raw data might include charts, graphs, drawings, and photographs of the changes you observed. If you display your experiment, make clear the question you are trying to answer, the variable you changed, the variable you measured, the results, and your conclusions. Explain what materials you used, how long each step took, and other basic information.

Related Projects You can undertake a variety of projects related to weather. For example, you might find out how seeding clouds produces rain. Or you could try an experiment with a pan of flour that will show you the different sizes of raindrops. Now that you have an anemometer, you might make a weather vane to determine wind direction, a rain gauge to keep track of rainfall, and a hydrometer to measure the humidity in the air.

For More Information

Ahrens, C. Donald. *Meteorology Today: An Introduction to Weather, Climate, and the Environment.* New York, NY: Brooks Cole, 2002.

Burt, Christopher C., and Mark Stroud. *Extreme Weather: A Guide and record Book.* New York, NY: W.W. Norton & Company, 2004.

Edheads. *Weather.* http://www.edheads.org/activities/weather/ (accessed on February 19, 2008). Interactive animations on weather and stories about professionals in the field.

The National Oceanic and Atmospheric Administration (NOAA) National Weather Service. *Jetstream: Online School for Weather.* http://www.srh.weather.gov/jetstream/ (accessed on February 18, 2008). Information and pictures of weather phenomena.

Web Weather for Kids. http://www.eo.ucar.edu/webweather/ (accessed on February 19, 2008). Information, activities, and safety information on weather.

96

Weather Forecasting

Weather sleuths everywhere Thousands of weather stations throughout the world communicate weather observations and data to international weather centers every three hours where the information is analyzed by meteorologists, who study the weather and the atmosphere. The weather stations consist of outdoor shelters, known as Stevenson screens, that house instruments such as thermometers, which measure air temperature, and anemometers, which record wind speed. All instruments at these stations are of the same type and accuracy.

Anemometers record wind speed.
PHOTO RESEARCHERS INC.

Weather stations also record many other weather elements, including types of clouds, humidity, air pressure, precipitation (rainfall or snowfall), and visibility. Instruments and equipment that record weather in the upper atmosphere include radar, satellites, radiosonde balloons, and planes. Radar tracks the path of storms, while satellites send back pictures of entire weather systems. The radiosonde balloons carry instruments that record weather conditions in the upper atmosphere and send the data back by radio. Planes with special meteorological equipment track storms and their weather patterns.

A supercomputer collects all this information, calculates how air pressure, moisture, and winds might affect each other, and produces a forecast for the next 24 hours.

Weather forecasting before computers The first weather forecasting guide was written about 2,000 years ago. A Greek naturalist named Theophrastus wrote the *Book of Signs,* a collection of 200 natural signs that indicated the type of

1283

Tornado watches are posted for a region when weather conditions are likely to form these destructive storms. CORBIS.

weather that was on its way. In 1687, John Tulley of Saybrook, Connecticut, published a farmers' almanac that included the first weather forecast made in the United States. In 1792, Robert Bailey Thomas of West Boyleston, Massachusetts, began writing an annual almanac, which he eventually called *The Old Farmer's Almanac.* Along with humorous stories, Thomas offered some of the nation's earliest long-range weather forecasts.

Instruments such as the weathervane, which indicates wind direction, were used at least 2,000 years ago in Athens, Greece. In the seventeenth century, more precise weather instruments emerged that could indicate humidity, temperature, and barometric pressure, as well as wind direction and rainfall. The real science of meteorology (pronounced ME-tee-or-ology), the study of the atmosphere and weather, began during this era.

Measuring the air's ups and downs One of the most important meteorological instruments was the barometer, which measures air pressure changes with a column of mercury that rises and falls. Air pressure differences between two adjoining areas of the atmosphere cause winds, and the barometer made it possible to predict wind velocity patterns. Many people worked on the design and theory of the barometer, but Evangelista Torricelli of Italy (1608–47) is generally credited with developing the first one in 1644.

Satellites can track deadly hurricanes, such as Hurricane Katrina, and alert those people who live in their path. AP IMAGES.

Dewpoint Temperatures

Dry Bulb Tempera-ture (°C)	Difference Between Wet-Bulb and Dry Bulb Temperatures (°C)														
	1	2	3	4	5	6	7	8	9	10	11	12	13	14	15
−20	−33														
−18	−28														
−16	−24														
−14	−21	−36													
−12	−18	−28													
−10	−14	−22													
−8	−12	−18	−29												
−6	−10	−14	−22												
−4	−7	−12	−17	−29											
−2	−5	−8	−13	−20											
0	−3	−6	−9	−15	−24										
2	−1	−3	−6	−11	−17										
4	1	−1	−4	−7	−11	−19									
6	4	1	−1	−4	−7	−13									
8	6	3	1	−2	−5	−9	−21	−14							
10	8	6	4	1	−2	−5	−14	−9	−28						
12	10	8	6	4	1	−2	−9	−5	−16						
14	12	11	9	6	4	1	−5	−1	−10	−17					
16	14	13	11	9	7	4	2	2	−6	−10	−17				
18	16	15	13	11	9	7	1	4	−2	−5	−10	−19			
20	19	17	15	14	12	10	4	8	2	−2	−5	−10	−19		
22	21	19	17	16	14	12	7	10	5	3	−1	−5	−10	−19	
24	23	21	20	18	16	15	10	13	8	6	2	−1	−5	−10	−18
26	25	23	22	20	18	17	12	16	11	9	6	3	0	−4	−9
28	27	25	24	22	21	19	17	18	14	11	9	7	4	1	−3
30	29	27	26	24	23	21	18	19	16	14	12	10	8	5	1

Dewpoint temperature chart.
GALE GROUP.

Weather maps and computers Weather maps have isobars, continuous lines that connect areas with the same air pressure. Meteorologists use isobars to observe the development of high and low pressure areas. A high pressure area is surrounded by winds that blow clockwise in the northern hemisphere and counterclockwise in the southern hemisphere. It usually brings dry weather. A low pressure area is surrounded by winds that blow counterclockwise in the northern hemisphere and clockwise in the southern hemisphere. It usually brings cloudy, wet, and windy weather.

Meteorologists also study the formation and movements of fronts, the front edges of moving masses of air. When cold air lies behind the edge, it is known as a cold front. When warm air lies behind, it is a warm front.

Computer forecasting techniques were first developed in the 1950s. The computer evaluates current weather conditions in a large area and then predicts changes that will occur in the next 10 minutes. This generates a new set of weather conditions, and the predictions continue until the computer has created a forecast for the next day's weather. With today's supercomputers, the several billion computations required for a single forecast can be worked out very quickly.

WORDS TO KNOW

Barometer: A device that measures air pressure.

Condensation: The process by which a gas changes into a liquid.

Control experiment: A set-up that is identical to the experiment but is not affected by the variable that will be changed during the experiment.

Dewpoint: The point at which water vapor begins to condense.

Front: The front edges of moving masses of air.

High air pressure: An area where the air is cooler and more dense, and the air pressure is higher than normal.

Hypothesis: An idea in the form of a statement that can be tested by observation and/or experiment.

Isobars: Continuous lines that connect areas with the same air pressure.

Low air pressure: An area where the air is warmer and less dense, and the air pressure is lower than normal.

Meteorologist: Scientist who studies the weather and the atmosphere.

Radiosonde balloons: Instruments for collecting data in the atmosphere and then transmitting that data back to Earth by means of radio waves.

Variable: Something that can affect the results of an experiment.

Weather forecasting: The scientific predictions of future weather patterns.

Weather forecasting: The scientific prediction of weather patterns, may look simple when we watch a television weather forecast on the local news, but it's not. That forecast was based on data collected and analyzed from many sources.

Warning people of hurricanes and tornadoes is an important function of weather forecasting. Understanding weather terms and the formation of storms can help you avoid surprises and stay safe. In the experiment that follows, you will learn more about why and when condensation forms. The project will enable you to build your own barometer to help you make your own weather forecasts.

EXPERIMENT 1

Dewpoint: When will dew form?

Purpose/Hypothesis This experiment deals with a principle of weather called dewpoint. Dew is the moisture that forms on plants and other objects when air is cooled sufficiently for the water vapor in the air to condense into liquid. The temperature at which dew forms is called the dewpoint temperature. If the dewpoint temperature is close to the air temperature, there is a high possibility of fog, rain, or snow during the next few hours.

In this experiment, you will first determine the dewpoint temperature for that day. Then you will use what you have learned to guess or predict whether dew will form on a cold glass left outdoors. Before you begin, make an educated guess about the outcome of this experiment based on your knowledge of weather. This educated guess, or prediction, is your hypothesis. A hypothesis should explain these things:

- the topic of the experiment
- the variable you will change
- the variable you will measure
- what you expect to happen

A hypothesis should be brief, specific, and measurable. It must be something you can test through observation. Your experiment will prove or disprove your hypothesis. Here is one possible hypothesis for this experiment: "If the dewpoint temperature is close to 32°F (0°C), dew should develop on a glass of ice water."

In this case, the variable you will change is the temperature of the glass, and the variable you will measure is the formation of dew. You expect dew to form on the glass of ice water if the dewpoint temperature for that day is near freezing.

As a control experiment, you will set up one glass of water at air temperature. That way, you can determine whether dew forms no matter what the temperature of the glass. If dew forms only on the cold glass, your hypothesis will be supported.

Level of Difficulty Easy.

Materials Needed

- thermometer (for safety, use an alcohol thermometer with red fluid inside)
- dewpoint temperature chart (illustrated)

What Are the Variables?

Variables are anything that might affect the results of an experiment. Here are the main variables in this experiment:

- the amount of water vapor present in the atmosphere
- the current weather conditions, including air temperature
- how fast the thermometer is swung during the experiment

In other words, the variables in this experiment are everything that might affect the dry bulb and wet bulb temperatures (and hence the dewpoint temperature). If you change more than one variable, you will not be able to tell which variable had the most effect on the dewpoint.

Materials for Experiment 1.
GALE GROUP.

- 1-inch (2.5-centimeter) square of cloth
- small rubber band
- water (at air temperature)
- ice
- 2 plastic or glass drinking cups (any size)

Approximate Budget About $10, if thermome-ters need to be purchased.

Timetable 30 minutes each day; experiment can be repeated each day for a week, if you wish.

Step-by-Step Instructions

1. Using the thermometer, take a reading of the outside air temper-ature and record it on a data sheet. This will be the "dry bulb temperature."
2. Place the cloth around the bulb at the bottom of the thermometer and wrap the rubber band around to hold the cloth securely. Wet the cloth thoroughly with tap water.
3. Wave the thermometer with the wet cloth in the air for one minute. Be sure to hold the thermometer at the top, at the opposite end of the cloth. Do not touch the thermometer stem.
4. Record the temperature shown on the thermometer. This will be the "wet bulb temperature."
5. On the data sheet, write the difference between the wet bulb and dry bulb temper-atures. Example: Dry Bulb Temperature is 61°F (16°C). Wet Bulb Temperature is 50°F (10°C). The difference is 11°F (6°C).
6. Using the data you have collected, refer to the dewpoint temperature chart. Locate the dry bulb temperature in the left col-umn. Locate the difference in wet and dry bulb temperatures across the top of the chart. Find where the two points intersect and record that number as the dewpoint temperature.

Step 2: Thermometer with cloth banded to the bottom. Wet cloth thoroughly. GALE GROUP.

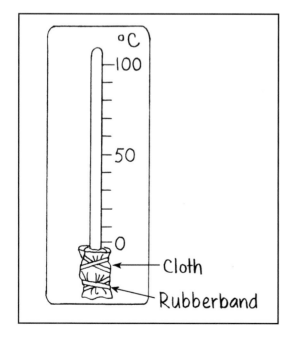

7. Fill one cup with water and ice cubes. The approximate temperature of the water will be 32°F (0°C). Fill the second cup (your control experiment) with water at normal tap water temperature.

8. Leave both cups outdoors in the shade for 30 minutes.

9. Check the outside of both cups for condensation. Record whether your hypothesis is correct. (The cup with ice water should always be below the dewpoint temperature and collect condensation. The cup at air temperature should remain dry unless the air temperature matches the dewpoint temperature.)

Troubleshooter's Guide

Here is a problem that may arise during this experiment, a possible cause, and a way to remedy the problem.

Problem: Condensation does not form on either glass.

Possible cause: The air does not contain enough water vapor. Place the cups in a different spot (outside or inside) or repeat the experiment on a different day.

Summary of Results Create a chart to organize your results. If you repeat this experiment for several days, notice if dew has formed on the cup surfaces each morning. Replace the ice every day.

Change the Variables You can vary this experiment in several ways. The air temperature and the amount of water vapor in the air change from day to day. If you change the locations or seasons in which you try this experiment, you can see different results. During spring and fall, high water vapor tends to be present. Indoor environments during the winter months often have less water vapor present.

PROJECT 2

Air Pressure: How can air pressure be measured?

Purpose/Hypothesis Changes in the atmosphere are the cause of most of our weather. The purpose of this project is to build a barometer that shows changes in air pressure. When air is warmed, it rises and the air pressure decreases. If the air is cooled, it sinks and air pressure increases. Low air pressure usually indicates stormy weather, and high air pressure usually indicates fair weather. By observing air pressure trends, you will be able to predict upcoming weather conditions.

Level of Difficulty Easy.

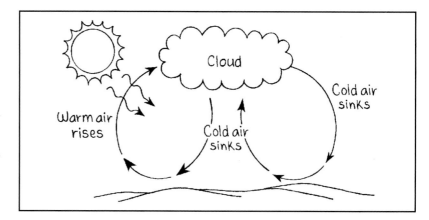

When air is warmed, it rises and the air pressure decreases. If the air is cooled, it sinks and air pressure increases. GALE GROUP.

Materials Needed

- wide-mouth jar without a lid
- 7-inch (17.5-centimeter) diameter round balloon
- plastic straw
- index card
- rubber cement
- scissors

Approximate Budget $1 for balloon.

Timetable 20 minutes to prepare barometer; 1 to 2 weeks to observe changes in air pressure.

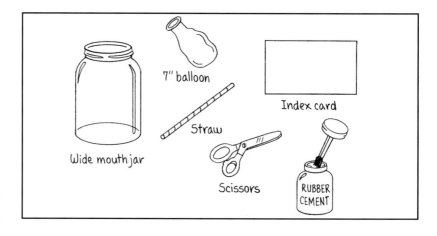

Materials for Project 2. GALE GROUP.

Step-by-Step Instructions

1. Cut end off the balloon and stretch the balloon over the mouth of the jar.
2. Use the rubber band to attach the balloon securely to the jar.
3. Rubber cement the straw horizontally to the center of the balloon, so most of it extends over the edge of the jar.
4. Prop up the index card behind the straw. Line up the straw with the middle of the index card, but not touching it.
5. Draw a line behind the straw and label it "baseline."
6. Draw a line 0.5 inch (1 centimeter) above the baseline and label it "high pressure—fair weather."
7. Draw a line 0.5 inch (1 centimeter) below the baseline and label it "low pressure—poor weather."
8. Place the barometer outdoors in the shade and watch for changes in air pressure.
9. Record your observations along with daily weather conditions.

Summary of Results Can you explain changes in the readings on your barometer? (If the air pressure outside increases, it presses on the balloon and causes the straw to rise. If the air pressure outside drops below the pressure in the jar, the balloon swells, and the straw points downward.) For a fun experiment, try monitoring the environment inside your home. Leave the barometer in different rooms and record the results.

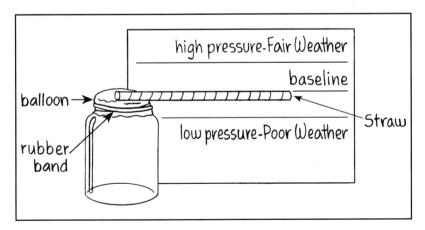

Illustration of completed barometer. GALE GROUP.

Troubleshooter's Guide

Here is a problem that may arise during this experiment, a possible cause, and a way to remedy the problem.

Problem: The straw on the balloon does not move.

Possible cause: If no change is noticeable, test the barometer by using a hair dryer to warm up the air in the jar. Adjust the balloon until the straw dips down.

Modify the Project You can extend this project by detailing the relationship between specific weather conditions and your barometer. After you do so for several weeks, you can use your barometer to predict the weather.

Follow the instructions for making your barometer. For the barometer in the project, you drew a 0.5 inch mark both above and below the baseline. Use the ruler to add lines every one-eighth of an inch both below and above the baseline. Make a chart listing wind speed, temperature, and precipitation.

Place your barometer outside in a safe spot where it can stay for several weeks. Every day note the change in the barometer and the weather conditions. Before and after any weather change, try to make a precise note of the mark on the barometer. News programs and weather Web sites can tell you the exact wind speed and temperature. If it rains, find out the amount it rained in your area and write it down in your chart.

After about a month take a look at your chart. What does the air pressure tell you about wind, temperature, and precipitation? Using your chart as a guide, use only the barometer to forecast the weather over the next week. How close can you come to actual weather events?

Design Your Own Experiment

How to Select a Topic Relating to this Concept The day's weather conditions affect your daily routine and sometimes your mood. Since weather is always changing and is different around the globe, it presents many study possibilities. Possible weather topics include precipitation, humidity, air masses, hurricanes, tornadoes, and El Niño.

Check the Further Readings section and talk with your science teacher or school or community media specialist to start gathering information on weather forecasting questions that interest you.

Steps in the Scientific Method To do an original experiment, you need to plan carefully and think things through. Otherwise, you might not be sure what question your are answering, what you are or should be measuring, or what your findings prove or disprove.

Here are the steps in designing an experiment:

- State the purpose of—and the underlying question behind—the experiment you propose to do.
- Recognize the variables involved, and select one that will help you answer the question at hand.
- State a testable hypothesis, an educated guess about the answer to your question.
- Decide how to change the variable you selected.
- Decide how to measure your results.

Recording Data and Summarizing the Results Experiments help us answer questions, so it is important to save your experiment results; keep a journal and jot notes and measurements in it. Your experiment can then be used by others and help answer their questions.

Related Projects When thinking about experimenting in weather, focus on one specific field. For example, if you decide to examine similarities in weather between New York City and London, England, you might compare weather patterns. When you start exploring possible projects, you will be amazed at the range of experiments and projects available.

For More Information

BBC. "Become a Weather Detective." *BBC Weather.* http://www.bbc.co.uk/weather/weatherwise/activities/weatherstation (accessed on February 6, 2008). Information and activities on weather forecasting.

Kerrod, Robin. *Young Scientist Concepts & Projects: Weather.* Milwaukee, WI: Garth Stevens Publishing, 1998. Offers a fact file and learn-it-yourself project book.

McVey, Vicki. *The Sierra Club Book of Weather Wisdom.* Boston: Little, Brown and Company, 1991. Includes dramatic weather stories from around the world, weather facts, and hands-on activities, games, and experiments.

National Oceanic and Atmospheric Administration. *National Weather Service.* http://www.nws.noaa.gov (accessed on February 6, 2008). Provides local weather conditions and forecasts.

Peacock, Graham. *Meteorology.* New York: Thompson Learning, 1995. Provides interesting information about weather and climate.

Taylor, Barbara. *Weather and Climate.* New York: Kingfisher Books, 1993. Outlines weather and geography facts and experiments.

97

Wood

Along with providing oxygen and beauty, trees also supply people with wood. Wood is the tissue of trees. We use wood to build houses, make paper, and provide fuel. It is a natural resource that has great use because of its strength and durability.

The hardwoods versus the softwoods There are two main group for categorizing different types of woods: hardwood or softwood. The difference between the two types of woods relates to how the tree reproduces.

Hardwoods are angiosperms, which are flowering plants. Angiosperm trees have their seeds within the flowers, and the seeds are protected by the ovary. A few examples of angiosperm trees are apple, oak, and walnut. A peach, apple, or other fruit from a tree develops around the seeds. Most hardwood trees are deciduous, meaning they lose their leaves when the season turns cool and they grow back when the weather warms. Deciduous trees have broad leaves.

Softwoods are trees that have their seeds exposed. These trees are called gymnosperms, which means "naked seed." Conifer trees are the most common types of gymnosperms and are often referred to as evergreens. These trees produce cones that contain the seeds and have needle-like leaves that can stay on the tree during cold weather. When the seeds do fall, they are exposed to air. Pine, spruce, and fir are examples of softwood trees.

A common rule of thumb is that a hardwood tree is harder and denser than a softwood. (The density of a wood is its mass for a certain volume.) But there are many exceptions to this rule. Balsa wood, for example, is categorized a hardwood yet it is one of the lightest woods in the world. It is commonly used to make model airplanes and other toys.

Inside the wood Outside of the tree is a layer of bark. The bark is made up of dead tissue that protect the tree from pests, harsh environment, and other possible damage. The "woody" inside tissue of trees carries water and nutrients throughout the tree. The layer directly next to

The oak tree is an example of an angiosperm tree. FIELD MARK PUBLICATIONS.

the bark is the phloem, which are living cells. The cells of the phloem form thin tubes that transport nutrients throughout the tree.

The neighboring inside layer to the phloem is the cambium. The cambium is where the tree's growth occurs. The cells in part of the cambium form the phloem, and the cells in the other part of the cambium form the wood tissue on the other side. As a tree grows and expands, the cambium layer move further from the center of the tree.

The wood tissue next to the cambium is also made up of layers. On the outer layer of the wood tissue is the sapwood. The sapwood transports the sap throughout the tree and it is usually a lighter color. When the sapwood cells die, they eventually become heartwood, the inner wood tissue of the tree. Although heartwood is dead, it is strong and provides the tree with support. Water does not move through the heartwood. Substances that form in the heartwood protect the wood from decay and also give the wood its distinctive color.

Wood properties The properties of wood mainly depend upon the type of tree. Yet even trees that are the same type can produce woods with different characteristics. The properties that people look for in wood depends upon the use of the wood. Common characteristics are wood color, strength, grain, and density. Some woods are more resistant to pests, and this would be important for wood that is outside. Flexibility can also be an important characteristic.

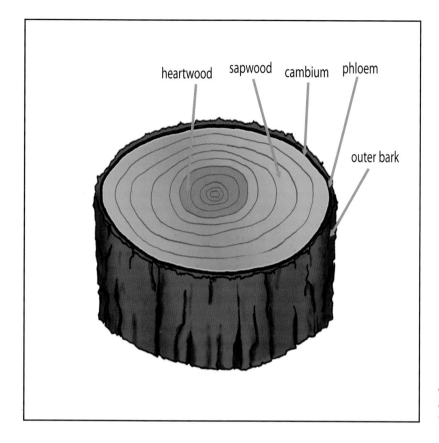

heartwood sapwood cambium phloem

outer bark

The wood tissue next to the cambium is also made up of layers. ILLUSTRATION BY TEMAH NELSON.

When selecting woods, wood strength is an important characteristic. The strength of wood depends upon the wood and the direction of the fibers. Wood fibers stretch up and down the tree and are visible from looking at the grain. The strength of wood is relatively high parallel to the grain, and relatively low perpendicular (across) the grain. Woods can also have a windy, curly grain. In general, the denser the wood, the stronger it is.

The fibers or grain of the wood also determines the pore size. Pores are the ends of the wood fibers. Some woods are open grain or porous, meaning they have large pores. Porous woods include oak and ash. Other types of wood are closed grain, and the pores are less visible. Closed-grain woods include cherry and maple.

Wood veneering and products Wood is considered a renewable resource because new trees can be grown. But some woods come from trees that take hundreds of years to fully mature. Veneering is one way to have the appearance of a unique or exotic wood while using only a sliver

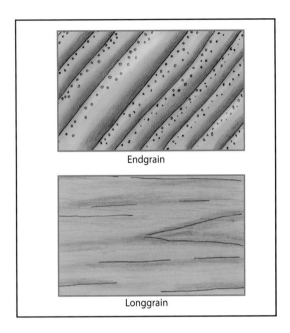

Endgrain

Longgrain

Wood grain. ILLUSTRATION BY TEMAH NELSON.

of the wood. A veneer is a thin slice of wood. The veneer is glued onto materials that are more available, such as plywood, giving the wood the appearance of the veneer wood type.

Plywood is a commonly used wood product that uses the principles of veneering. Plywood is made from gluing together many sheets of veneer with the veneer grains going in opposite directions. This produces an extremely strong material.

In the two experiments that follow, you will examine two properties of different woods: water absorption and hardness.

EXPERIMENT 1

Water Absorption: How do different woods absorb water?

Purpose/Hypothesis When wood absorbs water—from precipitation or moisture in the air—it can cause the wood to expand, then dry and possibly crack. How woods absorb water and how much each absorbs are key properties that help people select a type of wood. In this experiment, you will look at three or more types of woods. First you will examine how grain direction relates to water movement through the wood. You can place a piece of wood in dyed water, and measure if the water moves along the grain or across it (the end grain). Do you think the water will move in the same direction on each of the pieces of wood?

After you test water direction on each piece of wood, the dyed water will allow you to more easily examine the grain of each of the woods. Which wood is more open grain or closed grain? You will use this information to hypothesize which type of wood will absorb the most water. You can measure your hypothesis by weighing each piece of wood, before and after soaking the woods in water for 24 hours.

To begin the experiment, use what you know about wood and water to make an educated guess about how the water will move. This educated guess, or prediction, is your hypothesis. A hypothesis should explain these things:

- the topic of the experiment
- the variable you will change

WORDS TO KNOW

Angiosperm: A flowering plant that has its seeds produced within an ovary.

Cambium: The tissue below the bark that produces new cells, which become wood and bark.

Coniferous: Refers to trees, such as pines and firs, that bear cones and have needle-like leaves that are not shed all at once.

Deciduous: Plants that lose their leaves during some season of the year, and then grow them back during another season.

Density: The mass of a substance divided by its volume.

Hardwood: Wood from angiosperm, mostly deciduous, trees.

Heartwood: The inner layer of wood that provide structure and have no living cells.

Hypothesis: An idea phrased in the form of a statement that can be tested by observation and or experiment.

Mass: Measure of the total amount of matter in an object. Also, an object's quantity of matter as shown by its gravitational pull on another object.

Phloem: The plant tissue that carries dissolved nutrients through the plant.

Relative density: The density of one material compared to another.

Sapwood: The outer wood in a tree, which is usually a lighter color.

Softwood: Wood from coniferous trees, which usually remain green all year.

Variable: Something that can affect the results of an experiment.

Veneer: Thin slices of wood.

- the variable you will measure
- what you expect to happen

A hypothesis should be brief, specific, and measurable. It must be something you can test through observation. Your experiment will prove or disprove whether your hypothesis is correct. Here is one possible hypothesis for this experiment: "Water will move along the grain for all the woods, and the wood type with the most open grain will absorb the most water."

In this case, the variables you will change are the types of wood, and the variable you will measure is how water direction moves and which type of wood absorb the most water.

Level of Difficulty Moderate.

How to Experiment Safely

If the wood needs to be cut into pieces, have an adult cut the wood to size. You will be working with dyed water so this experiment can be slightly messy. Wash your hands after working with the dye.

What Are the Variables?

Variables are anything that could affect the results of an experiment. Here are the main variables in this experiment:

- the type of wood
- the environment in which the wood is kept
- the dryness of the wood
- the amount of time the wood is exposed to water

In other words, the variables in this experiment are everything that might affect the ability of the wood to absorb water. If you change more than one variable, you will not be able to tell which variable had the most effect.

Materials Needed

- 3 (or more) blocks of different types of wood, approximately 3 inches (7.6 centimeters) wide by 6 inches (15 centimeters) long, and $\frac{3}{4}$ of an inch thick. Oak, poplar, and pine work well; other wood types are walnut, cherry, and mahogany. (Available from building supply stores or scraps from a lumber yard or school shop. If you find wood that needs to be cut, have an adult cut the wood to size. The wood should all be approximately the same size but they do not need to match exactly.) Note: Avoid woods from trees you find outside as they likely contain more moisture than woods in stores.
- plastic container, large enough to fit the blocks of wood
- food coloring or dye, a dark color such as blue or green
- ruler
- watch or clock with a minute hand
- plastic or wooden stirrer
- gram scale
- wax paper
- gloves (optional)
- magnifying glass (optional)

Step 1a: Start with 3 (or more) blocks of different types of wood. ILLUSTRATION BY TEMAH NELSON.

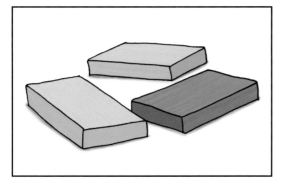

Approximate Budget Less than $5. (Assuming you can find the wood as scraps and you have or can borrow a gram scale.)

Timetable Approximately 45 minutes working time; 24 hours total time.

Step-by-Step Instructions

1. Place a piece of wax paper on the scale and weigh each of the three woods. Note the weight on a chart.

2. Fill the container about half way with warm water. Add several drops of the dye or food coloring. Stir and continue adding the dye until the water is a dark color.

3. At the same time, set each of the three pieces of wood in the water with the grain (length) facing up and down. Start timing for one minute.

4. Observe the water movement in each of the woods, looking at both the end grain and long grain. After one minute, measure where the water has reached in each of the woods. Measure on both the end and long grain. Note the results. (If you have gloves, you could wear them to avoid getting dye on your hands, or you could handle the wood with wax paper).

5. Set the woods back in the water and wait two more minutes, or until the water has reached close to the top of a wood. Measure how far the water traveled along the long and end grain, on each of the woods.

6. Set all the wood on a piece of wax paper. Examine each of the woods' grains up close or with a magnifying glass.

7. Form a hypothesis as to which type of wood will absorb the most water.

8. Set all the woods back in the container so they lie flat (with the long side left to right). The water should cover the pieces of wood. If it does not, add more water.

9. Wait about 24 hours.

10. Carefully drain the water.

11. Place a piece of wax paper on the scale. Hold one piece of wood above the container until it no longer drips and set the wood on it. You may want to pick the wood up with wax paper or wear gloves so as to not get dye on your hands. Note the weight of the wood.

Step 1b: Weigh each of the three woods. ILLUSTRATION BY TEMAH NELSON.

Steps 3 and 4: Set each of the three pieces of wood in the water with the grain (length) facing up and down and observe the water movement. ILLUSTRATION BY TEMAH NELSON.

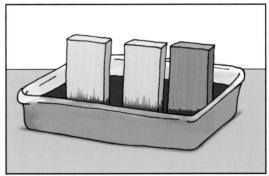

Troubleshooter's Guide

Here is one problems that may arise during the experiment and a way to remedy it.

Problem: One of the woods did not take up the dyed water at all.

Possible causes: The wood may have been too moist to start with. Woods are usually dried for long periods of time before they are available for use. Try another piece of wood, making sure it is not freshly cut, and repeat the experiment.

12. Weigh each of the pieces of wood, holding the pieces so they no longer drip before placing them on a fresh piece of wax paper.

Summary of Results Subtract the end weight of the wood from the starting weight. Which of the woods gained the most weight from the water? Did it relate to whether the wood had an open or closed grain? Was your hypothesis correct? How did the water travel along the grain of the wood? Did it differ depending upon the type of wood? Consider how water absorption would affect selecting a wood for a home or piece of furniture. Write a summary of your findings. You might want to sketch pictures of the water movement.

Change the Variables You can vary this experiment in several ways. You can focus on one type of wood, such as oak, and examine the water absorption properties of different types of oak. You can also change the amount of water available to each wood, to measure how much water the end grain or long grain can absorb. Another way to vary the experiment is to change the environmental temperature. How does humidity or cold affect water absorption?

EXPERIMENT 2

Wood Hardness: How does the hardness of wood relate to its building properties?

Purpose/Hypothesis In general, hardwoods are harder and denser than softwoods. The structure of the wood depends on the thickness and makeup of the cell walls. Many hardwoods have thicker cell walls (fibers) than softwoods. How hard or soft a wood is affects how the wood is used. For some soft woods, builders can pound nails into the wood without the wood cracking. A nail inserted into a hard wood may crack, and builders will use a drill before nailing wood together.

You can use a nail to determine the relative hardness or softness of three to four different woods. The woods you test will be a mix between hardwoods and softwoods. In order to compare them, you will need to use the same force when inserting the nail into the woods. The deeper the nail is driven into the wood, the softer the wood.

To form a hypothesis, you can first compare the heaviness of each wood to one another. Using this information, you can then make a hypothesis as to which nail will go in the least. You will then finish driving the nail into the wood with a hammer.

To begin the experiment, use what you know about wood and hardness to make an educated guess about how the heaviness of the wood will determine its hardness. This educated guess, or prediction, is your hypothesis. A hypothesis should explain these things:

- the topic of the experiment
- the variable you will change
- the variable you will measure
- what you expect to happen

A hypothesis should be brief, specific, and measurable. It must be something you can test through observation. Your experiment will prove or disprove whether your hypothesis is correct. Here is one possible hypothesis for this experiment: "The nail will move deeper into the woods that are lighter compared to the heavier woods, which may crack."

In this case, the variable you will change is the type of wood, and the variable you will measure is the depth the wood moves into the wood.

Level of Difficulty Moderate.

Materials Needed

- 3 or more different pieces of wood, minimum $\frac{3}{4}$-inch thick and approximately 6 inches (15 centimeters) square: at least 1 softwood (pine, cedar) and 1 hardwood (poplar, balsa, oak)
- 3 nails $\frac{3}{4}$-inch long with point, all the same diameter

What Are the Variables?

Variables are anything that might affect the results of an experiment. Here are the main variables in this experiment:

- the wetness of the wood
- the force with which the weight hits the nail
- the heaviness of the weight
- the size of the nail

In other words, the variables in this experiment are everything that might affect how far the nail is driven into the wood.

How to Experiment Safely

Be careful when using the hammer and nails. Have an adult help you with the hammering to make sure the wood cannot move around.

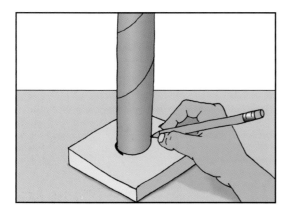

Step 6: Set the tubing in the middle of the lightest piece of wood and trace the circle onto the wood. ILLUSTRATION BY TEMAH NELSON.

Steps 7 and 8: Line up the paper circle over the wood circle. Place the nail on the center mark of the wood. ILLUSTRATION BY TEMAH NELSON.

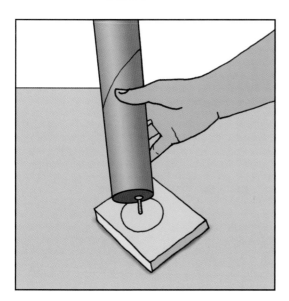

- cardboard or plastic tube, at least 30 inches (76 centimeters) long (wrapping paper rolls works well); if tubing is not available you can make tubing by taping together several sheets of thick paper
- full can or water bottle that fits tightly into the diameter of the tube
- hammer
- marker
- sharp pencil
- piece of paper
- scissors
- ruler with 0.06-inch increments

Note: The exact size of the wood is not important but when the tubing is on the wood there should be at least 2 inches (5 centimeters) of wood around the tube and the nail should be slightly shorter than the thickness of the wood.

Approximate Budget Less than $5. (Most, if not all, materials may be found in the average household.)

Timetable Approximately 30 minutes.

Step-by-Step Instructions

1. Lift each of the wood samples one at a time, then compare one to another in each hand. Place the woods in order, from the lightest to the heaviest.
2. Measure how long the nail is and note its length on a chart.
3. Use the marker and ruler to make small lines on each nail at 0.06-inch increments, about $\frac{3}{4}$ way up the nail.
4. Set the tubing on the paper and trace the circle. Follow your tracing to cut out the circle.
5. To find the center of the circle, fold the circle in half and then in half again.

Unfold and mark a dot where the fold lines intersect.

6. Set the tubing in the middle of the lightest piece of wood. Use the pencil to trace the circle onto the wood. Repeat this process with the other wood samples.

7. Line up the paper circle over the wood circle. Poke a small hole in the paper with the pencil to mark the middle of the circle on the wood.

8. Place the nail on the center mark of the wood and gently hammer it in until it reaches the second mark. The nail should be standing straight and not wobbling. If you can easily push the nail to its side, hammer it in to the next mark.

9. Set the wood on the floor.

10. Place the tubing on the circle mark. Hold the can or other circular object even with the top of the tubing and release. Retrieve the object and drop the can four more times, for a total of five times.

11. Repeat Steps 6–10 on the remaining types of wood.

12. Measure how far each nail went into the wood by measuring how much of the nail did not go into the wood. Note your results.

13. Finish driving the nail into the wood with the hammer. Hammer the nails gently and have an adult help you make sure the piece of wood is secure.

14. Note if any of the woods starts to crack.

Step 10: Hold the can or other circular object even with the top of the tubing and release. ILLUSTRATION BY TEMAH NELSON.

Summary of Results Subtract how much of the nail was still exposed from the length of the nail. Was your hypothesis correct? Was the lightest wood also the wood that the nail went into furthest? Compare the difference between the two types of the hardwood or softwood. Did any of the heavy woods crack or begin to crack? Write a summary of your results.

Change the Variables You can vary this experiment. Here are some possibilities. Try different types of either hardwood or softwood to compare them against one another. You could even try different types

Troubleshooter's Guide

Here are some problems that may arise during the experiment, some possible causes, and ways to solve the problem.

Problem: The nail fell over when the weight was dropped.

Possible causes:

1. The nail may have been too thin. Try using a slightly thicker nail with a sharp point, and repeat the experiment.

2. The weight may have hit the nail at an angle. The can, water bottle, or other circular object should fit snugly in the tube opening so that it cannot move around and hit the nail straight. Change the tube or object to there is no room for the can to move, and repeat the experiment.

Problem: The nail hardly went into the wood.

Possible cause: The weight you dropped is not heavy enough. If you are using a can or bottle, make sure it is full. See if you can find a heavier object that is the same diameter. You may also want to try a larger tube, and a larger (heavier) can, bottle, or other object.

of the same wood, such as oak. You can also experiment with driving the nail into the end grain instead of the long grain.

Design Your Own Experiment

How to Select a Topic Relating to this Concept
There are many experiments you could design to investigate the properties of wood and how people use it. Take a look at the wooden furniture, toys, sports equipment, or other pieces in your home or school and try to identify what type of wood it is. What about the home itself? Consider the properties of each piece. Can you see the grain or pores in the wood? Think about what woods you are curious about or you may want to investigate familiar wooden items. Why is a wooden bat, for example, made with a certain type of wood and how does this affect the bat's ability to hit a ball?

Check the Further Readings section and talk with your science teacher or school or community media specialist to start gathering information on questions relating to wood that interest you. You also may want to visit a lumberyard or store that sells different woods.

Steps in the Scientific Method To conduct an original experiment, you need to plan carefully and think things through. Otherwise, you might not be sure what question you are answering, what you are or should be measuring, or what your findings prove or disprove.

Here are the steps in designing an experiment:

- State the purpose of—and the underlying question behind—the experiment you propose to do.

- Recognize the variables involved, and select one that will help you answer the question at hand.

Experiment Central, 2nd edition

- State a testable hypothesis, an educated guess about the answer to your question.
- Decide how to change the variable you selected.
- Decide how to measure your results.

Recording Data and Summarizing the Results It is important to document as much information as possible about your experiment. Part of your presentation should be visual, using charts and graphs. You can also include samples of the woods. Remember, whether or not your experiment is successful, your conclusions and experiences can benefit others.

Related Projects If you are interested in experimenting more with wood and its properties, you can start collecting and examining different types of wood. You may want to start collecting woods you find outside and then purchase samples of other wood types. Compare properties of the different woods to one another. You can conduct an experiment on what gives wood its unique colors. Some woods, such as purpleheart, change or fade over time. How might oxygen or sunlight affect the color of wood? You can also explore the affect of disease and bugs on wood. In some cases, disease, worms, and bugs can leave marks that increase its beauty and value.

Another aspect related to wood you may also want to explore is wood finishes. Finishes can protect and affect the appearance of woods. Try an experiment in finishing the same type of wood with different finishes, such as a wax, oil, and shellac. How does each change the appearance and ability of the wood to withstand water? For a project, you can make different types of paper out of wood.

For More Information

Burnie, Davis. *Tree.* New York: DK Publishing, 2005. Information on trees and wood.

Gardner, Robert. *Science Projects Ideas about Trees.* Springfield< NJ: Enslow Publishers, 1997. Describes tree related projects for young people.

Wolke, Robert L. *What Einstein Didn't Know: Scientific Answers to Everyday Questions.* Secaucus, NJ: Birch Lane Press, 1997. Contains a number of interesting entries on the nature of water.

"Wood Cells." *Nikon.* http://www.microscopyu.com/galleries/confocal/woodcells.html (accessed on May 2, 2008). Close-up images of wood.

Budget Index

Chapter name in brackets, followed by experiment name. The numeral before the colon indicates volume; numbers after the colon indicate page number.

Experiment Central, 2nd edition

Level of Difficulty Index

Chapter name in brackets, followed by experiment name. The numeral before the colon indicates volume; numbers after the colon indicate page number.

EASY

Easy means that the average student should easily be able to complete the tasks outlined in the project/experiment, and that the time spent on the project is not overly restrictive.

EASY/MODERATE

Easy/Moderate means that the average student should have little trouble completing the tasks outlined in the project/experiment, and that the time spent on the project is not overly restrictive.

MODERATE

Moderate means that the average student should find tasks outlined in the project/experiment challenging but not difficult, and that the time spent on the project/experiment may be more extensive.

MODERATE/DIFFICULT

Moderate/Difficult means that the average student should find tasks outlined in the project/experiment challenging, and that the time spent on the project/experiment may be more extensive.

DIFFICULT

Difficult means that the average student wil probably find the tasks outlined in the project/experiment mentally and/or physically challenging, and that the time spent on the project/experiment may be more extensive.

Timetable Index

Chapter name in brackets, followed by experiment name. The numeral before the colon indicates volume; numbers after the colon indicate page number.

30 TO 45 MINUTES

Experiment Central, 2nd edition

2 HOURS

3 HOURS

Experiment Central, 2nd edition

General Subject Index

The numeral before the colon indicates volume; numbers after the colon indicate page number. **Bold** page numbers indicate main essays. The notation (ill.) after a page number indicates a figure.

I

Experiment Central, 2nd edition

O

W